Animal Ethics and Philosophy

Animal Ethics and Philosophy

Questioning the Orthodoxy

Edited by Elisa Aaltola and John Hadley

ROWMAN & LITTLEFIELD
INTERNATIONAL
London • New York

Published by Rowman & Littlefield International, Ltd.
Unit A, Whitacre Mews, 26-34 Stannary Street, London SE11 4AB
www.rowmaninternational.com

Rowman & Littlefield International, Ltd. is an affiliate of Rowman & Littlefield
4501 Forbes Boulevard, Suite 200, Lanham, Maryland 20706, USA
With additional offices in Boulder, New York, Toronto (Canada), and Plymouth (UK)
www.rowman.com

British Library Cataloguing in Publication Information Available
A catalogue record for this book is available from the British Library

ISBN: HB 978-1-78348-181-1
ISBN: PB 978-1-78348-182-8

Library of Congress Cataloging-in-Publication Data

Animal ethics and philosophy : questioning the orthodoxy / edited by Elisa Aaltola and John Hadley.
pages cm
Includes bibliographical references and index.
ISBN 978-1-78348-181-1 (cloth : alk. paper) — ISBN 978-1-78348-182-8 (pbk. : alk. paper) —
ISBN 978-1-78348-183-5 (electronic)
1. Animals (Philosophy) 2. Animal rights. 3. Animal welfare. I. Aaltola, Elisa, 1976– editor.
B105.A55A545 2015
179'.3—dc23
2014036000

∞™ The paper used in this publication meets the minimum requirements of American
National Standard for Information Sciences Permanence of Paper for Printed Library
Materials, ANSI/NISO Z39.48-1992.

Printed in the United States of America

Contents

Introduction

Questioning the Orthodoxy

John Hadley and Elisa Aaltola

In *Bourgeois Dignity: Why Economics Can't Explain the Modern World*, University of Illinois economist Deirdre McCloskey draws attention to a distinction between, on the one hand, *original* research and, on the other hand, *innovative* research.[1] According to McCloskey, original research is the application of existing knowledge to pressing problems and issues, and innovative research is the creation of altogether new knowledge. McCloskey's thesis is that the extraordinary improvement in living standards between 1800 to the present day cannot be explained by the workings of markets alone; instead, progress is the product of human ingenuity—that is, innovative research in a wide range of fields including the arts and humanities.

If McCloskey's distinction between original research and innovative research is sound, then there has been relatively little innovation in the field of animal ethics. Indeed, even the most respected and widely cited philosophers in the field, such as Peter Singer and Tom Regan, have not produced genuinely innovative research to any substantial degree. After all, Singer and Regan are, respectively, utilitarian and deontological philosophers first and animal ethicists second. That is to say, they have each applied existing theories to the problem of human relations with other animals but have not created new knowledge as such. In other words, they have produced merely original research, and they have not produced innovative research.

To say that a philosopher has produced merely original research, as opposed to genuinely innovative research, sounds like casting aspersions. But our point is not to slight the considerable achievements of the many dozens of philosophers who have contributed to animal ethics theory; rather, we aim to draw attention to the nature of the discipline and the idea of progress within it. If McCloskey's distinction is sound, very few philosophers create new knowledge because we all, to some extent, respond to what others say or we disagree with someone else's interpretation of another theorist's work. While it is true that there is a sense in which new knowledge is created when we identify a hitherto overlooked

1

implication of an existing theory, the innovativeness in such cases remains derivative of the initial creativity and, thus, more the product of
effort rather than ingenuity.

Of course, it is open to readers to reject McCloskey's distinction, but
we think it is useful for thinking about the state of play in animal ethics
and the future of the discipline. It goes without saying that the editors of
this collection are as guilty as any other philosophers of producing what
McCloskey would suggest is merely original research.

BEYOND EXTENSIONISM?

The creation of this volume was motivated by the nagging thought that
very little of what passes for innovative research in animal ethics is deserving of the label. As anyone familiar with the literature knows, the
field is, by and large, a site for "moral extensionism". Moral extensionism
is the extension of existing moral and political theory across the species
barrier to nonhuman animals. Research in animal ethics is invariably a
case of taking an established theory and applying it to the plight of animals: Singer takes utilitarian theory and extends it to all sentient beings;
Regan extends deontological theory; Hursthouse extends virtue theory;
Rowlands extends contractarian theory; Cochrane extends Razian theory;
Donaldson and Kymlicka extend sovereignty theory, and so on. In effect,
animal ethics philosophers are in the business of pointing out that previous thinkers have misunderstood, wrongly applied, or overlooked a feature of an established theory. In all such instances, assuming that there is
some important insight captured by McCloskey's distinction, research in
animal ethics is not genuinely innovative but instead merely works with
existing materials. An obvious question arises: Why do we need any
more theory of this kind?

As well as an innovation deficit, another problem of extensionism is
that any theory that is spawned by it, however original it may be, is
ultimately vulnerable to the same problems as the established theory.
Thus, any utilitarian animal ethics theory faces the nearest and dearest
objections, such as the scope problem, that arise after extending the theory to nonhuman animals. Similarly, any deontological animal rights theory faces the familiar conflict of duties problem, and any virtue theory
approach to animal ethics faces the conflict of virtues problem. While it is
true that there are responses to these problems in the literature, they are
by no means decisive and the seeming intractability of the problems casts
a metalevel shadow over claims to authority in animal ethics, or more
broadly animal philosophy. Most proponents of moral extensionism,
with the exception of Tom Regan in *The Case for Animal Rights*,[2] pass over
metaphilosophical problems quickly or proceed as if these problems have
no bearing on debates about human and animal relations. But clearly, it is

open to someone to reject, say, Singer's utilitarian theory by claiming that, just like all utilitarian theories, it is too demanding or epistemically flawed, without even reading what he says about sentience, factory farming and animal experimentation. Likewise, someone could reject Regan's, or McMahan's,[3] theory on the grounds that intuition ought to play no role in ethical theorizing, without seriously countenancing the "postulate of inherent value" or "convergent assimilation", respectively.

Uncertainty about criteria for evaluating moral theories is not the only metalevel problem that hangs over animal ethics theory. Indeed, there is a roll call of metaethical and metaphilosophical controversies: the nature and scope of the psychological capacities necessary for moral status; the epistemological status of claims about animal mindedness; the role of intuitions in moral theory; the metaphysics of intrinsic value; the individualist versus relational moral status debate; the concept of truth; and representational versus nonrepresentational theories of meaning, to name just a few. Our aim in this volume was to highlight how these contentious issues relate to animal ethics with the goal of moving the field beyond simple moral extensionism.

Our original call for chapters asked for contributions that self-consciously examined these problems against the background of the existing animal ethics literature, broadly construed. We were hoping to get chapters that addressed questions like: How is existing animal ethics theory impacted upon by the metalevel problems? With an appreciation of the metalevel problems and controversies, what informative taxonomical boundaries within the field of animal ethics come into view? Among the leading animal ethics theorists, who are the naturalistic moral realists, the non-naturalists, and the noncognitivists? Is truth or rational consensus a goal in animal ethics, or is human and nonhuman animal relations best thought of as an expressive domain? Notice that we, too, were inviting contributors to engage in extensionism, albeit metamoral extensionism. The rationale was that metalevel analyses would open up new pathways towards research that would be genuinely innovative.

We hope that by looking at familiar issues from novel perspectives and asking questions that have thus far remained not only unaddressed but often unuttered, the chapters in this collection will help to guide animal ethics towards philosophically stimulating directions—the type of directions that spark truly innovative research. It is also hoped that such research will facilitate a broader social change in our attitudes towards other animals, sorely required in an era that is witnessing a continuous intensification of animal industries.

THE CONTRIBUTIONS IN THIS VOLUME

Part I of this collection features four chapters that focus on the most important concept in animal ethics theory: sentience or the capacity to experience pleasure and pain. John Hadley takes issue with orthodox sentience-based versions of animal rights theory. Hadley's is a distinctively metalevel analysis that focuses on the "supervenience relation" that is attendant upon the central animal rights tenet that moral status or "direct value" is grounded upon sentience. Proponents of animal rights theory betray their true evaluative commitments, Hadley argues, when they make a distinction among the class of sentient beings between persons and nonpersons. This act of moral categorization, Hadley claims, is undertaken for the express purpose of reconciling animal rights theory with commonsense intuitions: "[B]y marking out sub-groups within the group of directly valuable individuals, and then using the sub-group device to resolve theoretical problems . . . proponents of animal rights undermine the sense that animal rights theory is, fundamentally, an 'equalizing' project that is meant to be consistent with the spirit of a normative claim implicit in Darwin's famous words".

Far from reflecting a post-Darwinian view of human-nonhuman animal psychological continuity, a close analysis of the moral metaphysics of animal rights reveals, Hadley argues, a pre-Darwinian axiological theory in line with which human and nonhuman animal psychology *is* different in kind. The end result, Hadley claims, is that orthodox versions of animal rights are plagued by a theoretical tension explicable in terms of an "inconsistent triad" problem.

In "Against Moral Intrinsicalism", Nicolas Delon is also critical of orthodox animal ethics approaches to intrinsic value and moral status. According to orthodox intrinsic value theory, moral status is dependent on mental capacities, and extrinsic factors do not affect the moral status of nonhuman animals; indeed, in line with moral individualism (or, as Delon calls it, "moral intrinsicalism"), only the intrinsic properties of the individuals in question can have a bearing upon moral status. Delon rejects this view and asserts that both intrinsic and extrinsic factors ought to be taken into account.

In line with Delon's position, moral status is dependent upon factors such as mental capacities *and* relationships, with the latter having "status-enhancing" properties. Delon gives special attention to vulnerability as a morally relevant relational or extrinsic factor. In contrast to fragility, vulnerability is defined in relation to external harms, and it gains its moral significance from positive, relational duties to protect special others from those harms. Using the example of companion animals, Delon maintains that their vulnerability is an extrinsic factor that renders them dependent upon special relations and enhances their moral status—thus, the moral status of companion animals is higher than that of many other animals, and there are grounds for partiality on their behalf. This example, again, Delon claims to have broader implications that count against intrinsical-ism.

Morten Tønnessen and Jonathan Beever argue that animals are more psychologically sophisticated than is ordinarily assumed by proponents of sentience-based theories. In "Beyond Sentience: Biosemiotics as Foundation for Animal and Environmental Ethics", they point to an animal's capacity to make its way around the environment, or, as they put it, its "unique worlds of subjective experience". Drawing upon the Umwelt theory of pioneering ethologist Jakob von Uexküll, Tønnessen and Beever focus on signalling processes—the aspects of an animal's biological life associated with navigation and communication. In Uexküllian terms, all living beings have *semiotic agency* (the capacity to make use of signs in one's environment). Tønnessen and Beever argue that the moral implications of human impacts upon the environment register most profoundly as human interference with the semiotic agency of living things, and, therefore, semiotic agency, and not sentience, should be the basis of moral status.

Tønnessen and Beever's chapter can be understood as an attempt to address the so-called scope problem of sentience—the charge that sentience is an arbitrarily narrow criterion for intrinsic value or moral status. Insofar as their theory comprises a positive case for the value of life alongside a negative case directed at sentience as a criterion of status, then Tønnessen and Beever's theory can be regarded as a revival of the kind of biocentric environmentalism associated with Paul Taylor[4] and, more recently, Nicholas Agar.[5]

Zipporah Weisberg is concerned with how animals are characterized in both philosophical theory and political advocacy. In "Animal Agency: What It Is, What It Isn't, and How It Can Be Realized", she is critical of contrasting conceptions of the agency of nonhuman animals. First, a neo-Kantian conception of agency, Weisberg claims, depicts other animals as having a lesser ontological status due to their presumed passivity—a depiction that, again, seems to suggest nonhuman animals cannot be active participants in decision making that directly impacts their own lives. Secondly, Weisberg is critical of conceptions of agency that are implicit in recent animal studies and posthumanist literature. Her critique here could just as easily be made of other theorists in this collection, such as Tønnessen and Beever, and Williams, who aim to extend intrinsic value to all living things. Indeed, Weisberg singles out von Uexküll's Umwelt theory for special attention: "[I]t is one thing to recognize the vitality, dynamism, and activity of the natural world and all its nonhuman constituents, but it is quite another to suggest that every single entity, from microorganisms to elephants, is an agent. By spreading the concept of agency so thinly, the concept loses its ethical potency".

While generally sympathetic to their project of political enfranchise-ment, Weisberg reserves special criticism for Donaldson and Kymlicka's *Zoopolis*.[6] At bottom, however, her criticisms are not so much directed at *Zoopolis* as the liberalism that constitutes its theoretical backdrop. First, Weisberg is concerned with bias: so-called liminal animals may be vul-nerable to exploitation and demonization because they are not afforded the first-class status enjoyed by domesticated animals; secondly, she claims that citizenship theory is by definition "inadvertently anthropo-centric" insofar as only animals who enjoy close relations with human beings enjoy citizenship status; and her final criticism is a reiteration of the familiar charge against liberalism made by theorists such as Ted Ben-ton[7] and Barbara Noske.[8] Here the essential criticism is that, while the liberal preoccupation with individual agency may be theoretically worth-while, a focus on moral status overlooks how substantive change for nonhuman animals can only come about through changes to the econom-ic system that does so much to influence how those animals are treated in the real world.[9]

Uexküll's theory was of interest to French phenomenologist Maurice Merleau-Ponty, whose theory of embodied perception informs Wayne Williams's contribution to Part II of this volume. In "Enchanted Worlds and Animal Others", Williams, like Tønnessen and Beever, is critical of psychology-based approaches to value on the grounds of their purport-edly narrow scope. Williams uses Tom Regan's concept of inherent value as his stalking horse, arguing that Regan's attempt to secure for moral patients the kind of moral worth ordinarily reserved for moral agents is incomplete. In line with the strategy employed by Tønnessen and Beever, Williams argues that greater appreciation of the connection between an animal and her environment lends support to broadening the scope of nonrelational value or moral status. From an appreciation of humans and other animals as embodied subjects, Williams invokes not only Merleau-Ponty's philosophy but also John McDowell's influential theory of values as secondary qualities, and recent work by Burwood, Lennon and Gil-bert.[10] In line with McDowell's theory, we can think of valuing as analo-gous to colour perception—it is not that values are projected onto the world by a sentient creature; rather, they are a feature of a two-way interaction between a perceiver and the environment which is, as Williams argues, inclusive of both notions of value and appropriate re-sponses toward value-invoking qualities.

The chapters in Part II focus upon epistemological issues in animal ethics theory. At issue are the conceptual definitions, theoretical presup-positions and methodologies that shape how philosophers understand other animals and address human-nonhuman animal ethical relations. In "'The Flesh of My Flesh': Animality, Difference, and 'Radical Commu-nity' in Merleau-Ponty's Philosophy", Jonathan D. Singer explores hu-man-animal relations from the viewpoint of Merleau-Ponty's phenomenology. The background question for Singer is whether seeing subjectivity in other animals is an anthropomorphic projection, and he seeks to answer this question by showing how doubt over animal subjectivity is incoherent. Using Merleau-Ponty, Singer maintains that a thorough grasp of subjectivity includes understanding that the living body is entwined with a mind and expresses mental contents—indeed, means those contents—to such an extent that scepticism becomes absurd. For Merleau-Ponty, we exist in a community with nonhuman others, sharing with them what he terms *intercorporality*, within which embodied subjects coconstitute each other. Here Merleau-Ponty's famous notion of "Flesh" emerges as a key concept: Flesh is the mode of existence in which coconstituting subjectivity, experience, and perception takes place: it forms the basis for our understanding of others, and for our social relations with those others. The Flesh enables one to pay heed to both similarity and complete difference, thus rendering the notion of anthropomorphic projection ever more distant; according to Singer, Flesh thereby offers grounds for an animal ethic, which is based on lived experience that comes with a sense of community with other animals while also respecting the specificity of those animals. Indeed, Singer claims that Merleau-Ponty's philosophy allows us to include nonhuman animals in the "radical community" from which ethics stems. Singer concludes that a phenomenological alternative to anthropocentric ethics can be grounded in a reflective epistemology, within which one seeks to become aware of one's coconstitution and interbeing with other animals, thus expanding the boundaries of "we".

In "The Problem of Speaking for Animals", Jason Wyckoff draws upon Edward Said's notion of "orientialism" to address the issue of speaking on behalf of people and animals who cannot speak for themselves. According to Wyckoff, the problem of speaking for animals involves an appreciation of how the social embeddedness of language bears upon the search for answers to epistemological, ethical and practical questions. Wyckoff introduces "dominionism" as a parallel concept to orientialism, and takes it to include—among other factors—the presumption that other animals are objects or resources to be used. Wyckoff suggests that dominionism rests on the way in which knowledge claims concerning nonhuman animals depend on the social context and, in an anthropocentric society, reflect normatively loaded binaries and homogenizations. Dominionism renders speaking for other animals integrally difficult, since the language used for such speaking is typically coloured by anthropocentrism (as one example, Wyckoff refers to advocacy, which emphasizes similarities between humans and other animals, thereby presuming humanity to be the reference point for value). Speaking for nonhuman animals must, therefore, include careful reflection on the normative connotations of the words being used, together with attention on the position one is speaking from and to whom one is speaking—this, again, will necessitate a radical transformation of advocacy discourse in a way that will enable direct challenging of dominionism. On these grounds, Wyckoff argues in favor of a paradigm shift in our very animal imagery.

Elizabeth Foreman's chapter, "Doing Without Moral Rights", represents something of a departure from the rest of the collection. Foreman's concern is not so much with the theoretical underpinnings of arguments for animal rights, but rather with rights themselves, as normative instruments. Foreman calls rights "unfortunate outgrowths" of a conception of morality as a legislative domain within which the concept of moral standing plays the same functional role as the notion of "standing to complain" in law. Foreman's suggestion is to do away with rights altogether and instead develop normative theory around the notion of "appropriate attitudes".

The Respect Principle, a key element of Regan's theory of rights, is a focus of Foreman's critique. She argues that the normative significance of the idea of respecting inherent value is, at bottom, an injunction to show a proper attitude towards a creature meriting it. It is thus mistaken, Foreman argues, to think of a *right to* respect; instead, we should view respect in terms of attitudes and duty. To illustrate her case, she discusses the wrongness of torturing kittens, and suggests that what emerges as pivotal is our capacity to orientate toward nonhuman animals caringly; if such care is lacking, we harbour a misconceived grasp of what it is to be an animal. Foreman argues against the objection that an ethic based on attitudes is anthropocentric, and she acknowledges the political, legal and rhetorical power of appeals to rights, but she concludes that "thinking in terms of rights actually runs counter to the goals of the animal rightist, since the notion of rights is fundamentally anthropocentric".

The focus of Part III is moral psychology; specifically, contributors aim to challenge ethical rationalism—the methodology of most orthodox animal ethics theory. Emotions such as empathy, love and disgust are discussed with contributors drawing upon empirical data from recent social psychology research into the role of emotions in moral judgement and behaviour. The main suggestion is that rationalist approaches to moral psychology afford a very limited view of how moral and political judgements about nonhuman animals are made.

While he does not explicitly mention John McDowell's theory, in "Disgust and the Collection of Bovine Foetal Blood" Robert William Fischer argues that our emotional responses to the treatment of other animals can point to the morality of the associated actions. So, for Fischer, like McDowell, moral judgement involves a perceiver detecting an evaluative feature that is in some sense independent of them. Fischer claims a reaction of disgust, in certain circumstances, acts as a moral heuristic and can provide a "defeasible reason" for thinking the associated action is wrong. This is a controversial claim, and Fischer defends it with reference to a case study many readers may find disgusting. Echoing Hume's theory of moral sentiments,[11] Fischer argues that our negative reaction to what is being done to an animal is directed at the character traits of the abuser and the negative impact such traits are likely to have on the good of the community as a whole. For Fischer, disgust does not trace objective values and is not to be followed as an infallible moral compass; however, it is helpful as a heuristic tool, and capable of providing strong grounds and premises for moral deliberation.

As with Fischer's chapter, the focus in Angela Coventry and Avram Hiller's chapter is our emotional responses to what is been done to nonhuman animals. In "Hume on Animals and the Rest of Nature", they argue that Hume's theory of moral sentiments can be the basis for a thoroughgoing environmental ethic. Coventry and Hiller are critical of rival theorists who employ Humean concepts, most notably leading environmental philosopher J. Baird Callicott[12]—an important figure in animal ethics because of his use of moral sentiments theory for the protection of whole ecosystems and [some] animals. After surveying the recent literature on Hume, Coventry and Hiller argue that Callicott and others have overlooked key elements of Hume's corpus that could be given a normative application in animal and environmental ethics. Drawing upon a diverse range of Hume's texts, Coventry and Hiller argue that Hume's views about our judgements of the beauty of material objects, such as tables and chairs, can be readily extended to ecosystems and nonsentient organisms. Just like Fischer in his theory of disgust, Coventry and Hiller show that the key element of the extension of moral sentiments theory to ecosystems and plants is the connection Hume makes between sentiment and the good of society at large.

In "The Politicization of Animal Love", Tony Milligan argues that love holds out the promise of challenging familiar political terminology and sparking political imagination concerning other animals. Next to standard political concepts such as rights, equality and justice, love, Milligan claims, can help to prepare the ground for changing the political status of nonhuman animals to fellow citizens. For Milligan, rights can entwine with love, and indeed need to do so. The backbone of his account is an Aristotelian conception of citizenship. In line with this conception, the interests of fellow citizens are held as part of a common good and, ultimately, as a manifestation of friendship. In Aristotle's theory, other people emerge to us as "another self", with whom we can identify, and whose good thereby matters to us, and it is here that love as *philia* plays a prominent role. Indeed, love emerges as a central aspect of not only human life but also the *polis*, and it is thereby a politically charged concept, which helps to illuminate the application of standard political terminology to the animal context. Milligan criticizes the idea that love requires shared humanity, Kantian personhood or reciprocity: regardless of their species and lack of moral agency, Milligan claims nonhuman animals can love, and can be loved. If we accept love of animals, and love for animals, then the borders of the Aristotelian polis, and more broadly our shared community with its notions of rights and justice, are opened for nonhuman creatures.

"The Rise of Sentimentalism and Animal Philosophy" is Elisa Aaltola's contribution to the debate between sentimentalism and rationalism in contemporary animal ethics. Against the backdrop of the current revival of sentimentalism in both philosophy and social psychology, Aaltola defends the claim that possessing an emotional capacity is a necessary criterion for moral agency, and a sufficient criterion for moral status. First, in explaining why emotions are required on a general level, Aaltola argues that rationalism struggles to explain why "reason-responding" is necessary for moral judgement. Secondly, in mapping out which specific emotions bear moral relevance, Aaltola concentrates on affective empathy—the form of empathy celebrated not only by Hume but also by many contemporary empirical scholars. The sentimentalist approach, Aaltola demonstrates, has far-reaching metaethical implications for reason-based analytical approaches to animal issues. Aaltola also argues that sentimentalism is evident in societal attitudes towards nonhuman animals, and that the care tradition, which has underlined the importance of emotions in human-nonhuman animal relations, makes a mistake in not taking into account the counterside of sentimentalism—the limiting impact that positive emotions like love (see Milligan's contribution to this volume) and negative emotions like hate and disgust (see Fischer's contribution to this volume) commonly have on such attitudes. It is partly for this reason that the relevance and role of emotions need to be further explored in animal philosophy.

NOTES

1. Deirdre N. McCloskey, *Bourgeois Dignity: Why Economics Can't Explain the Modern World* (London: University of Chicago Press, 2010).

2. Tom Regan, *The Case for Animal Rights* (Berkeley: University of California Press, 1983).

3. Jeff McMahan, *The Ethics of Killing: Problems at the Margins of Life* (Oxford: Oxford University Press, 2002).

4. Paul Taylor, *Respect for Nature* (Princeton: Princeton University Press, 1986).

5. Nicholas Agar, *Life's Intrinsic Value* (New York: Columbia University Press, 2001).

6. Sue Donaldson and Will Kymlicka, *Zoopolis: A Political Theory of Animal Rights* (Oxford: Oxford University Press, 2011).

7. Ted Benton, *Natural Relations: Ecology, Animal Rights and Social Justice* (London: Verso, 1993).

8. Barbara Noske, *Beyond Boundaries: Humans and Animals* (Montreal: Black Books, 1997).

9. For a discussion of this criticism, see Alasdair Cochrane, *An Introduction to Animals and Political Theory* (London: Palgrave McMillan, 2010).

10. John McDowell, "Values as Secondary Qualities", in *Morality and Objectivity*, ed. Ted Honderich (London: Routledge and Keegan Paul, 1985), 110–29; Stephen Bur-

wood, Kathleen Lennon and Paul Gilbert, *Philosophy of Mind* (London: University College London Press, 1998).

11. David Hume, "Affection of Humanity: The Foundation of Morals", in *Ethics*, ed. Peter Singer (Oxford: Oxford University Press, 1994).

12. See, for example, J. Baird Callicott, "Animal Liberation and Environmental Ethics: Back Together Again", in *The Animal Rights/ Environmental Ethics Debate: The Environmental Perspective*, ed. Eugene C. Hargrove (Albany: State University of New York Press, 1992).

Part I

Intrinsic Value and Moral Status: Rethinking Sentience

ONE

A Metalevel Problem for Animal Rights Theory

John Hadley

In this chapter I argue that a leading form of animal rights theory is vulnerable to a fundamental logical inconsistency. The inconsistency takes the form of the well-known "inconsistent triad" problem: three principles that appear sound in isolation, when combined in a single theory, are logically incompatible, thus rendering the theory as logically unstable. The three incompatible principles that are constitutive of the relevant form of animal rights theory are: the psychology or sentience principle (hereafter, the psychology principle); the same kind or equality principle (hereafter, the same kind principle) and the evolution or genomic plasticity principle (hereafter, the evolution principle).

For the purposes of the following analysis, by "animal rights theory" I mean to refer to theories in which particular moral "goods", such as utility-trumping rights or the principle of equal consideration of interests, are extended to nonhuman animals on the grounds of sentience or, strictly speaking, the possession of a psychology above a threshold level of complexity marked by sentience. Accordingly, the target animal rights theories are "naturalistic" theories — that is, they identify or analyse evaluative properties (intrinsic value, inherent value, moral considerability, etc.) as natural properties (specifically, psychology or sentience). Notable examples of animal rights theorists who presuppose metaethical naturalism and, if the argument to follow is sound, are vulnerable to the inconsistent triad problem include Peter Singer, Tom Regan, Gary Francione, David DeGrazia, Mark Rowlands, Julian H. Franklin, Evelyn Pluhar,

Gary Varner, Alasdair Cochrane, Robert Garner, Will Kymlicka—indeed, most animal rights theorists who write in the so-called analytic tradition.

Other nonpsychology-based theories—for example, life-ethic, biocentric or relational theories—may also extend rights or equal consideration to nonhuman animals, but these are not "animal rights theories" in the sense relevant for this analysis. For the purposes of this analysis, an animal rights theory is a sentience- or psychology-based theory. Moreover, insofar as a psychology-based theory of moral entitlements or status does not maintain a commitment to some version of the person-nonperson distinction or the equality of persons, it is also not an "animal rights theory" in the relevant sense. It is only because animal rights theories extend rights or equal consideration to animals on the grounds of sentience, while also maintaining the person-nonperson distinction and the equality of persons, that they are exposed to the triad problem. The person-nonperson distinction pits the psychology principle against the same kind principle, and the equality of persons pits the psychology principle against the evolution principle.

Below, I will briefly explain each principle and then show how important elements of the psychology principle, specifically, the person-nonperson distinction and the equality of persons, are at odds with the same kind principle and the evolution principle, respectively.

It is important to note that the inconsistent triad problem is a distinctly theoretical or metalevel problem pointing to the underlying logical structure of animal rights theory. This entails that it is not a viable response to the inconsistency charge to argue that, in comparison to rival nonpsychology-based theories of direct value or moral status, such as biocentric or life-ethic theories, animal rights theory is in good shape in terms of its conformance with commonsense intuitions about the normative significance of suffering and the moral status of persons and severely cognitively impaired human beings. The only viable response to an inconsistent triad problem is to abandon, or at least amend, one or more of the principles or related concepts so as to remove the incompatibility.

THE PSYCHOLOGY PRINCIPLE

> Direct value, moral considerability or moral status supervenes upon psychological complexity, irrespective of species.[1]

Whether expressed in terms of "intrinsic value", "inherent value", "noninstrumental value", "moral considerability", or "moral status", the kernel of animal rights theory is the idea that, ultimately, what matters and ought to entitle an individual to particular moral "goods" (utility-trumping rights, equal consideration of their interests, etc.) is sentience—that is, a threshold level of psychological complexity at which the individual is capable of experiencing pleasure and pain. For proponents of animal rights theory, psychological complexity is ordinarily explicated along "folk psychological" lines. Folk psychology is the network of common-sense or intuitive concepts and principles, chief among them beliefs and desires, used by normal people to make sense of the behaviour of other persons and, perhaps, the so-called higher animals.[2]

It is commonplace in philosophy of mind and animal ethics literature for the domain of folk psychology to be divided up between, on the one hand, cognitive or rationalist elements and, on the other hand, hedonistic or phenomenological elements.[3] Accordingly, while it might be acceptable, consistent with some proponents of animal rights theory, to say that the less psychologically complex animals have beliefs and desires pertaining to hedonistic aspects of their psychology—for example, an animal may desire to be relieved of pain and suffering—any further attribution of cognitive content to such animals is regarded as controversial.[4] Indeed, some proponents of animal rights theory refer to animal beliefs and desires as "proto" or "pseudo" beliefs or desires,[5] or they argue that animal beliefs lack forward-looking or reflexive content able to be explicated in propositional terms.[6] Proponents of animal rights theory reflect the purported difference in psychological complexity between human and nonhuman animals by maintaining a distinction between persons and nonpersons or, more commonly, moral agents and moral "patients".[7]

THE SAME KIND PRINCIPLE

> In virtue of having the same kind of psychology, human and sentient nonhuman animals ought to be grouped together, for ethical purposes, into the same kind, set, class, category, or group.

The same kind principle reflects the post-Darwin scientific orthodoxy that human beings and animals from other species have the same naturalistic origins. In a passage cited by almost every proponent of animal rights as having serious ethical implications,[8] Darwin unwittingly laid out the descriptive foundation for a theory of cross-species normative equality: "There can be no doubt that the difference between the mind of the lowest man and that of the highest animal is immense. . . . Nevertheless the difference in mind between man and the higher animals, great as it is, certainly is one of degree not kind".[9]

In line with Darwin's claim, proponents of animal rights theory hold that as the differences in psychological complexity between Homo sapiens and animals from other species are purportedly differences of degree not kind, as far as ethical theorizing is concerned there can be no naturalistic grounds for viewing humans and other animals as fundamentally different. Accordingly, the same kind principle is a normative principle about membership of a moral grouping or class and is not simply a descriptive claim about the scope of psychological complexity in the natural world. In other words, for proponents of animal rights theory, Darwin's claim stands as an implied act of moral categorization. This act of categorization is popularized in applied ethics literature as the idea of including animals within the "sphere of moral concern". Thus, animal rights theory, insofar as it takes its lead from Darwin, is at bottom an equalizing project; its rationale is to promote or reflect equality between all sentient ("directly valuable") individuals.

It is important to note that while the same kind principle implies a measure of equality between humans and other sentient animals, it does not entail radical egalitarianism or identical attributions of value or status across species boundaries within the morally significant grouping. As will become clear below, within animal rights theory there are distinct subgroupings within the group of directly valuable individuals.

THE INCONSISTENCY BETWEEN THE PSYCHOLOGY PRINCIPLE AND THE SAME KIND PRINCIPLE

For proponents of animal rights theory, a point exists along the psychological complexity continuum above which direct value ceases to vary (and moral status equalizes), and yet below which the distribution of value remains variable. In other words, in line with animal rights theory, direct value is a natural property that has both categorical and admit-of-degree manifestations.[10] This upshot of the psychology principle has been noted by some of its proponents as a potential source of embarrassment. McMahan, for example, concedes:

> If certain psychological capacities are to be the basis of a person's worth, it seems that the possession of those capacities to a markedly higher degree ought to give a person a higher degree of worth. The idea that there is a threshold beyond which worth ceases to vary with the capacities that are its basis may seem an arbitrary, ad hoc stipulation motivated entirely by a desire to salvage our egalitarian intuitions.[11]

While the invariance of direct value above a threshold level of complexity enables the long-standing norm of the moral equality of persons to be maintained within animal rights theory, it generates a tension with the same kind principle that jeopardizes the overall theoretical coherence of the theory. As is well known, personhood has long been associated with so-called higher-order psychological capacities, which have frequently been invoked as markers of fundamental differences between humans and other animals.[12] To use personhood capacities as a marker of distinct subgroupings within the morally significant group or class, however, calls into question the inclusion of the same kind principle within animal rights theory. Imagine a variant of Nozick's Experience

Machine.[13] Would we say that two individuals, a nonperson Fido and a person Susan, are members of the same kind on the basis of having the same kind of psychology, if life in the experience machine represents a good life for Fido but a poor life for Susan? In other words, if a good life for Fido was to be adjudged solely with reference to how his life "feels from the inside" but a good life for Susan required "actual contact with a deeper reality", then it would be reasonable to conclude that the degree of difference between their respective psychologies warrants locating them within altogether different kinds. To invoke a distinction I mentioned earlier between the cognitive and the phenomenological elements of folk psychology, it would be reasonable to say that Susan's psychology is best categorized as rationalist, while Fido's is best described as hedonist. What is needed to reflect the idea of "sameness of kind" and to render credible the claim that all sentient animals, human and nonhuman, are members of the same group or class is a conception of psychological complexity that meshes the hedonistic elements with the rationalist elements in a less strikingly demarcated way.

An objection from proponents of animal rights theory is that the differences between persons and nonpersons are not so great as to warrant placing each in different groupings. On this view, there is nothing inconsistent about having two individuals who have different psychologies within the same group or class. Two responses can be made to the objection: if the objector is talking about distinctions per se, then she is right. The mere fact that persons and nonpersons differ in terms of psychological complexity does not warrant that they should be regarded as members of different groups. Two buildings or two ladders can differ immensely in terms of tallness; yet both remain members of the kind "tall buildings" and "tall ladders", respectively. But if the differences between human and animal psychological complexity are explicated along folk psychological lines, then there is a danger that the appeal to sameness of *normative* grouping will ring hollow. The myriad ways in which the distinction between humans and animals is ordinarily invoked—persons versus nonpersons, agents versus patients, desires versus proto desires, desires versus preferences, and interest in continuing to live versus interest in avoiding pain—serve to reinforce axiological division. In other words, the claim that human and animal psychology can be a shared basis for value is undermined by a folk psychological vocabulary that readily draws attention to differences between human and animal mental states.

Ironically, most proponents of morally enfranchising animals *do* indeed draw sharp dividing lines through the class of psychologically complex animals, even while maintaining a steadfast commitment to the evaluative claim for cross-species equality that is implicit in the same kind principle. In utilitarian theory, for example, the greater psychological complexity and, by entailment, superior moral importance of persons over nonpersons is reflected in the distinction between the morality of killing and the morality of causing pain.[14] In his three-tier hierarchy of interests, Gary Varner likewise draws a line when he allows the categorical desires of persons to trump the noncategorical desires of nonpersons.[15] Similarly, Julian Franklin, in his treatment of so-called lifeboat cases,[16] and Mark Rowlands, in his analysis of the harm of death,[17] also draw demarcatory lines among the class of psychologically complex and, thereby, directly valuable beings. Finally, in his worse-off principle, Tom Regan enjoins that in cases of unavoidable killing we should kill a million nonpersons before we kill one person.[18]

These theorists may respond that we should not read too much about direct value or moral importance from what are logically distinct concepts or principles that find a place in only tangential elements of their theories. Indeed, theorists such as Peter Singer and James Rachels may argue that there is no concept sufficiently analogous to direct value that plays a role in their theories. A related objection is that an increase in psychological complexity marks a difference in interests, but this difference in interests does not entail a change in value or status. In line with this objection, perhaps it is logically coherent to argue that two individuals equal in direct value have differing status, or that two individuals with different interests have the same status.

But while the notion of direct value may play no *explicit* role in certain psychology-centred theories, it is reasonable to suggest that judgements about direct value are *implicit* in the theories when concepts such as "moral standing", "moral status" and "moral considerability" play a role in their theories in strongly analogous fashion to the functional role played by direct value in animal rights theory. After all, in Singer's utilitarian theory, for example, an individual is entitled to equal consideration if they are sentient. It makes sense to say, then, that an animal's entitlement to the moral "good" equal consideration supervenes upon psychological complexity. Similarly, in Regan's theory, an individual has *inherent* value if they possess the [folk] psychological capacities constitutive of what he refers to as the "subject-of-a-life" criterion.[19] But it is implausible to suggest that use of personhood capacities by some theorists to solve supposedly only tangential theoretical problems is not reflective of a broader axiological commitment, particularly considering that the "tangential" problems include hypothetical life and death cases. It is fair to say, then, that the orthodox approach in animal rights theory has been to include animals within the morally significant group or class, but then to locate them along with human nonpersons within a distinct subgroup with "second-class" status. In commenting on neo-Kantian theories that, analogously, employ higher and lower subgroupings, Arneson expresses the worry this way:

If the capacity for rational agency is a capacity that varies continuously in magnitude, one wonders how one picks out some threshold level of the capacity such that variations in rational agency capacity above the threshold do not generate corresponding differences in fundamental moral status. On the face of it, the Kantian account of rational agency is like an account of moral status that identifies height as the characteristic of living beings that determines their moral status, proclaims that tall is better than short, and identifies beings over six feet tall as the first-class citizens of the moral universe.[20]

Is there a problem with proponents of animal rights theory drawing sharp lines within the normative grouping of individuals who possess direct value? After all, if psychology is a sound basis for value, then the fact that animals are included at all is a significant improvement on anthropocentric theories that exclude animals altogether. The concern is that by marking out subgroups within the group of directly valuable individuals, and then using the subgroup device to resolve theoretical problems with the aim of bringing animal rights theory into line with intuitions, proponents of animal rights undermine the sense that animal rights theory is fundamentally an "equalizing" project that is meant to be consistent with the spirit of a normative claim implicit in Darwin's famous words. With an old time higher-lower psychological complexity hierarchy in place, animal rights theory does not represent a major progression from the pre-Darwinian era.

THE EVOLUTIONARY PRINCIPLE

The best explanation for evolutionary change via natural selection is genomic plasticity or "adaptive variation".

For many philosophers and evolutionary biologists, a cornerstone of evolutionary theory is adaptive variation—more specifically, the idea that evolutionary change via natural selection is driven by genomic plasticity.[21] Genomic plasticity, its adherents argue, explains two basic ideas of evolutionary theory: the mutability of species, and trait variation within distinct populations of the very same species.[22] Taken together, species mutability and trait variation serve to undermine metaphysical essentialism.[23] Metaphysical essentialism is the idea that natural kinds such as species have fixed essences—necessary and sufficient conditions—possessed by all and only members of the kind.[24] Okasha expresses the anti-essentialism entailed by adaptative variation:

[M]odern biology offers no grounds whatever for supposing that intraspecific variation is confined to some particular set of "accidental" traits, leaving an invariant shared essence. On the contrary, Darwinism leads us to expect variation with respect to all organismic traits, morphological, physiological, behavioural and genetic. For genetically based phenotypic variation is essential to the operation of natural selection. If selection is to cause a species to evolve adaptations, and eventually to evolve into different species, as Darwinian theory asserts, then there must be variation within the species for selection to operate on. Intra-specific variation with respect to all organismic traits, and thus the lack of species specific essences, is fundamental to the Darwinian explanation of organic diversity.[25]

Some may consider any attribution of the evolution principle to animal rights theory as controversial. But if attributing the evolution principle to animal rights theory is a misrepresentation, it is not because any proponents of animal rights theory have explicitly rejected the antiessentialism that, in line with the orthodoxy in Darwinian metaphysics,[26] I presuppose is a corollary of genomic plasticity; rather, the evolutionary principle might seem out of place in animal rights theory because, to date, proponents of the theory have not explicitly addressed the implications of Darwinian metaphysics for animal ethics. The relevant test for the reasonableness of any attribution of the evolution principle to animal rights theory ought to be not whether proponents of the theory explicitly mention genomic plasticity, but instead whether we can nonarbitrarily attribute the evolution principle to animal rights theory given the prominent place that naturalism and evolution occupy within analytic theories of animal rights.

Some might argue that it is open to proponents of animal rights theory to argue that ethical theorizing does not have to reflect genomic plasticity. But if animal rights theory floated free of Darwinian naturalism, two problems would arise: First, it would amount to aligning animal rights theory with outliers in the philosophy of biology, ostensibly for the sake of maintaining intuitions that proponents of animal rights themselves acknowledge are likely to be infected with species bias. Secondly, even though it may be possible to claim that without the evolution principle, animal rights theory is still consistent with the spirit (though perhaps not the letter) of Darwinian naturalism, given that they would be seen to be rejecting a contemporary Darwinian orthodoxy, the only option proponents of animal rights theory would have for demonstrating their Darwinian credentials would be rhetorical appeals to the same kind principle.

It might be objected that moral groupings like the class of all individuals who possess direct value, and morally significant natural groupings like the class of all individuals who are psychologically complex, are fundamentally different from the kinds that concern philosophers of biology. But if the philosophy of biology is not to guide us through the moral categorizations we make in response to the normative pull of psychological complexity, then what is the alternative? A possible answer is ethical theorizing without reference to biology but, as many proponents of animal rights have pointed out, the intuitions that guide our determinations of moral groupings are likely to be suspect vis-à-vis the scope of value in the natural world.

THE INCONSISTENCY BETWEEN THE PSYCHOLOGY PRINCIPLE AND THE EVOLUTION PRINCIPLE

In *Darwin's Dangerous Idea*, Daniel Dennett describes the theoretical implications of evolution as akin to a very corrosive acid: "[I]t eats through just about every traditional concept, and leaves in its wake a revolutionized world view, with most of the old landmarks still recognizable, but transformed in fundamental ways".[27] Dennett's point is that evolution (specifically, adaptive variation driven by genomic plasticity) will have profound implications for our understanding of moral concepts if, in reductive fashion, we identify value with descriptive properties like psychological complexity. Like an acid, evolution will act to erode the traditional ways of understanding moral concepts and principles and change the ways in which they can be meaningfully applied.

For animal rights theory, a reductive theory that identifies direct value or moral status with sentience or psychological complexity, the implication of adaptive variation is clear and striking: the purported equality of value above the threshold level of complexity marking the boundary between personhood and nonpersonhood is at odds with the basic mechanics of evolution. Simply put, the capacities upon which personhood and, in turn, direct value, purportedly supervene admit of degree above the threshold at which proponents of animal rights theory claim value is categorical. The implication is that while the *boundary* of the value-psychological complexity supervenience relation may faithfully reflect or be concordant with the distribution of psychological complexity in the natural world, the *internal dynamics* of the supervenience relation appears strikingly discordant with Darwinian naturalism.

A supporter of animal rights theory may object that theorists need some instrument for making finely tuned judgements about value or status, and thresholds or tiers are the ideal instrument. In line with the objection, thresholds and tiers allow us to paper over differences in complexity between groups and subgroups, thereby helping to address problems relating to vagueness. But while thresholds and tiers may be useful for delineating *between* groups and subgroups, the objection does not explain the purported stability of value above thresholds *within* groups or subgroups.

A possible response is to appeal to the function of thresholds and tiers. Not only do they help to delineate, but they also serve to economize. In the case of their place within animal rights theory, thresholds and tiers help to economize value attributions among the kind or group consisting of all sufficiently psychologically complex animals. In line with the objection, proponents of animal rights theory employ a threshold or tier in order to delineate between the self-conscious and the merely conscious or sentient. Thus, logically, the objection continues, value cannot vary above thresholds or tiers because variation within kinds or subkinds would undermine the economizing impact of the threshold employed to distinguish them. Accordingly, the supervenience relation does not need to be so finely tuned as to reflect variance in value above the threshold or tier delineating the subkind consisting of persons or self-conscious animals.

But such a conception of thresholds or tiers does not easily fit within a naturalistic account of world. A threshold, after all, marks a threshold level of X, where X stands for a noncategorical property that individuals can possess to a more or less degree such that it is meaningful to say they can be placed over or below a line of demarcation. Indeed, conceiving of thresholds in such a way accounts for why line drawing is such a fraught enterprise. In the absence of variations in value above thresholds, however, proponents of animal rights theory suggest that thresholds carve reality at radical breaks, and this implies that threshold determinations are not being made on grounds consistent with genomic plasticity.

It might be objected that the above analysis betrays a fundamental flaw. According to the objection, proponents of animal rights theory, indeed many ethicists, philosophers of mind, and ethologists have made a mistake interpreting Darwinism and have misconstrued the descriptive picture that follows from descent via natural selection. In line with this objection, it is simply wrong as a matter of descriptive fact to accept the orthodoxy and explicate psychological complexity in terms of a continuum of gradually increasing complexity. As two commentators recently put it:

> There is no single dimension of cognitive complexity along which all species can be arrayed. In different lineages, according to the specific developmental/metabolic/structural constraints existing within the lineage and according to the specific adaptive demands generated by the environment in which the lineage lives, natural selection builds different cognitive adaptations. The evolution of life is tree like and different branches of the tree can point in different directions, making it impossible to identify a single evolutionary ladder.[28]

But consistent with the purposes of this chapter, my intention has been not to defend animal rights theory but rather to offer a constructive critique after fairly explaining its basic tenets. Insofar as a picture of psychological complexity in terms of a continuum is a constitutive feature of animal rights theory, then it is reasonable to talk in terms of continuums and thresholds. Suffice to say also that if a continuum is, as a matter of fact, an inaccurate account of psychological complexity, then this will constitute a problem for the animal rights theory only to the extent that it renders the group- and subgroup-based classification system as redundant. It may be that for the purposes of descriptive and normative theorizing, groups and subgroups, although not thresholds, remain descriptively accurate, to say nothing of their explanatory usefulness in thinking about the supervenience of value upon psychology.

Why should it matter if in the course of ethical theorizing proponents of animal rights theory paper over descriptive features of the world and leave an ostensibly pre-Darwinian hierarchical axiological order intact? In other words, why does it matter if at the metalevel animal rights theory is logically inconsistent? If there is no requirement for ethical theory to trace descriptive features of the world, then floating free of nature is not in itself a problem. Proponents of animal rights theory, indeed proponents of any reductionist ethical theory that includes the equality of persons, can explain away the odd supervenience relation as a metaphysical quirk of moral categorization and the price to pay for bringing ontology into line with commonsense intuitions. But presumably philosophers who allow for value ascriptions to float free of reality cannot claim the virtue of having their judgements about value checked for partiality by an independent standard. One of the theoretical virtues of reduction is that the descriptive boundary acts as a check upon the exercise of unconscious biases during value ascriptions. As a number of proponents of animal rights theory have made plain, as social creatures our intuitions about the mindedness of other animals are bound to be shaped by our upbringings in societies in which animal exploitation is long-standing and omnipresent to the point of being mundane. Without affording substantial revision of pre-Darwinian axiological priorities, animal rights theory cannot yield theory that provides a template for reforming everyday valuing practices and norms. Suffice it to say also that a commitment to the value-conferring power of psychological complexity could also be called into question, if value attributions trace time-honoured human-centred boundaries at a time when best science indicates it should be more widely and randomly distributed in progressive fashion.

RESOLVING THE INCONSISTENCY

It was stated at the outset that because the inconsistent triad problem is a distinctly theoretical or metalevel problem, the only way to resolve the inconsistency is to replace or amend one, or more, of the incompatible principles. One option, therefore, would be to abandon the equality of persons and thereby reconcile the psychology principle with the evolution principle. But it is fair to say that dropping the equality of persons would be too high a price to pay for bringing animal rights theory strictly into line with nature, particularly considering that it is already starting from behind, so to speak, in terms of its conformance with commonsense intuitions.

Short of abandoning the equality of persons, another option would be to amend the psychology principle by changing how psychological complexity and personhood is analysed. For example, the orthodox folk psychological understanding of complexity could be dropped in favour of an alternative account that is consistent with both the same kind principle and the evolution principle. What might such an account look like?

One suggestion would draw upon artificial intelligence or computational models of mind and explicate psychological complexity in terms of information-processing capacities. Suitably constrained by an evolutionary account of mindedness, an information-processing story could be consistent with both the same kind principle and the evolution principle.[29] In line with an information-processing account of animal minds: just like human cognition, animal cognition involves structure and numerical processing and is explicable in terms of algorithms or laws of thought. An animal's sense of smell, vision, and hearing would all be explicated in terms of libraries of nonlinguistic symbols. Sensory stimuli from the environment would be catalogued cognitively and associated with the respective experiential "inputs", allowing the animal to build a set of rules for syntax (that predator will bite me—that prey will not, etc.). The syntax for the computations and the rules associated with them could then be expressed statistically. Any further elaboration than this would appeal, in typically Darwinian fashion, to the adaptiveness of particular design elements in response to environmental, including social, pressures.

A second approach could be to adopt what might be called a "minimal psychological theory". A minimal psychological theory would be an analysis of psychological complexity in distal evolutionary terms. Such an account would eschew mention of proximate folk psychological terms, such as *beliefs* and *desires*, which may have wide currency but also carry connotations at odds with the moral aspirations for cross-species equality implicit in animal rights theory; instead, the minimal account would stress commonalities between human and animal mental states in a manner that reflects common evolutionary origins. Nicholas Agar's recent conceptual analysis of life in terms of "representationally guided movement" goes part of the way towards illustrating what a minimal psychological theory might involve.[30] Starting with an evolutionary story about the development of the simplest organisms, Agar proceeds to array all living things on a spectrum in terms of their capacity to detect and respond to changes in the environment. The minimal psychological theory story would be faithful to Agar's account up to a point just prior to his analysis of representationally guided movement as "desire-like". At this point the minimal story would cease tracing Agar's theory and instead reiterate earlier "distal" parts of his narrative that served to reflect the common evolutionary origins of humans and animals from other species. Dennett alludes to the relative theoretical safety of explicating psychological complexity in distal terms:

> There haven't always been minds. We have minds, but we haven't existed forever. We evolved from beings with simpler minds (if minds they were), who evolved from beings with still simpler candidates for minds. And there was a time, four or five billion years ago, when there weren't minds at all, simple or complex—at least, not on this planet. Which innovations occurred in what order, and why? The major steps are clear, even if the details about dates and places are speculative. Once we've told that story, we will at least have a framework in which to try to place our quandaries.[31]

An obvious concern with approaches that eschew explicit reference to beliefs and desires, however, is that they will lack moral pull. Some may argue that if the psychology-value supervenience relation is explicated without familiar valuing notions like beliefs and desires taking centre stage, then theories of value will have little motivational impetus in the real world.[32] But while it is true that any alternative to folk psychology will be starting from behind insofar as its ability to resonate with people is concerned, a transitional phase to a new evaluative vocabulary might be a fair price to pay for having a theory that does not face the inconsistent triad problem. So long as evaluative vocabularies are not hardwired into us, there is reason to think that over time new terms that are part and parcel of alternative accounts will start to resonate with people.

CONCLUSION

The triad problem is not, strictly speaking, a problem only for animal rights theory but also for any theory that grounds value or status upon psychology while maintaining the person-nonperson distinction and/or the equality of persons. Thus, theories in which rights possession and interest consideration are based upon a level of psychological complexity above mere sentience, such as contractarian or agency-based theories, are also vulnerable to a logical incompatibility problem. For such theories, the equality of persons will be at odds with the evolution principle in precisely the same way that these principles conflict in animal rights theories.

While it is fair to say that the triad problem applies to most, if not all, theories that include the three principles, animal rights theories have been singled out here for two reasons: First, animal rights theory is frequently held up as the proper ethical response to the theory of evolution. By pointing out how even theorists who are most enthusiastic to have ethical theory reflect evolution nonetheless remain wedded to putatively "pre-Darwinian" theorizing, I was able to lay bare the triad problem in a more striking way than simply by pointing out that all psychology-based theories fall prey to it. Second, while I'm sufficiently familiar with nonanimal rights psychology-based theories to assuredly claim that they, too, are vulnerable to the charge of inconsistency, I am more familiar with the animal rights theories and, thus, more confident that the material presented above best illustrates the problem. Accordingly, it is in a spirit of constructive criticism and critical self-reflection, and with the sincere hope that animal rights theory will ultimately be strengthened by addressing the triad problem that this critique is put forward.

A number of other theorists have alluded to the problem that this chapter lays bare.[33] But it is one thing to charge proponents of animal rights theory with "perfectionism", "essentialism" or "latent anthropocentrism"; it is another to articulate why, without begging the question against the orthodox versions of the theory, such charges ought to be read as pejorative in the sense of pointing to a serious problem with the underlying theoretical structure. It is fair to say also that previous analyses have taken place at the normative level, or, in the case of Arneson's influential discussion of human equality,[34] have called into question just a single principle in the triad without discussing its implications for other theoretical elements. The shortcoming of previous analyses has meant that the central theoretical tension between key structural elements in nonanthropocentric value theories has remained opaque. The hope is that the above metalevel analysis highlighted the problem in a transparent way and thus allows for pinpointing the precise location of the logical incompatibility.

To conclude: in the above I have argued that animal rights theory has a serious logical problem with its underlying or metalevel theoretical structure. The problem takes the form of an inconsistent triad. An inconsistent triad problem is when three principles that appear sound in isolation are combined in a single theory and are shown to be incompatible. The above analysis suggests the incompatibility in animal rights theory is traceable to how proponents of animal rights conceptualize psychological complexity in a way that allows for the maintenance of the person-nonperson distinction and the equality of persons. The former undermines the claim by proponents of animal rights that for ethical purposes humans and animals from other species are members of the same kind or group. And the equality of persons calls into question the idea that animal rights theory is consistent with orthodox evolutionary theory.

NOTES

1. Direct value is value in virtue of what the individual is like—that is, in virtue of a particular capacity deemed to be the grounds for the attribution of utility-trumping rights or equal consideration of interests. Direct value stands in contrast to indirect value, which is value in virtue of being cared about by others or by being related to

them in some way. The distinction is also commonly referred to as between nonrelational value and relational value. Supervenience is a concept widely discussed in metaphysics, metaethics and philosophy of mind. The term *supervenience* is used to refer to the relationship between two sets of properties. This relationship is sometimes referred to as *reductive* or *reduction*, but supervenience is often used to denote a relationship between two sets of properties that is not reductive. In this chapter, the relevant properties are psychological properties, specifically, sentience or psychological complexity and evaluative properties—that is, direct value or moral status. Readers unfamiliar with the terminology can simply understand the term *supervenience* as the same phenomenon referred to in lay terms as "based upon" or "grounded upon".

2. Paul M. Churchland, "Folk Psychology (2)", in *A Companion to the Philosophy of Mind*, ed. Samuel Guttenplan (Oxford: Blackwell, 1995), 308–16.

3. Nicholas Agar, *Life's Intrinsic Value: Science, Ethics and Nature* (New York: Columbia University Press, 2001), 16.

4. Colin Allen and Michael Trestman, "Animal Consciousness", in *The Stanford Encyclopaedia of Philosophy* (Summer Edition), ed. E. N. Zalta, http://plato.stanford.edu/archives/sum2014/entries/consciousness-animal/, accessed 1 August 2014.

5. David DeGrazia, "Self-Awareness in Animals", in *The Philosophy of Animal Minds*, ed. Robert W. Lurz (Cambridge: Cambridge University Press, 2009), 201–17, 205.

6. Michael Tooley, *Abortion and Infanticide* (Oxford: Clarendon Press, 1983); Peter Carruthers, *The Animals Issue* (Cambridge: Cambridge University Press, 1992), 134.

7. Jeff McMahan, *The Ethics of Killing: Problems at the Margins of Life* (Oxford: Oxford University Press, 2004); Peter Singer, *Practical Ethics* (Cambridge: Cambridge University Press, 1993); Gary Varner, *In Nature's Interests? Interests, Animal Rights and Environmental Ethics* (Oxford: Oxford University Press, 1998); Tom Regan, *The Case for Animal Rights* (Berkeley: University of California Press, 1983). It is worth stressing the point about the target theories for this analysis: insofar as a theory does not draw distinctions between persons and nonpersons or, by corollary, human and nonhuman desires, then it is not an "animal rights theory" for the purposes of the analysis.

8. See Regan, *The Case for Animal Rights*, 18; James Rachels, *The Moral Implications of Darwinism* (Oxford: Oxford University Press, 1990), 57; Singer, *Practical Ethics*, 72.

9. Charles Darwin, *The Descent of Man* (London: Penguin Classics, 2004 [1871]), 150.

10. Two notable exceptions, arguably, are Tom Regan, *The Case for Animal Rights*, and Gary Francione, *Introduction to Animal Rights: Your Child or the Dog?* (Philadelphia: Temple University Press, 2000), who both argue that the property they refer to as "inherent value" is a thoroughgoing categorical property possessed by all bearers equally. I argue above that Regan's distinction between moral agents and moral patients, which Francione also adopts, is grounds for thinking that, contrary to their assertions, their key value concept does admit of degree. (For a related discussion of Regan's concept of inherent value, see Lilly-Marlene Russow, "Regan on Inherent Value", *Between the Species* 4 (1988): 46–54.) But note: even if we accept Regan's and Francione's claim that inherent value does not admit of degree, then their theories, like others that maintain the equality of persons, are at odds with the third principle in the triad, the evolution principle.

11. McMahan, *The Ethics of Killing*, 249.

12. Aristotle, "How Humans Differ from Other Creatures", in *Animal Rights and Human Obligations*, ed. Tom Regan and Peter Singer (Englewood Cliffs, NJ: Prentice-Hall, 1976), 53–55; Alasdair Cochrane, "Do Animals Have an Intrinsic Interest in Liberty?" *Political Studies* 57 (2009): 660–79, 667; Carruthers, *The Animals Issue*, chapter 6.

13. Robert Nozick, *Anarchy, State, and Utopia* (Oxford: Basic Books, 1974).

14. Singer, *Practical Ethics*, chapter 4.

15. Varner, *In Nature's Interests?*, 93–97.

16. Julian H. Franklin, *Animal Rights and Moral Philosophy* (New York: Columbia University Press, 2005), 105.

17. Mark Rowlands, *Animals Like Us* (Verso: London, 2002), 70–99.

18. Regan, *The Case for Animal Rights*, 327.

19. Ibid.

20. Richard Arneson, "What, if Anything, Renders All Humans Morally Equal?" in *Singer and His Critics*, ed. Dale Jamieson (Oxford: Blackwell), 103–28, 106–7.

21. Daniel C. Dennett, *Darwin's Dangerous Idea* (New York: Simon and Schuster, 1995); Richard Dawkins, *The Selfish Gene* (Oxford: Oxford University Press, 2006), 17.

22. Elliot Sober, "Evolution, Population Thinking and Essentialism", *Philosophy of Science* 47 (1980): 350–83; Philip Kitcher, "Giving Darwin His Due", in *The Cambridge Companion to Darwin*, ed. Jonathan Hodge and Gregory Radick (Cambridge: Cambridge University Press, 2009), 455–76.

23. Samir Okasha, "Darwinian Metaphysics: Species and the Question of Essentialism", *Synthese* 131 (2002): 191–213.

24. Elliott Sober, "Metaphysical and Epistemological Issues in Modern Darwinian Theory", in *The Cambridge Companion to Darwin*, ed. Jonathan Hodge and Gregory Radick (Cambridge: Cambridge University Press, 2009), 302–22, 309.

25. Okasha, "Darwinian Metaphysics", 197.

26. Okasha, "Darwinian Metaphysics"; Kitcher, "Giving Darwin His Due".

27. Dennett, *Darwin's Dangerous Idea*, 63.

28. M. Mameli and L. Bortolotti, "Animal Rights, Animal Minds and Human Mindreading", *Journal of Medical Ethics* 32 (2006): 84–89, 86.

29. See Daniel C. Dennett, *Content and Consciousness* (Oxon: Routledge, 2010 [1969]), chapter 3; Dennett, *Darwin's Dangerous Idea*, chapter 4. I would like to thank Bruce Long for assistance with explicating a computational theory of animal minds.

30. Nicholas Agar, *Life's Intrinsic Value*.

31. Daniel C. Dennett, *Kinds of Minds* (New York: Basic Books, 1996), 18.

32. Nicholas Agar, *Life's Intrinsic Value*, 62.

33. See Francione, *Introduction to Animal Rights*, 215, n.61; Val Plumwood, *Environmental Culture: The Ecological Crisis of Reason* (London: Routledge, 2002), chapter 5; Gary Steiner, *Animals and the Moral Community: Mental Life, Moral Status, and Kinship* (New York: Columbia University Press, 2009), chapter 4.

34. Arneson, "What, if Anything, Renders All Humans Morally Equal?"

TWO

Against Moral Intrinsicalism

Nicolas Delon

Human beings tend to treat the following animals quite inconsistently. Pet mice, lab mice, and "pest" mice enjoy wildly different treatments: at one end of the spectrum, mice are named, cherished, treated like friends or companions; in the middle, they are handled in batches and anonymously, yet carefully, cared for, and some of them named, before suffering and dying as experimental subjects; at the other end of the spectrum, mice are ignored, fended off, busted or destroyed. Most people also believe domesticated animals are entitled to our assistance in a much larger range of situations than animals in the wild; among the former, cattle is normally slaughtered and consumed, while many among Western people would consider eating pets as grossly immoral and tend to consider them like family. Finally, billions of sentient nonhumans are killed and experimented upon every year for food or research, while few of us, if any, recommend doing so on any sentient human being.[1]

Advocates of the moral status of nonhuman animals believe that at least some, if not all, of these practices are wrong, because these animals have similar *interests* in virtue of their physiological and psychological *capacities* to have various sorts of experience. But what are the relevant similarities between these animals that make it wrong to treat them differently? Aren't there any relevant differences that equally make it permissible to treat them differently aside from their capacities?

In this chapter I challenge a widespread, if tacit, assumption of animal ethics—namely, that the only properties of entities that matter to their moral status are intrinsic properties (typically psychological or cognitive capacities such as sentience or consciousness) that are independent of their context, species or relations. This view is sometimes called *moral individualism.*[2] The rejection of speciesism has long relied on the so-called Argument from Marginal Cases,[3] which points to the absence of intrinsic morally relevant differences between infants, comatose, senile or severely mentally impaired humans, on the one hand, and nonhuman animals with allegedly comparable capacities, on the other hand, to argue that our speciesist practices are inconsistent. Accordingly, relationships, arbitrary group memberships (gender, race, species, nations), and emotional or spatial distance have become unreliable moral standards.

Moral individualism, McMahan writes, "is a thesis about the justification of judgments concerning how individuals may be treated. The basic idea is that how an individual may be treated is determined, not by considering his group memberships, but by considering his own particular characteristics".[4] So construed, moral individualism has been taken for granted by most "animal rights" theorists—consequentialists,[5] rights theorists,[6] contractarians,[7] capabilities theorists[8]—in their search for *morally enfranchising characteristics*.

Disputes about the relevance of relations such as love and affection, or species membership, are actually as old as animal ethics. So-called "Singer-Regan theories" have long been opposed on this ground.[9] Indeed, many accounts of our obligations to animals have focused on, or made room for, some relationships.[10] For instance, Wittgensteinians and care ethicists have challenged moral individualism, whether or not they call it so, arguing instead for the importance of nonbiological ideas such as "fellow creatures",[11] "being human",[12] "an animal",[13] or "some mother's child".[14] Below, I will use the very concepts of mainstream animal ethics to undermine the default assumption that moral individualism lays bare.

Although these debates may seem well worn, capacities and relations have too often been understood as mutually exclusive, the notion of what counts as "morally arbitrary" too often taken for granted by moral individualists, and the relevance of relationships too loosely related to moral status by critics. My goal here is twofold: pinpointing the specific assumptions underlying the denial of morally relevant relationships and highlighting the compatibility of the latter with a genuine account of moral status. I will argue that, while it is true that some intrinsic capacities central to flourishing are fundamentally relevant, the principled exclusion of extrinsic properties (in virtue of their extrinsicness) is unwarranted, some relations are relevant to some obligations, and such obligations are a part of an animal's status. The argument rests on an analysis of moral status in terms of supervenience, final value and the connection between value and obligations. First, I further explain what moral individualism is. Then I spell out my analysis of moral status and address the assumption, which I will label *intrinsicalism*. The negative part of the argument, here, is that the assumption is not implied by the most plausible analysis of moral status. In the final section, I build a positive case for the relevance of extrinsic properties to moral status based on vulnerability and the reasonableness of partiality.

MORAL INDIVIDUALISM

The motivation for the focus on intrinsic properties is understandable. Consider Lori Gruen's apt reminder:

> Extrinsic considerations such as popularity, usefulness to others, political expediency, and social prejudice can be set aside. . . . No one should be denied the possibility of exercising their capacities and satisfying their interests simply because of inegalitarian social conventions or discriminatory traditions. These sorts of relational properties have a long history of being used to exclude members of "out" groups, and appeals to such relational properties have led to ethically unacceptable practices and policies.[15]

Moral individualism is a formal, or metanormative, rather than a substantive, thesis about our obligations. Basically, it is a requirement of impartiality across relevantly comparable individuals. It is based upon three central claims: (1) the moral status of an individual is a normative consideration for all agents; (2) moral status is an agent-neutral consideration; (3) extrinsic properties cannot be the basis for agent-neutral reasons. Hence, insofar as relations provide only agent-neutral reasons, they cannot ground moral status.

The notion of moral status is central to both animal ethics overall and moral individualism.[16] A "status-conferring intrinsic property", according to McMahan, is "a property that gives its possessor a moral status that is a source of 'agent-neutral' reasons".[17] Properties that qualify as status conferring may be sentience,[18] being a "subject-of-a-life",[19] variable sets of cognitive abilities,[20] central capabilities,[21] or, for those who tend to deny animals direct moral standing, higher-order consciousness,[22] language[23] and rational agency.[24]

While McMahan acknowledges that some special relationships (e.g., this child being's *my* child) may provide significant reasons,[25] such reasons, he claims, are merely agent-relative. Agent-neutral reasons, in contrast, arise from intrinsic properties and normally trump the former. He writes, "It is foundational to . . . moral individualism that . . . only intrinsic properties can be status-conferring and give rise to agent-neutral moral reasons".[26] Let me call *intrinsicalism* this "foundational" assumption of moral individualism. This assumption, I will argue, is not uncontroversial. For instance, Elizabeth Anderson writes that "[m]oral considerability is not an intrinsic property of any creature, nor is it supervenient on only its intrinsic properties, such as its capacities. It depends, deeply, on the kind of relations they [e.g., an individual with severe Alzheimer's] can have with us",[27] while Ronald Sandler remarks that "something might, owing to its particular history, be due gratitude and loyalty, whereas a like entity with a different history is not due these. Thus, morally considerable entities can have different (and multiple) types of moral status".[28] I want to build on these insights to strengthen and formalize the links between extrinsic properties and moral status.

Consider two animals with roughly comparable psychological capacities (say, the same levels of sentiency or cognitive capacities such as memory, self-awareness, empathy, etc.). Consider now that two such individuals have different relational properties insofar as they may serve different purposes, or be bonded to human agents through affection or proximity. The question is: Are some of those relational properties morally relevant too? According to proponents of moral individualism, the answer is no, and to think otherwise an agent must be confused by irrelevant factors such as species bias, economic profit, emotional bonds or other forms of cognitive or sociological biases. Thus, McMahan writes:

> A rough guide to what we owe to animals is this: we owe to them whatever kind of treatment we believe the severely retarded would be owed in virtue of their intrinsic natures by morally sensitive Martians. We should, in short, treat animals no worse than we believe severely retarded human beings with comparable capacities should be treated *by moral agents who are not specially related to them.*[29]

As Anderson writes, "In this individualistic framework individuals must earn entitlements on their own merits, independently of their membership in generally meritorious groups". In sum, biological comembership is morally *irrelevant* (species, gender, race), while nonbiological comembership is associative and accordingly either merely *agent-relative* (family, friends, fellow citizens) or morally *insignificant* (wealth, social or geographical origin, religion, sexual orientation).[30]

McMahan's view is typical of other proponents of moral individualism who do not defend the basic assumption that only intrinsic properties matter; instead, the significance of properties is invoked to argue against relational views. The very claim that intrinsic properties are what matters is never directly addressed. But it does not follow from the irrelevance of some relational properties that all relational properties are irrelevant to considerations of moral status. It may be that when the full gamut of relational properties are laid bare then there will be some that have a bearing upon moral status, that some extrinsic features of an individual are relevant to the individual herself, or to moral agents, in a fashion that affects moral status. I believe vulnerability is one such relational property, and that reasonable partiality provides another source of extrinsic value relevant to status, but before I proceed to argue for the relevance of such extrinsic properties, I need to posit some machinery.

MORAL STATUS DOES NOT IMPLY INTRINSICALISM

A common understanding of moral properties (e.g., value) is that they "supervene" on natural properties, such as the capacities of animals emphasized so far. According to a standard definition, *a class of properties B supervenes on a class A just when, necessarily, if x and y are A-indiscernible, they are B-indiscernible.* That is, *no B-difference without an A-difference.* Supervenient properties (e.g., mental, aesthetic, moral) are said to supervene on base properties (e.g., physical, natural). The supervenience relation provides a framework to illuminate standards of consistency and universalization in moral reasoning, whereby like individuals in relevant respects ought to be treated alike.

Importantly, the same relation can apply to supervenience on nonintrinsic properties. Suppose R is one (and the only) morally relevant relation among a given set of individuals:[31] *if x and y are indiscernible in respect of their one-place nonmoral properties, if x and y are discernible in respect of their moral properties, then they must be R-discernible.* It is compatible with the form of justification ("because") we expect when reasoning about moral differences. If that is correct, then taking account of relationships need not preclude the admittedly essential standards expressed by the supervenience relation.

Moral status is among the moral properties an entity can have. Morally considerable entities, writes Mark Bernstein, are those "toward whom moral behaviors can be intelligibly addressed".[32] But considerability is only a first step to determinate status. It is a threshold and range concept: it applies equally to all those that meet a given criterion above a given threshold. In a classic definition, Mary Ann Warren writes:

> To have moral status is to be morally considerable, or to have moral standing. It is to be an entity toward which moral agents have, or can have, moral obligations. If an entity has moral status, then we may not treat it in just any way we please; we are morally obliged to give weight in our deliberations to its needs, interests, or well-being. Furthermore, we are morally obliged to do this not merely because protecting it may benefit ourselves or other persons, but because its needs have moral importance in their own right.[33]

Three points are worth emphasizing. First, Warren is concerned with *direct* moral status, which entities have "in their own right" rather than in virtue of the status of other entities to which they may be related. For instance, a pig with direct moral status does not matter simply as a piece of livestock with instrumental value; he matters because he has needs and interests. Insofar as one is dealing with direct status, failing to perform one's duties wrongs the entity itself; duties are *owed to* the entity itself rather than to some other being with moral status or merely *with regard to* the entity (i.e., indirect duties). This is because only entities with "needs, interests, or well-being" (those for which things can go well or ill, better or worse, those which can be benefited or harmed) can have status. As Elizabeth Harman writes:

> A harm to a being "matters morally" just in case there is a reason not to perform any action that would cause the harm and the reason exists simply in virtue of its being a harm to that thing, and simply in virtue of the badness of the harm for that thing. A thing has moral status just in case harms to it matter morally.[34]

Following this account of moral harm, moral status derives from the importance of harms, which is a function of their *badness for the entity*. The moral individualist might then infer: an entity's status is strictly a function of its cognitive capacities. But note that this account does not rule out something's badness-for a being arising from nonintrinsic factors, such as the being's environment, relationships or others' expectations and attitudes. For instance, suppose our "nearest and dearest" give us stronger reasons than others; there may be corresponding claims that these individuals make on us. Thus, failing to meet their expectations is bad for them and makes them worse off in a distinctive way. Others do not have similar claims, and our failing to do unto them as we ought to do unto others is a different sort of harm. I will revert to such cases later. If they are plausible, then Harman's conditions for moral harms remain compatible with a broader basis for status.

Second, Warren conceives of moral status as "a tool", "a means of specifying those entities towards which we believe ourselves to have moral obligations, as well as something of what we take those obligations to be".[35] Moral status is not so much *world guided* (a reflection of entities' natures) as *action guiding* (constraining our responses to their natures). Moral status, in other words, has a *function*. It provides agents with reasons for action. It has this function insofar as it works as a placeholder, covering the bundle of our obligations towards its bearer.[36] When considering a given entity, it ought to be sufficiently clear that its status affords reasons to treat it in certain ways rather than others. It ought to be a salient component of a pig's status that, and why, kicking him in the head, beating him with an iron stick, castrating him without anesthesia as a piglet, or not providing for his complex social needs harm him. And it ought to be at least epistemically accessible to the agent why this is so — because the pig is sentient, has a complex emotional life, flourishes in a complex social environment, revels in play, foraging, mud cooling, and so on. It ought to be clear, in other words, that the pig has his status in virtue of *his* characteristics.

Third, moral status has a specific axiological underpinning. If something has status, then it is meaningful to say that it is valuable, and the way we value something that has status is, typically, in Kantian terms, as an end rather than as a mere means. Final valuing is thus built into the concept of moral status, as opposed to instrumental valuing. This difference parallels, to some extent, the difference between direct and indirect moral status. Hence, I believe, moral status implies final value.[37] The phrase *in their own right* in Warren's definition is a mark of final value. When we perform our duties directly to the pig, because he has moral status, we take him into account "for his own sake" — not instrumentally or for the sake of anything else. As Warren notes, something cannot have direct moral status if it matters *only* because the way we treat it affects another entity's well-being, or because we value something external, to whose value it contributes. For instance, breaking a vase harms the owner, not the vase, whereas kicking a pig harms the pig, not only or primarily his owner.

Final value is (1) *nonderivative* (i.e., not derived from the value of something else) and (2) *noncontributory* (i.e., its bearer is not valuable merely as a part of a valuable whole). (1) A finally valued object is therefore the primary bearer of value, from which other objects derive their secondary (that is, instrumental) value. For instance, the value of a tool derives from the value of what it helps one achieve; the value of a biological species, from an "animal rights" perspective, derives from the value of its individual members. (2) Animal rights theorists, broadly construed, believe animals are not valuable merely in virtue of the species they belong to, while environmentalists typically believe natural wholes have final value, to which individual parts contribute.

Final value can apply to a variety of objects: human and nonhuman animals, natural wholes, biological species, artworks, monuments. However, writing on the concept of moral status, Frances Kamm marks a distinction between entities counting *in their own right* (e.g., a painting) and those *for whose sake* (i.e., welfare) we can act (e.g., a bird).[38] And having a sake seems required for having moral status in the relevant sense, even though morality also pertains to things and acts that are finally valuable but lack moral status. Artworks, monuments, precious artefacts and natural wholes can count noninstrumentally, but they cannot be harmed; rather, they can be hurt, damaged, destroyed, or caused to disappear.[39] Nothing is owed *to* Leonardo's *Mona Lisa*, the Parthenon, or the Grand Canyon, even though we ought, plausibly, not to treat them as mere means or dispensable commodities.

The latter distinction is important because it is highly plausible that final value can supervene on extrinsic properties (being rare or precious, having a historical or symbolic role),[40] including the value of natural entities such as rare specimens, endangered or fragile species or ecosystems, unique landscapes, forests or canyons.[41] If final value implied moral status, my claim would be easily supported: entities whose value supervenes at least in part on their extrinsic properties would have moral status. And provided, as is likely, that moral status and final value depend on the same properties, such entities would also have moral status based on their extrinsic properties. However, final value does *not* imply moral status, and I still need to substantiate the claim that they both depend on the same properties among a given entity's properties.

The first step in the argument is: final value can supervene on extrinsic properties. Concrete objects or events can have final value in virtue of their uniqueness, rarity or history, such as athletic records, biological species, landscapes or ecosystems, national monuments, artworks, precious artefacts, delicacies, and more. But this is also true of some entities that qualify for moral status. People (e.g., friends, lovers, children) and other animals (pets, certain zoo, lab, work or wild specimens) can have special final value in virtue of special relationships to valuers (shared history or commitments, being unique, parental or other special responsibilities). That is, final value can supervene on properties that two intrinsically similar entities, or duplicates, need not share. Now, there remains to be shown that their moral status depends on such properties.

First, note that this special sort of value certainly provides some agents with additional reasons and likely generates additional duties of care and assistance. Yet moral individualists would remark, such reasons and duties are merely agent-relative—that is, they bind only the participants in the relationships. My cat makes stronger claims on me than other cats and on other people. If my cat has moral status, then the specific responses and attitudes (e.g., care) that her value warrants and calls for are based on precisely those features of hers on which my obligations to her are based. Thus, I finally value my cat in a distinctive way in virtue of the features that entitle her to specific treatment. These features may include: her being my *cat*, the fact that I rescued and adopted her, my responsibility in her present situation, her dependency, and so on.

Even responding appropriately to specially finally valuable things such as a painting of Vermeer's or the California redwoods—the value of which is based in part on the fact that such things are not related to the world like intrinsically similar things—involves the recognition of significant *agent-neutral* constraints against damaging, destroying or replacing them for the sake of other things. And these constraints stem from the relational properties of those things. With respect to such entities, therefore, valuing comes closely tied with *actions* required by the properties that ground value (rarity, uniqueness, wildness, naturalness, history, etc.).

When it comes to the special final value of my cat or my child, however, more fine-tuning is required to show that such value leads to special status in the agent-neutral sense. For one thing, reasons not to harm any child are surely agent-neutral, but they are also independent of a child's relational properties; on the other hand, *our own* children yield mainly agent-relative reasons, as remarked above. Still, overlooked by the moral individualist is the fact that any parent's ability to provide for her children critically depends on a wider context of institutions, schools, health care, family and social support and, crucially, anybody's and society's recognition that parents are allowed and obliged to care first and foremost for their children's essential needs. Hence, on the top of agent-relative constraints, special relationships generate agent-neutral, second-order reasons to enable people to act upon their reasonable agent-relative reasons. Now, the obligations that relate to these reasons are not merely owed to the ones taking care—they are also owed to the ones cared for. The next section will elaborate on this claim.

MORAL STATUS, PARTIALITY AND VULNERABILITY

Moral status has an irreducibly relational component but still involves agent-neutral considerations. Thus, my view differs, on the one hand, from purely relational, contractarian accounts of status according to which status can, in principle, be reduced to any given pair of individuals bound by possibly asymmetrical moral considerations, such as my friend's status *to me*.[42] On the other hand, it differs from individualist views according to which relationships cannot bear on moral status since they are merely agent-relative. Finally, my view is not simply that relationships matter in addition to, or instead of, moral status based on capacities; I show how moral status breaks down into two distinct but possibly interacting components. And now for the positive argument.

Agent-neutral reasons for status based on extrinsic properties, I believe, have two main sources: (1) the "reasonable" character of partiality and special relationships; (2) vulnerability. First consider "reasonable partiality". This is the view that agents may appeal to agent-relative "restrictions" and "prerogatives"[43] or are allowed to give priority to their own good, or the good of their "near and dear". Special relationships such as love, friendship, family, and expectations generated by shared commitments and projects can ground partiality, the reasonableness of which is grounded in the contribution of special relationships to the flourishing of all those who partake in them. This much has been widely acknowledged by a variety of authors,[44] including with respect to pet keeping and domesticated animals overall.[45] Even consequentialists have acknowledged indirect, impartiality-based reasons to allow for a degree of partiality in human undertakings and cares so as to address the "nearest and dearest" objection, and to the extent that partiality has optimal consequences overall.[46] To my knowledge, however, no one has noticed how such considerations bear on direct moral status, as analysed in this chapter, and emphasized the relevance of extrinsic final value.

Regarding pets, an indirect case for partiality can be rested on maximizing utility: absolute impartiality would require people to give up on some of their most significant commitments and attachments, deprive them of valuable experiences, and, at least until extinction, make millions of animals worse off than they would be under the practice of pet keeping. This is, in a nutshell, what motivates the consequentialist response to the "nearest and dearest" objection. But the case can also be made on the basis of direct considerations. Insofar as reasonable partiality is justified, pets provide their caretakers with agent-relative reasons to care for them more than they care for *other* animals. But the final value of the pet to her related caretaker is justified precisely in virtue of the fact that the relationship instantiates a finally valuable aspect of human and nonhuman lives. My cat and I—or cats and people in general—can benefit from the multispecies community they give rise to,[47] with all the particular features of each relationship (uniqueness, shared history, past commitments) resonating in a distinctive way with the general features of the typical pet-human relationship. Insofar as caretakers have special obligations to their pets, and as anyone has some obligations not to disregard, impede, or interfere with the relationships giving rise to them, the caretaker's failure to specially care for her pet *wrongs* the pet—which anyone ought to recognize and has reasons to prevent, or at least regret or blame.

Finally, note that reasonableness is essential. For radical partiality would allow one to discount an animal's status according to morally irrelevant factors such as disgust, comfort or self-interest. For instance, being a "pest" is a relational property, but intrinsic capacities matter too. In hard cases, conflicts of interest must be settled with due consideration of all relevant factors, not just one's negative partiality towards certain groups.

Consider now the concept of vulnerability. One explanation for the special wrongness of harming certain beings lies in the extrinsic disposition of vulnerability. Children and domesticated animals plausibly have different rights than their adult or wild counterparts, respectively, either because of a lesser degree of autonomy (regarding, for example, voting) or as a means of protection (regarding, for example, driving), though the diminished capacities that account for this fact also account for the increased protection they deserve when children or domesticated animals cannot fend for themselves. The special status of children and domesticated animals is therefore based on both *intrinsic* properties (their actual capacities) and *extrinsic* properties (vulnerability, dependency).

To be vulnerable means to be able to be harmed in a certain context. Jennifer McKitrick has convincingly shown that dispositions are not necessarily intrinsic.[48] Among examples of extrinsic dispositions, she cites weight, visibility or vulnerability. An intrinsic disposition is shared by perfect duplicates (e.g., the fragility of a vase, grounded in its internal physical properties), and its *manifestation* (breaking) depends on given *circumstances* (e.g., being struck), whereas an extrinsic disposition is not shared by perfect duplicates since the circumstances of its manifestation can vary if the environment changes (e.g., disability or vulnerability are a function of how context allows individuals to achieve some of their goals or avoid being harmed). Importantly, vulnerability is a central feature of most domesticated animals, especially farm and research animals that have been specifically designed to remain dependent and sometimes vulnerable to specific harms (e.g., cancer for the infamous Harvard Oncomouse).[49] More straightforwardly than partiality, vulnerability generates agent-neutral reasons to protect the vulnerable. Protection is owed directly to them—that is, the corresponding obligation is based on extrinsic properties. Hence, at least part of their moral status depends on their extrinsic properties. Plus, insofar as attending to vulnerability implies special care and related attitudes, it implies recognition of a special kind of value: vulnerable beings, unlike intrinsic duplicates, are those by the sake of which our protection ought to be directed. Again, there is an internal relation between valuing and acting as status requires, which shows that wherever there is moral status and special final value, there is *special moral status*, since value and status depend on the same properties. More accurately, value supervenes on an entity's morally relevant properties, including sometimes her extrinsic properties, and determines the kind of status that it has in virtue of those very properties.

CONCLUSION

Moral status, I pointed out at the onset, is not the whole truth about moral obligations. Warren writes:

> Many of our obligations are based not only upon the moral status of those towards whom we are obliged, but also upon situational factors, such as a promise we have made, a personal relationship in which we are involved, a civil or criminal law that has been justly enacted, or a wrongful past action of our own that requires restitution or compensation.[50]

As I showed, however, obligations are not strictly speaking "based upon" status; status *consists in* certain obligations. And obligations based on personal relationships are among such obligations insofar as they bind agents beyond those involved in such relationships.

From widely shared starting points, I explicated moral status in terms of supervenience, final value and direct obligations; then I linked the possibility of extrinsic, or special, final value with moral status to show that the latter can depend on extrinsic properties; finally, I offered two sorts of relational properties on which special final value supervenes, which in turns determines special status. In sum, animals to which we are specially related have a twofold special status: one is agent-neutral (vulnerability), another is agent-relative but binds all agents in an agent-neutral way (partiality).[51] This status consists in duties directly owed to the animal, and each of its aspects is based on an extrinsic property on which a distinctive final value supervenes. *Contra* moral individualism, some extrinsic properties give rise to agent-neutral reasons. Following a plausible analysis of moral status, such reasons bear on moral status. Hence, moral status is not a mere function of capacities, along with separate, additional obligations; instead, moral status is best understood as a (variable) set of obligations depending on capacities *and* context, yet binding agent-neutrally, thus meeting both requirements of relational accounts and those of impartiality (captured by the idea of the supervenience of final value on extrinsic properties).

At the beginning of the third section above, I claimed that the intrinsic and extrinsic components of moral status possibly interact. By this I mean two things: first, capacities affect what relationships one can take part in, or what harms one is vulnerable to; second, that which morally relevant capacities typically support—for example, needs and expectations—can also be affected (e.g., strengthened) by context (e.g., domestication). This dual-source status is therefore compatible with impartiality since intrinsically comparable animals can still have different expectations and interests depending on context.

NOTES

1. The inconsistencies of our current practices and attitudes are nicely described by Harold A. Herzog, *Some We Love, Some We Hate, Some We Eat: Why It's So Hard to Think Straight About Animals* (New York: Harper, 2010).

2. The label was coined and championed by James Rachels and more recently defended by Jeff McMahan. See James Rachels, *Created from Animals: The Moral Implications of Darwinism* (Oxford and New York: Oxford University Press, 1990); Jeff McMahan, "'Our Fellow Creatures'", *Journal of Ethics* 9, no. 3–4 (2005): 353–80. This view, however, is central to much of mainstream animal ethics.

3. For a specific use of the argument to deny morally relevant cross-species differences in our treatment of nonhumans, see Peter Singer, *Animal Liberation: A New Ethics for Our Treatment of Animals* (New York: Random House, 1990).

4. McMahan, "'Our Fellow Creatures'", 335.

5. Singer, *Animal Liberation*; Rachels, *Created from Animals*; Jeff McMahan, *The Ethics of Killing: Problems at the Margins of Life* (Oxford and New York: Oxford University Press, 2002); Alastair Norcross, "Puppies, Pigs, and People: Eating Meat and Marginal Cases", *Philosophical Perspectives* 18, no. 1 (2004): 229–45.

6. Tom Regan, *The Case for Animal Rights* (Berkeley: University of California Press, 1983); Gary L. Francione, *Introduction to Animal Rights: Your Child or the Dog?* (Philadelphia: Temple University Press, 2000).

7. Mark H. Bernstein, *On Moral Considerability: An Essay on Who Morally Matters* (Oxford: Oxford University Press, 1998); Mark Rowlands, *Animal Rights: Moral Theory and Practice*, 2nd ed. (New York: Palgrave Macmillan, 2009).

8. Martha Craven Nussbaum, *Frontiers of Justice: Disability, Nationality, Species Membership*, The Tanner Lectures on Human Values (Cambridge, MA: The Belknap Press, 2006). Nussbaum's view is actually ambiguous: she argues against Rachels's moral individualism for the relevance of a "Species Norm", but her focus on species-specific capabilities does not carry over to other extrinsic properties such as social context and membership. Whether her view qualifies as intrinsicalist depends on whether species norms are intrinsic or extrinsic.

9. Cora Diamond, "Eating Meat and Eating People", *Philosophy* 53, no. 206 (1978): 465–79.

10. See, for example, Mary Anne Warren, *Moral Status: Obligations to Persons and Other Living Things*, Issues in Biomedical Ethics (Oxford and New York: Oxford University Press, 1997); Elizabeth Anderson, "Animal Rights and the Values of Nonhuman Life", in *Animal Rights: Current Debates and New Directions*, ed. C. R. Sunstein and M. C. Nussbaum (Oxford and New York: Oxford University Press, 2004), 277–98; Elisa Aaltola, "Animal Ethics and Interest Conflicts", *Ethics & the Environment* 10, no. 1 (2005): 19–48; Josephine Donovan and Carol J. Adams, *The Feminist Care Tradition in Animal Ethics: A Reader* (New York: Columbia University Press, 2007); Clare Palmer, *Animal Ethics in Context* (New York: Columbia University Press, 2010); Sue Donaldson and Will Kymlicka, *Zoopolis: A Political Theory of Animal Rights* (Oxford: Oxford University Press, 2011).

11. Diamond, "Eating Meat and Eating People"; Raimond Gaita, *A Common Humanity* (London: Routledge, 2000); Alice Crary, "Humans, Animals, Right and Wrong", in *Wittgenstein and the Moral Life: Essays in Honor of Cora Diamond*, ed. Alice Crary (Cambridge, MA: MIT Press, 2007), 381–404; "Minding What Already Matters: A Critique of Moral Individualism", *Philosophical Topics* 38, no. 1 (2010): 17–49.

12. Cora Diamond, "The Importance of Being Human", *Royal Institute of Philosophy Supplement* 29 (1991): 35–62.

13. Crary, "Minding What Already Matters".

14. Eva Feder Kittay, "At the Margins of Moral Personhood", *Ethics* 116, no. 1 (2005): 100–131.

15. Lori Gruen, *Ethics and Animals* (Cambridge: Cambridge University Press, 2009), 66.

16. Rachels, however, suggests we might dispense with the notion, which is redundant, cumbersome, or inaccurate: assessing precisely what treatment a given individual is entitled to in virtue of its own characteristics is done by considering the latter rather than its species-specific status, though talk of moral status can be convenient "for purposes of public policy". See James Rachels, "Drawing Lines", in *Animal Rights: Current Debates and New Directions*, ed. C. R. Sunstein and M. C. Nussbaum (Oxford and New York: Oxford University Press, 2004), 170–3. Here Rachels seems to me to be hinting at R. M. Hare's two levels of moral reflection: "critical", on the one hand, and "intuitive", on the other hand. See Richard M. Hare, *Moral Thinking: Its Levels, Method, and Point* (Oxford: Oxford University Press, 1981).

17. McMahan, "'Our Fellow Creatures'", 355.

18. Singer, *Animal Liberation*; Steven F. Sapontzis, *Morals, Reason, and Animals* (Philadelphia: Temple University Press, 1987); Francione, *Introduction to Animal Rights*.

19. Regan, *The Case for Animal Rights*.

20. David DeGrazia, *Taking Animals Seriously: Mental Life and Moral Status* (Cambridge: Cambridge University Press, 1996).

21. Nussbaum, *Frontiers of Justice*.

22. Peter Carruthers, *The Animals Issue: Moral Theory in Practice* (Cambridge: Cambridge University Press, 1992).

23. R. G. Frey, *Interests and Rights: The Case against Animals* (Oxford: Oxford University Press, 1980); Michael Leahy, *Against Liberation: Putting Animals in Perspective* (New York: Routledge, 1991).

24. John Rawls, *A Theory of Justice* (Cambridge, MA: Harvard University Press, 1971), §77; Jan Narveson, "Animal Rights", *Canadian Journal of Philosophy* 7, no. 1 (1977): 161–78.

25. McMahan, *The Ethics of Killing*, 231–2; "'Our Fellow Creatures'", 354.

26. "'Our Fellow Creatures'", 357.

27. Anderson, "Animal Rights and the Values of Nonhuman Life", 289.

28. Ronald L. Sandler, "Enhancing Moral Status", *On the Human*, 23 May 2011, http://onthehuman.org/2011/05/enhancing-moral-status/, accessed 25 July 2014.

29. McMahan, *The Ethics of Killing*, 227. My emphasis.

30. Anderson, "Animal Rights and the Values of Nonhuman Life", 281.

31. Relational properties can be intrinsic (e.g., part/whole relations), but here "relational" is always nonintrinsic.

32. Bernstein, *On Moral Considerability*, 9.

33. Warren, *Moral Status*, 3.

34. Elizabeth Harman, "The Potentiality Problem", *Philosophical Studies* 114, no. 1–2 (2003): 173.

35. Warren, *Moral Status*, 9.

36. Also see David DeGrazia, "Moral Status as a Matter of Degree?", *Southern Journal of Philosophy* 46, no. 2 (2008): 181–98; Christopher W. Morris, "The Idea of Moral Standing", in *The Oxford Handbook of Animal Ethics*, ed. Tom L. Beauchamp and R. G. Frey (Oxford: Oxford University Press, 2011), 255–75.

37. This feature is stressed, for instance, in Frances M. Kamm, *Intricate Ethics: Rights, Responsibilities, and Permissible Harm* (New York: Oxford University Press, 2007), 227–36; Morris, "The Idea of Moral Standing"; Agnieszka Jaworska, "Caring and Full Moral Standing", *Ethics* 117, no. 3 (2007).

38. Kamm, *Intricate Ethics*, 28.

39. This claim is more controversial with respect to natural entities such as species and ecosystems, depending on one's value perspective (i.e., ecocentric, biocentric, zoocentric). Environmentalists believe such entities can be harmed in a genuine sense. Indeed, they believe the value of individuals derives from the value of those wholes.

40. Christine M. Korsgaard, "Two Distinctions in Goodness", in *Creating the Kingdom of Ends* (Cambridge: Cambridge University Press, 1996), 249–74; Wlodek Rabinowicz and Toni Rønnow-Rasmussen, "A Distinction in Value: Intrinsic and for Its Own Sake", *Proceedings of the Aristotelian Society* 100, no. 1 (2000): 33–51; Shelly Kagan, "Rethinking Intrinsic Value", *Journal of Ethics* 2, no. 4 (1998): 277–97; Jonas Olson, "Intrinsicalism and Conditionalism About Final Value", *Ethical Theory and Moral Practice* 7 (2004): 31–52.

41. The *locus classicus* is John O'Neill, "The Varieties of Intrinsic Value", *The Monist* 75 (1992): 119–37. Also see Dale Jamieson, "Animal Liberation Is an Environmental Ethic" and "Values in Nature" in *Morality's Progress: Essays on Humans, Other Animals, and the Rest of Nature* (New York: Oxford University Press, 2002).

42. Christopher W. Morris, "Moral Standing and Rational-Choice Contractarianism", in *Contractarianism and Rational Choice: Essays on David Gauthier's "Morals by Agreement"*, ed. Peter Vallentyne (Cambridge: Cambridge University Press, 1991), 76–95; Andrew I. Cohen, "Contractarianism, Other-Regarding Attitudes, and the Moral Standing of Nonhuman Animals", *Journal of Applied Philosophy* 24, no. 2 (2007): 188–201.

43. Samuel Scheffler, *The Rejection of Consequentialism* (New York: Oxford University Press, 1982).

44. See Michael Stocker, "The Schizophrenia of Modern Ethical Theories", *Journal of Philosophy* 73, no. 14 (1976): 453–66; John Cottingham, "Partiality, Favouritism and Morality", *The Philosophical Quarterly* 36, no. 144 (1986): 357–73; Thomas Nagel, *Equality and Partiality* (Oxford: Oxford University Press, 1991); Susan Wolf, "Morality and Partiality", *Philosophical Perspectives* 6 (1992): 243–59; Samuel Scheffler, *Boundaries and Allegiances* (Oxford: Oxford University Press, 2001); Niko Kolodny, "Which Relationships Justify Partiality? General Considerations and Problem Cases", in *Partiality and Impartiality: Morality, Special Relationships and the Wider World*, ed. Brian Feltham and John Cottingham (Oxford: Oxford University Press, 2010), 169–93.

45. Keith Burgess-Jackson, "Doing Right by Our Animal Companions", *Journal of Ethics* 2, no. 2 (1998): 159–85; Robert Heeger, "Reasonable Partiality to Domestic Animals", *Ethical Theory and Moral Practice* 8, no. 1–2 (2005): 123–39; Bernard E. Rollin, "Reasonable Partiality and Animal Ethics", *Ethical Theory and Moral Practice* 8, no. 1–2 (2005): 105–21; Tony Milligan, "Dependent Companions", *Journal of Applied Philosophy* 26, no. 4 (2009): 402–13; Steve Cooke, "Companion Animals", *Res Publica* 17 (2011): 261–74.

46. Hare, *Moral Thinking*; Peter Railton, "Alienation, Consequentialism, and the Demands of Morality", *Philosophy & Public Affairs* 13, no. 2 (1984): 134–71; Frank Jackson, "Decision-Theoretic Consequentialism and the Nearest and Dearest Objection", *Ethics* 101, no. 3 (1991): 461–82; Brad Hooker, *Ideal Code, Real World: A Rule-Consequentialist Theory of Morality* (Oxford: Clarendon Press, 2002), 126–41.

47. Note that my argument generalizes over individual and collective relations.

48. Jennifer McKitrick, "The Case for Extrinsic Dispositions", *Australasian Journal of Philosophy* 81, no. 2 (2003): 155–74.

49. For a general theory of vulnerability as a context-dependent disposition to be harmed, see Robert E. Goodin, *Protecting the Vulnerable: A Reanalysis of Our Social Responsibilities* (Chicago: Chicago University Press, 1985). For two philosophical accounts of vulnerability/dependency-based obligations towards animals, see Palmer, *Animal Ethics in Context*, and Donaldson and Kymlicka, *Zoopolis*. For a sociological account of vulnerability, see Leslie Irvine, *Filling the Ark: Animal Welfare in Disasters* (Philadelphia, PA: Temple University Press, 2009). For an anthropological account of domestication and the creation of dependency, see Tim Ingold, "From Trust to Domination: An Alternative History of Human-Animal Relations", in *Animals and Human Society: Changing Perspectives*, ed. A. Manning and J. Serpell (London: Routledge, 1994), 1–22; and Juliet Clutton-Brock, *A Natural History of Domesticated Mammals* (Cambridge: Cambridge University Press, 1999).

50. Warren, *Moral Status*, 9.

51. Kittay claims that parents or caretakers should be entitled to the whole community's help and care to provide for their disabled children. But she has a fully relational analysis of status and avoids relying on properties to ground status. See Eva Feder Kittay, "The Personal Is Philosophical Is Political: A Philosopher and Mother of a Cognitively Disabled Person Sends Notes from the Battlefield", *Metaphilosophy* 40, no. 3–4 (2009): 606–27.

THREE

Beyond Sentience

Biosemiotics as Foundation for Animal and Environmental Ethics

Morten Tønnessen and Jonathan Beever

In this chapter we argue that biosemiotics can be framed to serve as a foundation for animal ethics, particularly with regard to justifying attribution of moral status to nonhumans. Further, this biosemiotic approach can help us better understand value relationships in the wider context of environmental ethics. Our contribution rests on the contemporary semiotic interpretation of the *Umwelt* theory[1] of Baltic-German biologist Jakob von Uexküll (1864–1944), one of the founding fathers of ethology whose influence on biosemiotic theory cannot be overstated.[2] The resulting approach, biosemiotic particularism, problematizes contemporary sentience-based accounts of moral relevance in important ways and opens the door to a reconsideration of the scope and justification of moral considerability.

BIOSEMIOTICS

The developing interdisciplinary theories of biosemiotics are driven by what neurolinguist Don Favareau calls "the primordial scientific question: *'What is the relation between mental experience, biological organization, and the law-like processes of inanimate matter?'*"[3] Functionally, biosemiotics is an approach to biology that considers living organisms in terms of semiosis, or sign exchange. Favareau defines biosemiotics as "the study of the myriad forms of communication and signification observable both within and between living systems. It is thus the study of representation, meaning, sense, and the biological significance of *sign processes*—from intercellular signaling processes to animal display behavior to human semiotic artifacts such as language and abstract symbolic thought".[4] Much of the language taken up by biosemiotics appears also in traditional biological contexts, but it is taken as somehow metaphorical. In this context, such language is nonmetaphorical: biosemiotics takes seriously the idea that representation, meaning and interpretation have functional roles in the interactions of nonhuman living organisms. Semiotician Paul Cobley succinctly states, "The endeavour of biosemiotics encompasses a number of projects. One of these is the attempt to introduce a greater sense of the phenomenon of 'meaning' in biology".[5]

Relatedly, biosemiotics is interested in *meaning for*—that is, in the subjective experiences that ground, necessarily, the semiotic relationship. In some ways the biosemiotician pushes uncomfortably against the conceptual wheelhouse of philosophical moral theory, boldly claiming that subjective experience is "an undeniably ubiquitous characteristic of all living systems".[6] On this reading of "subjective experience", we are asked to "not conceptually reduce the rich multiplicity of organismic experience to the evolutionary anomalous and biologically minority instance of self-conscious, language-employing *human* 'subjective experience'".[7] Certainly phrases like these are meant to be introductory and deserve the much closer analysis and conceptual clarification that contemporary scholars continue to develop. However, the *idea* of subjective experience is intended to shake off the trappings of an anthropocentric phenomenology and to force us to confront these very questions about the scope and justification of that experience.

UMWELT THEORY

Theoretical description of the nonanthropocentric experiential component of meaning has been drawn from Jakob von Uexküll's Umwelt theory, which asserts that each living being has its own unique world of experience. Humans and animals alike have experiences and thus subjective worlds. But we do not necessarily have experiences all the time. The tick, for instance, Uexküll's famous model creature, hangs inert on the tip of a branch in a forest clearing for much of its existence, and in this interval "the world stands still"[8]—and we humans have cognitively inactive periods (as well as dreams) during sleep. Uexküll argues that all organisms, except plants and fungi, have unique *Umwelten*, or worlds of subjective experience.[9] In a vaguer sense, he attributes subjective (or quasi-subjective, as we shall call it) experience also to plants and fungi, whose worlds are characterized as "dwelling places".

Even at the very most basic level, semiosis functions to distinguish life from nonlife. According to Uexküll, "The complex perception and production of effects in every animal subject can . . . be attributed to the cooperation of small cellular-machine operators".[10] (Uexküll opposes what he see as an overtly physicalist machine metaphor of life with his own claim that if the physical organism is machinelike, then there is also always a[n internal] machine operator involved, "each one possessing only one perceptive and one effective sign".)[11] In other words, an organism's Umwelt or experiential life-world is foundationally driven by biosemiosis, even at the cellular level. Much of Uexküll's theoretical work has been taken up on the contemporary scene, especially by those interested in expanding the world of subjective experience to nonhumans. Among them, semiotician Thomas Sebeok worked to develop the idea that the Umwelt of each species is unique, and so needs to be understood in its own terms. As Favareau describes, "[s]tarting in 1977 and continuing well into the 1990s, Sebeok published in-depth critiques of the various underestimations, overestimations, anthropomorphism and machino-morphism being then attributed to animal cognition".[12]

Uexküll's Umwelten play an important conceptual role, placing all life on a continuum of experience from more to less restricted or planned, as phenomenologist Merleau-Ponty describes it. "The Umwelt is less and less oriented toward a goal and more and more toward the interpretation of symbols. But there is not a break between the planned animal, the animal that plans, and the animal without plans".[13]

For Uexküll, the Umwelt extends consideration of semiosis, or sign interpretation, much farther down the phylogenetic or organizational hierarchy than an account based on, say, creature consciousness[14] would allow us. Consciousness, on Uexküll's reading, is merely one mode or variation of subjective experience. As Merleau-Ponty concludes, "Uexküll himself posits the Umwelt as a type of which the organization, the consciousness, and the machine are only variations".[15] We are not warranted, on this view, to uphold one variant above another. In terms of biological functioning, a central assumption of Uexküll's is that "[a]ll animal subjects, from the simplest to the most complex, are inserted into their environments to the same degree of perfection. The simple animal has a simple environment; the multiform animal has an environment just as richly articulated as it is".[16] The number of objects with a particular functional tone that an animal is able to distinguish equals the number of actions it is capable of carrying out.[17] "Every Umwelt of a normal animal", according to von Uexküll—alluding to his familiar musical metaphor—"is a faultless composition of nature—you only have to understand how to look for its theme and its notes".[18] However, as pointed out in "Umwelt Transitions: Uexküll and Environmental Change",

[i]n our world of massive ecological degradation, not least in form of habitat loss, we cannot but observe how many beings today face increasing difficulties performing their all-to-natural Uexküllian duets—obstructed, in effect, by the expansion of the human habitat. Their struggle to maintain their ways of life amounts to a struggle for survival of a kind that . . . Uexküll [did not foresee].[19]

While Uexküll held a static view of nature in which harmony and order defined the ecological situation, we know today that most environments, if not all, undergo cycles of change. On this point the Umwelt theory is in Uexküll's original version outdated, and our generation thus needs to develop an Umwelt theory for our time. The notion of *Umwelt transition*, one element in such an endeavour, can be defined as "a lasting, systematic change, within the life cycle of a being, considered from an ontogenetic (individual), phylogenetic (population-, species-) or cultural perspective, from one typical appearance of its Umwelt to another".[20] To invoke an environmental crisis is in effect to invoke a change in the conditions for life. As stated in the same article, "[i]f not before, then at least by inflicting planetary climate change, our current anthropogenic ecological crisis has reached a global scale, thus entitling us to talk about a global Umwelt transition, changing the conditions for life for all or most life forms".[21]

While approaches utilizing Uexküll's Umwelt theory need to adapt to contemporary scientific and social frameworks, the underlying conceptual framework remains intact; specifically, Uexküll's biological view compels an understanding of forms of life on a continuum, with no sharp biological or, extending farther, ethical delineations. This opening up of a continuum of living beings problematizes contemporary sentience-based approaches to questions of moral considerability.[22]

SENTIENCE AS MORALLY RELEVANT

Sentience, commonly understood as the capacity to experience pleasure or pain,[23] has been held up by several philosophers and ethicists as a (perhaps *the*) morally relevant capacity.[24] Sentience-based approaches to moral considerability have their roots in the work of eighteenth-century British jurist and philosopher Jeremy Bentham, who suggested, famously, that suffering, not reasoning or speaking, was what mattered morally.[25] This passage, from Bentham's 1789 treatise *An Introduction to the Principles of Morals and Legislation*, outlines a now-familiar capacities-based account of moral standing. On Bentham's view, neither colour of skin nor reason, nor even language, hold up as an exemplar of a morally relevant capacity. Instead, *suffering* is held up as the moral exemplar: a capacity shared by not only all (normally functioning) human beings but also a wide range of nonhuman animals. In an unpublished penal code penned around 1780, Bentham outlines the practical output of his view. There, he notes that we ought to be legally restrained from cruelties to animals for the offender's sake and the sake of other men, as well as for the sake of the animals themselves: "[L]et any one say that can, why other animals in proportion to their susceptibility of pain and pleasure should have less claim to his attention than other men".[26]

Later adopters of the sentience-based view of moral considerability, Peter Singer key among them, further developed the view and its applicability. For Singer, "the capacity for suffering and enjoyment is *a prerequisite for having interests at all*, a condition that must be satisfied before we can speak of interests in a meaningful way".[27] Sentience is a capacity held by a wide range of living things but no nonliving things. Moral considerability, then, stops somewhere along the spectrum of life. To find its limits, we can rely on a range of evidence from behavioural studies, evolutionary developmental theory and neural/cognitive physiology and chemistry. Some level of bullet biting by the staunchest of proponents of such an approach has even allowed for a moral priority to be given to some nonhumans even at the expense, *ceteris paribus*, of some human individuals. Singer, for instance, argues that it is a perfectly consistent and coherent position to put the interests of a fully functioning dog first against the interests of an anencephalic infant, a severely mentally handicapped teenager, or a brain-dead elderly human. But in no case, Singer claims, can we utilize sentience to justify the moral considerability of, say, plants. Neither behavior nor neurology, nor even evolution, offers evidence that plants experience pain.[28] Language used to describe nonsentient life is at best metaphorical, according to Singer.

> We may often talk about plants "seeking" water or light so that they can survive, and this way of thinking about plants makes it easier to accept talk of their "will to live", or of their "pursuing" of their own good. Once we stop, however, to reflect on the fact that plants are not conscious and cannot engage in any intentional behavior, it is clear that all this language is metaphorical; one might as well say that a river is pursuing its own good and striving to reach the sea, or that the "good" of a guided missile is to blow itself up along with its target.[29]

Such metaphorical language misleads, on this view, as it seems to imply a sentient capacity not only in nonsentient life but also in nonsentient nonliving mechanisms like missiles and rivers. Thus, Singer's sentience-based account restricts the scope of moral considerability to all human and some subset of nonhuman animals.

Singer's project is concerned with the practical—social and legal—implications for an expanded moral circle, and so argues for consistency with starting conditions of moral considerability that are already intuitively supported. If we think the experience of pain is bad and have an obligation not to cause it to other humans, and some nonhumans can also experience pain, we ought not cause pain in those nonhumans. But what properly justifies this basic assumption that both Bentham and Singer hold—namely, that the capacity to experience the satisfaction or dissatisfaction of interests is fundamental to moral relevance? This question represents a fundamental problem about the role of intuitions in ethical theory.[30] Questions about the justification for claims like these open space beyond sentience in which we seek to sow the seed of semiosis as a broader and yet still morally relevant criterion on which to base recognition of moral considerability. Our claim is in this context twofold: that our account of semiosis as foundational for attribution of moral status *supports* the view that sentience is morally relevant, and that it *criticizes* the view that sentience is the most basic (or even the only) morally relevant capacity.

From the perspective of biosemiotics, Singer's account of sentience, bound up with interests, consciousness and intentional behaviour, defines these concepts too restrictively. Environmental philosopher Holmes Rolston offers a similar criticism, noting that "[i]n Singer's dichotomy, there seem to be only two metaphysical levels: conscious experiencers and merely physical processes".[31] On Singer's view,[32] to anyone and anything that is not sentient there is nothing that we can do that could possibly make any difference to its well-being—a view regarding nonsentient organisms that the biosemiotician does not share.

SENTIENCE AND UMWELT

The line between those things that morally matter and those things that do not is still standardly drawn along the boundary between sentient and nonsentient beings. Following Uexküll's biological Umwelt theory, the approach we develop here argues that sentience is not exhaustively descriptive of subjective experience. Rather, that sort of experience is a more fundamental necessary condition for the comparatively rarer experience of pleasure and pain—that is, for sentience. In an Uexküllian sense, all living beings, even unicellular beings, have subjective experience by having *semiotic agency*, the capacity to make use of signs in their environment. This implies, among other things, a capacity to be affected by the environment, in a manner that depends on environmental events including the actions of its various inhabitants (humans included). The reason why moral status (general moral considerability) should be attributed to all living beings is that all living beings have semiotic agency, and are thus ultimately affected by our actions. The assertion that all living beings have semiotic agency implies that

1. there is a world of experience that means something to each living creature based on its interpretation of signs in its environment, and

2. all living beings, through their semiotic capacity, are capable of distinguishing between what attracts them, what repulses them, and what has no function for them.

The difference between attractive to the human organism and attractive to a bacterium is a function of the scope and complexity of each organism's respective Umwelten, but both are semiotically driven. Our actions might affect the well-being of any living creature insofar as they affect its world of experience and action. Whereas sentience has traditionally been understood in relation to the moral weight of suffering and pain in particular, our approach involves an acknowledgement of the wider ground of which sentience stands: the reality of subjective experience omnipresent in the realm of living organisms generally.

Scientific questions, such as how widespread is sentience in the animal kingdom?, are limited in that they implicitly direct us to stop inquiry into the scope of moral value at a certain organizational level. What we suggest is that we start out by recognizing what is common to all living organisms—namely, their semiotic agency—and that this capacity can inform not only biological but also ethical discourses.

Attribution of moral status can be done at different levels of biological organization. We hold that moral status and value should be attributed at various levels simultaneously. Our basic premise is that the capacity for semiosis is a justifiably broader foundation for attributing moral status and value. This approach suggests a certain (but not exclusive) emphasis on *subjective experience* and thus on the level of the organism/individual, where applicable. However, *individuality* is no simple notion, and the organism's character of being already ecological—internally as already a system of microorganisms and externally as a member of a larger ecological network—points to valuation of ecological levels too. An account of animal ethics, on this relational view, demands a complementary account of valuation of those environmental relations as well.

Given this ecological perspective, we propose *biosemiotic particularism*.[33] Particularism, on our view, claims that normative assessment should be based on a living being's own merit, or its particular fulfillment of its semiotic capacity (again, a morally relevant capacity of which sentience is a particular case).[34] Such capacity fulfillment varies so much that it makes sense neither to value all living beings evenly nor to rank them hierarchically. To paraphrase Uexküll, each animal ought to be treated according to its needs, which are just as richly articulated as the animal itself is. Proper treatment of different living beings has to be case specific and take species-specific and other needs into consideration.[35] Facilitating the fulfillment of the needs of the living to the greatest extent possible is a core normative component of ethics.

Avoidance of pain is normally one of the needs of sentient organisms. In Uexküll's view, it can generally be observed that "pain inhibits the act that causes pain".[36] In other words, the purpose of pain, in biological terms, is to motivate the animal in pain to avoid what inflicts pain, so as to pursue what is in its interest. On this view, an Umwelt bereft of pain is not ideal, nor is one dominated by (perhaps paralysed by) pain. Uexküll's observation with regard to the purpose of pain further enables us to distinguish between pain that serves a biological function (meaningful pain) and pain that does not serve any biological function (senseless pain). We assume that the moral significance of inflicting or otherwise causing senseless pain is in some cases radically different from the moral significance of inflicting meaningful pain in this sense. One criterion for what qualifies as meaningful pain could thus be that the pain in question must give the animal different options with regard to behavioural response—in other words, the animal in question must be free to (re-)act as it prefers to. As we see, fulfilling the needs of sentient animals partly amounts to respecting their autonomy. This respect for autonomy is a central aspect of the proper treatment of sentient beings, whether human or nonhuman. The difficult translation of concepts like autonomy and preference to nonsentient living organisms is made easier by understanding sentience as one instance of complex semiotic agency that is itself morally relevant. Such a conceptual shift works to deny the charge of equivocation on terminology such as autonomy and agency that would otherwise hold.

ON THE RELATION BETWEEN SEMIOTIC AGENCY AND MORAL CONSIDERABILITY

All living beings—that is, all organisms—have semiotic agency: the capacity to make use of signs in their environment. Given that biosemiosis always involves a subject that, in an endeavour to make sense of its environment, interprets, chooses and responds, this implies that all organisms are experiential—that all organisms have subjective (or quasi-subjective—see below) experience. Since we postulate that semiotic agency is a morally relevant property, it follows that all living beings have moral status (that is to say, they are deserving of moral consideration). But the ways in which living beings are capable of relating to signs are manifold, and this section is devoted to detailing the major categories of semiotic agency.

If you were asked to think of an animal, you would probably think of a sentient one. Such a model creature would be one that is engaged in (a) intraorganismic semiosis, within its body, (b) interorganismic semiosis, insofar as it engages with other organisms directly, and (c) extraorganismic semiosis, insofar as it perceives the surroundings at large. This model creature would, given its sentience, be able to feel (1) its own body internally, (2) other bodies, and (3) the surroundings at large. But what is more, it would be a proper subject—a being whose experience is one whole (undivided) experience.

While a human being, a bird, and a snake would all qualify as model creatures in the above-mentioned senses, albeit with different sensory capabilities, there are many creatures that would not. Plants, for example, are diffuse and noncentralized in their semiotic functioning. Proper subjects are *one* in experiential/semiotic terms in a way that plants are not. While no plants and no fungi are subjects in this strict sense, some animals, too, are noncentralized in experiential/semiotic terms and thus not proper subjects on this account. An example treated by Uexküll is the sea urchin, which he characterizes as a "reflex republic"[37] in which numerous quills "perform their reflex tasks without central direction, each on its own".[38]

With this biosemiotic foundation we should distinguish between the moral status of proper subjects—living beings that are *one* (or whole) experientially—and the moral status of living beings that have a diffuse or decentralized semiotic interpretative capacity and thus also diffuse or decentralized experience. Given that organism-level experience is always underpinned by biosemiosis at lower (bodily) and higher (ecological) levels of biological organization, most biosemioticians would say that experience proper presupposes centralized, cohesive semiotic agency. In this sense, experience, which occurs at the level of the organism as a whole, is a complex instance of the semiotic capacity for interpretation, which occurs at all levels of biological organization from the cell to the ecosystem. Proper subjects stand out with regard to moral concern because their lives have another dimension—namely, unified, cohesive experience of their surroundings, which quasi-subjects lack. Quasi-subjects such as plants, fungi and animals with decentralized bodies also have semiotic agency and quasi-experience, but only proper subjects have cohesive, integrated experience. These differences are clearly morally relevant, since they are very much telling of how different beings are affected by the way we treat them. This is not to say that quasi-subjects do not have moral status, but their "subjectivity" is different, and thus their needs.

One apparent paradox in this context is that some unicellular beings are *one* experientially and thus proper subjects, whereas much more complex organisms such as trees are not. In one sense there is a dimension to the amoeba's life, of cohesive semiotic experience, that is not present in the life of the tree. The paradox of the amoeba and the tree cannot be resolved by distinguishing between sentient beings and nonsentient beings, since neither is sentient. But the semiosis of the tree is much more complex, and this is what distinguishes it in terms of needs and ability as well. As the example also shows, it is not the case that the only thing that matters is whether a living being is a proper subject or a quasi-subject. The complexity of the biosemiosis involved is more central.

To sum up so far, there are at least three organizational aspects of organisms that are morally relevant given our perspective: whether they are proper subjects or quasi-subjects, whether they are sentient, and, last but not least, how complex their semiosis is.

Another conceptual distinction related to moral relevance can be made: that between *semiotic* and *semiosic*—a distinction that is central to philosopher/semiotician John Deely.[39] So far we have used *semiotic* as that which is sign-mediated. However, a finer distinction can be made, according to which "semiosic" denotes the capacity to interpret and make use of signs, whereas the "semiotic" denotes the awareness of the sign-character of that which is sign-mediated. This distinction underlies Deely's notion of the "semiotic animal"—the human being—and other, merely "semiosic animals". In his perspective, while animals only *make use of* signs, human beings stand out by being the only creatures that *understand* signs *as* signs. In our context the latter attitude might have unfortunate implications, since it might lead to reestablishing the idea of human exceptionalism, on the grounds of semiotics. Such an anthropo-centric tendency is also a limitation of "semioethics".[40]

This being said, Deely's distinction between semiotic and semiosic could come to play a more constructive role if we do away with the assumption that only human beings are capable of being aware that signs are signs. Elsewhere,[41] Tønnessen analyses two incidents of cat play, where one cat, Muki, played with the ray of light from a torch, and another cat, Maluca, played with the stream of water from a garden hose. On this interpretation, both cats were able to distinguish between a solid, physical object—a cat-thing that you can snatch with your claws—and a ray of light or flow of water. What they were playing was that the light, or the water, was in fact something that they could catch with their claws. The object of their play, in other words, was in a sense the very notion of solidity. Tønnessen argues that Muki and Maluca, in those play situa-tions, were not merely semiosic but further semiotic animals, displaying semiotic as well as semiosic agency. In semiotic parlance, the ray of light and the stream of water, respectively, were perceived by the cats as signs of something that they in fact were not.[42]

The question is what moral difference the capacity for semiotic (rather than semiosic) agency makes. Should human beings be treated better, because we are self-consciously aware that signs are signs? Should cats, insofar as they understand that signs are signs? Taken to the extreme, Deely's line of thinking would imply that semioticians deserve better treatment than others—hardly a defensible position. On the other hand, it is indeed reasonable to inquire into whether or not, in different situa-tions, the capacity for semiotic understanding (rather than mere semiosic action) makes a difference with regard to how a living being is affected by the actions of human beings. This discussion, which we will not take further here, partly overlaps with discussions within ethics about what difference the capacity for self-consciousness makes in the context of attributing moral status. [43]

ATTRIBUTION OF MORAL STATUS AT VARIOUS LEVELS
OF BIOLOGICAL ORGANIZATION

At first glance, the biosemiotic ethic that we outline here appears to be applicable on the individual level only. But from an Uexküllian perspective, a living being is, in a sense, what it relates to—in other words, its entire existence rests on the ecological relations it partakes in, and it cannot meaningfully be viewed in isolation from these. Semiotic agency is a function of the individual's semiotic web, the network of overlapping Umwelten that shape the interpretations and experiences of the organism. It is therefore meaningless, or at the very least exceedingly difficult, to make the claim that only individual organisms have moral status. Even the claim that only human individuals have moral status, as some would argue, is ultimately futile in this sense, for how can we value and protect a human organism without valuing and protecting the nonhuman biological diversity that thrives within it? We are, by our constitution, more-than-human, and further depending on larger networks of relations that sustain us. These are ontological assertions with moral implications, even prior to our unbiased consideration of the interests and well-being of others.

A biosemiotic ethic likewise starts from the claim that all organisms, humans and nonhumans alike, are constituted by and dependent on their larger network of relations. Semiotic agency, the capacity that grounds moral considerability on this view, moves beyond the limited scope of sentience to the interpretative and experiential worlds of all living things. Further, a biosemiotic ethic argues that moral consideration demands taking an ecological view, taking into account the ways in which particular organisms are engaged in their larger semiotic webs of relations. From sentient animals to Uexküll's tick to plants and single-celled organisms, all living organisms are morally relevant. Conflicts between competing needs are to be adjudicated not in isolation but in community. On the sentience-based account as described above, neither the tick nor the plant have properties we ought to acknowledge as morally relevant. Our obligations, vis-à-vis either, are limited to our acknowledging its potential usefulness as an instrument for sentient beings. On the biosemiotic account, however, the tick and the plant share a basic semiosic capacity, albeit more or less complex. Thus both have moral considerability; neither is a mere object. [44]

If in a thought experiment we let first the unicellular organisms deteriorate, and then the nonsentient animals, and then plants and fungi—if we do not speak out against any of this simply because none of them are sentient beings, then in the end there would not be many left to support and sustain the lives of sentient animals. They, too, would certainly perish.

Rather than focusing on established ethical dilemmas, such as having to choose between two individuals or species in some lifeboat scenario, a biosemiotic ethic can contribute to reframing the way we look at value conflicts. In a geological era now named the Anthropocene due to the evident human dominance of ecosystems, humankind cannot always win out, neither with regard to resources nor with regard to space and opportunity. We do not need an ethic that designates winners and losers in a hegemonic competitive perspective. If we are to thrive as a species in a biosphere that will necessarily have to be characterized by long-term human-nonhuman conviviality, we have to be companionable and cultivate strategies that allow for solving dilemmas by allowing for fulfillment of the basic needs of as many as possible. All organisms need nutrition and space, but almost all other needs vary from life form to life form. The overlapping Umwelten in and through which all living organisms exist constitute the vast web of ecological relations. Understanding the nature and value of those webs of relations from a biosemiotic perspective will move animal and environmental ethics beyond sentience.

CONCLUSION

While still supporting the positive moral implications of sentience-based ethical perspectives, the biosemiotic particularist does not think that sentience is a prerequisite for having interests. For the Uexküllian biosemiotic ethic advanced here, the question is not "Can they reason?", nor is it "Can they talk?" or even "Can they suffer?" Instead, it is "Can they navigate in a world of meaning?"—that is, interpret signs in their environment. On this biosemiotic view, all living beings—plants and animals alike—have semiotic agency—a capacity to make use of signs, including to distinguish between what is good for them and what is bad for them, and consequently all living beings have interests and, arguably, moral status. This particularist view further differs from the sentience-based ethicist in holding that intentionality is not necessarily tied to consciousness—nonconscious creatures are intentional too, in that they systematically, by way of making choices, pursue their specific agendas, many of which are associated with basic biological functioning. A biosemiotic ethic likewise begins from being, from a scientifically driven study of biosemiosis to understand both the nature of and the relationships between the human and the nonhuman and, from there, to make clearer the nature and scope of moral considerability.

It does matter to sentient animals how we treat them—but it also matters to semiotic beings beyond sentient ones—to living beings at large. In the view advanced here there are at least four organizational aspects of organisms that are morally relevant: whether they are proper subjects or quasi-subjects, whether they are sentient, how complex their semiosis is, and whether they are capable of understanding signs *as* signs rather than merely making use of them. Given all these dimensions of the life of the living, we claim that biosemiotics can serve as a foundation for an animal ethics that is bound up in a broader environmental/ecological context. We further point to biosemiotic particularism, the view that proper treatment of different living beings has to be case specific and take species-specific and other specific needs into consideration, as a reasonable normative approach.

ACKNOWLEDGEMENTS

We would like to acknowledge the editors of this volume for their insightful comments on earlier drafts of this chapter. Tønnessen's work in this project has been supported by the research project "Animals in Changing Environments: Cultural Mediation and Semiotic Analysis" (EEA Norway Grants/Norway Financial Mechanism 2009–2014 under project contract no. EMP151).

NOTES

1. Jakob von Uexküll, *A Foray into the Worlds of Animals and Humans: With a Theory of Meaning* (Minneapolis: University of Minneapolis Press, 2010).

2. Our use of the Umwelt theory is, in this context, very different from Uexküll's own use or abuse of it. Elsewhere, we point to a key caveat emptor for further ethical work that might draw on Umwelt theory:

> Uexküll's 1917 essay ultimately reminds the reader that continued work that draws on Umwelt theory in support of an ethical theory or normative evaluation should be aware that Uexküll's cultural and historical context led him to apply a rich biological theory in defense of a contestable theory of moral development and standing. While Uexküll's scientific work in biology has helped the contemporary reader develop important new ecological understandings of the place of the human animal in the natural world, it has also lead [sic] to wildly different results in terms of its normative implications. (Jonathan Beever and Morten Tønnessen, "'Darwin und die Englische Moral': The Moral Consequences of Uexküll's Umwelt Theory", *Biosemiotics* 6, no. 3 (2013): 446.)

Following his lead in extending consideration to a wide host of nonhuman organisms and living systems, a small but growing number of philosophers and semioticians have begun exploring whether and to what extent Umwelt theory might inform animal and environmental ethics: see Jesper Hoffmeyer, "Biosemiotics and Ethics", in *Culture and Environment: Interdisciplinary Approaches*, ed. Nina Witoszek and Elizabeth Gulbrandsen (Oslo: Centre for Development and the Environment, 1993), 152–76; Jesper Hoffmeyer, "Biosemiotics and Ethics", in *Biopolitics: A Feminist and Ecological Reader on Biotechnology*, ed. Vandana Shiva and Ingunn Moser (London: Zed, 1995), 141–61; Kalevi Kull, "Biosemiotics and the Problem of Intrinsic Value of Nature", *Sign Systems*

60 *Morten Tønnessen and Jonathan Beever*

Studies 29, no. 1 (2001): 353–65; Morten Tønnessen, "Umwelt Ethics", *Sign Systems Studies* 31, no. 1 (2003): 281–99; Marc Champagne, "Axiomatizing Umwelt Normativity", *Sign Systems Studies* 39, no. 1 (2011): 9–59; Jonathan Beever, "Meaning Matters: The Biosemiotic Basis of Bioethics", *Biosemiotics* 5, no. 2 (2012): 181–91; Ralph R. Acampora, "The (Proto-)Ethical Significance of Semiosis: When and How Does One Become Somebody Who Matters?" in *The Semiotics of Animal Representations*, ed. Kadri Tüür and Morten Tønnessen (Amsterdam/New York: Rodopi, 2014, 343–62); and so on. The account given here builds on those prior efforts, arguing for the investigation into the implications of taking the moral relevance of semiotic agency seriously.

3. Donald Favareau, *Essential Readings in Biosemiotics* (Dordrecht: Springer, 2010), vi.

4. Favareau, *Essential Readings*, v.

5. Paul Cobley, "The Cultural Implications of Biosemiotics", *Biosemiotics* 3, no. 2 (2010): 225–44, 225.

6. Favareau, *Essential Readings*, 2.

7. Favareau, *Essential Readings*, 2.

8. Uexküll, *Foray*, 51–52.

9. We note that Uexküll's account of subjective experience always involves more than what is actually experienced—that is, what is sensed as happening (at the very least anticipation of events, in many cases also memory and fantasy). In Uexküll's words (*Foray*, 119), "The search image, the tracing of the most familiar path, and the demarcation of territory already constitute exceptions to [the rule that Umwelten are the products of perception signs triggered by external stimuli], since they could be ascribed to no sort of external stimuli but represented free productions of the subject". Thus, subjective experience includes not only sensing of direct encounters but also sensing of what is perceived as having happened and what is perceived as desirable, and so on. Overall, experience, in the manifold living realm, might be considered as being on a continuum from reflex-like interpretation of stimuli all the way up to complex experiential semiosis.

10. Uexküll, *Foray*, 47.

11. Uexküll, *Foray*, 47.

12. Favareau, *Essential Readings*, 38.

13. Maurice Merleau-Ponty, *Nature: Course Notes from the Collège de France*, ed. Dominique Séglard, trans. Robert Vallier (Evanston: Northwestern University Press, 2003), 176.

14. For example, Mark Bernstein, "Contractualism and Animals", *Philosophical Studies: An International Journal for Philosophy in the Analytic Tradition* 86, no. 1 (1997): 49–72; Peter Carruthers, *Consciousness: Essays from a Higher-Order Perspective* (New York: Oxford University Press, 2005); Thomas Nagel, "What Is It Like to Be a Bat?" *The Philosophical Review* 83, no. 4 (1974): 435–50.

15. Merleau-Ponty, *Nature*, 168. On Merleau-Ponty, cf. J. Singer, this volume.

16. Uexküll, *Foray*, 50.

17. Uexküll, *Foray*, 96.

18. Jakob von Uexküll, "The New Concept of Umwelt: A Link between Science and the Humanities", trans. Gosta Brunow, *Semiotica* 134, no. 1/4 (2001): 120.

19. Morten Tønnessen, "Umwelt Transitions: Uexküll and Environmental Change", *Biosemiotics* 2, no. 1 (2009a): 48.

20. Tønnessen, "Umwelt Transitions", 49.

21. Tønnessen, "Umwelt Transitions", 49–50.

22. This step from a discussion of a biological capacity to a morally relevant one is here taken too quickly. There is a central premise in the argument that we set aside for our purposes here. But this central premise is a necessary condition for the conclusion that one might draw. That premise is that semiosis is a morally relevant capacity. In order to draw a strong or valid conclusion, one would need to argue this point more thoroughly than the thesis of this chapter allows. In this work, we accept semiosis as a morally relevant capacity while recognizing that this premise is controversial and that

accepting it presupposes rethinking of basic terms including *subjectivity, agency, mind* and *perception*. If these terms are understood in their mainstream, anthropocentric sense, where they are predominantly associated with *human* subjectivity, agency, mind-set and perception, our case will undoubtedly appear a nonstarter. But our biosemiotic endeavour principally aims to change the way we think about such phenomena in order to acknowledge the manifold real occurrences of interpretation, experience, agency and the like in nature that might very well in many cases surpass current human comprehension or imagination. For our claim to make sense, our habitual human bias must be avoided.

23. Although such a definition is common across many if not all sentience-based accounts of animal ethics, other normative welfare accounts take sentience more broadly or more narrowly (see John Webster, *Animal Welfare: Limping towards Eden* [Oxford: Blackwell, 2008], 5–11). Given our focus on accounts of animal ethics, we do not directly address these broader normative accounts. Our goal in this chapter is to critique and unpack the conditions of this broader view via a biosemiotic account.

24. For another critique of sentience-based approaches, see Williams, this volume.

25. Jeremy Bentham, *An Introduction to the Principles of Morals and Legislation*, ed. J. H. Burns and H. L. A. Hart (London: Methuen, 1982 [1789]), 235–36 footnote.

26. Jeremy Bentham, "Penal Code—Cruelty to animals. MSS LXXII 214", in *Bentham and the Oppressed*, ed. Lea Campos Boralevi (New York: Walter de Gruyter, 1984 [1780]), 228–29.

27. Peter Singer, *Animal Liberation* (New York: Random House, 2002 [1975]), 9.

28. Singer, *Animal Liberation*, 262.

29. Peter Singer, *Writings on an Ethical Life* (New York: HarperCollins, 2000), 99.

30. See, for example, Peter Singer, "Ethics and Intuitions", *Journal of Ethics* 9 (2005): 331–52; John Doris and Stephen Stich, "As a Matter of Fact: Empirical Perspectives of Ethics", *The Oxford Handbook of Contemporary Analytic Philosophy*, ed. Frank Jackson and Michael Smith (Oxford: Oxford University Press, 2005), 114–52; and Steven D. Hales, "The Problem of Intuition", *American Philosophical Quarterly* 37, no. 2 (2000): 135–47.

31. Holmes Rolston III, "Respect for Life: Counting What Singer Finds of No Account", *Singer and His Critics*, ed. Dale Jamieson (Malden, MA: Blackwell, 1999), 249, 247–68.

32. Singer, *Animal*, 8.

33. Not to be confused with "moral particularism"; see Richard Mervyn Hare, *Freedom and Reason* (Oxford: Clarendon, 1963), and Margaret Olivia Little, "On Knowing the 'Why': Particularism and Moral Theory", in *Ethical Theory: An Anthology*, ed. Russ Shafer-Landau (Oxford: Blackwell, 2007), 775–84.

34. Emotional capacity might be another particular case of semiotic agency. Cf. Aaltola, this volume.

35. Singer (*Animal*, 2) is on to something similar when he notes that "[s]ince a man cannot have an abortion, it is meaningless to talk of his right to have one. Since dogs can't vote, it is meaningless to talk of their right to vote". And further (399): "Concern for the wellbeing of children growing up in America would require that we teach them to read; concern for the well-being of pigs may require no more than that we leave them with other pigs in a place where there is adequate food and room to run freely".

36. Uexküll, *Foray*, 76.

37. Uexküll, *Foray*, 76–77.

38. Uexküll, *Foray*, 76.

39. Augusto Ponzio, Susan Petrilli and John Deely, *The Semiotic Animal* (Ottawa: Legas, 2006).

40. See Susan Petrilli, "Semioethics, Subjectivity, and Communication: For the Humanism of Otherness", *Semiotica* 148, no. 1/4 (2004): 69–91, and John Deely, "From Semiosis to Semiotics: The Full Vista of the Action of Signs", *Sign Systems Studies* 36, no. 2 (2008): 437–92.

41. Morten Tønnessen, "Abstraction, Cruelty and Other Aspects of Animal Play (Exemplified by the Playfulness of Muki and Maluca)", *Sign Systems Studies* 37, no. 3/4 (2009b): 558–79.

42. Cognitive ethologists continue to develop frameworks for understanding how animals use signs as signs in acts of communication. See, for instance, W. J. Smith, "Animal Communication and the Study of Cognition", in *Cognitive Ethology: Essays in Honor of Donald R. Griffin*, ed. Carolyn A. Ristau, 209–30 (New York: Psychology Press, 2014).

43. Cf. Singer's observation that even though anticipation, memory and greater knowledge in some cases mean that we should value a human being's suffering higher, "[s]ometimes animals may suffer more because of their limited understanding" (Peter Singer, *Practical Ethics*, 2nd ed. [Cambridge: Cambridge University Press, 1993], 60); for instance, when a wild animal is not capable of distinguishing between a "friendly" attempt to overpower and confine it from an attempt to kill.

44. There is further work to be done on how the biosemiotic account might deal with the variety of priorities problems at the systems or species level. The work defining the priority of principles that Paul Taylor does in *Respect for Nature* (Princeton: Princeton University Press, 2011 [1986]) resembles the sort of work that must be done in the context of biosemiotic ethics.

FOUR

Animal Agency

What It Is, What It Isn't, and How It Can Be Realized

Zipporah Weisberg

Animal agency—what it consists of, and what ethical and political import it has, if any—has inspired significant debate among animal studies scholars in recent decades. Animal theorists typically approach the question of animal agency in one of four ways, all of which respond to the Kantian claim that agency is grounded in reason and is therefore restricted to human beings. The first approach, taken by Tom Regan, among others, is to concede that animals do not qualify as agents in the Kantian sense, but to insist that they are nevertheless worthy of moral consideration as moral "patients".[1] The second approach, which is especially popular among posthumanist scholars, is to take the opposite tack. These scholars not only reject the Kantian conception of agency but also redefine it so broadly as to attribute it to virtually every being and every *thing*, including matter, microorganisms and technical artefacts. This trend was initiated by Gilles Deleuze and Félix Guattari in the late 1980s and reformulated in the late 1990s by Bruno Latour and N. Katherine Hayles. It has more recently been rearticulated by posthumanists with an interest in animal and environmental ethics, such as Myra Hird.[2] The third approach, also adopted by a number of contemporary posthumanist scholars such as Donna Haraway, is to conflate animals' isolated acts of resistance with full-fledged agency. The fourth approach, which is taken by animal scholars inspired by phenomenology such as Traci Wartenkin and political theorists of animal rights such as Sue Donaldson and Will Kymlicka, is to redefine agency in nonanthropocentric terms, on the one hand, while limiting it to human and nonhuman animals, on the other. There are two layers to this fourth approach: the first is to redefine agency to apply to human and nonhuman animals and leave it at that; the second is to redefine it and *politicize* it. I argue here that the latter approach is the optimal one.

Regan's approach makes sense strategically—why bother redefining agency when we can simply downplay its importance in determining animals' moral worth?—but it ultimately does a disservice to animals by reducing them to passive recipients of moral consideration. The posthumanist impulse to radically decentre the human is well justified given the catastrophic outcome for other animals. The specifically materialist and vitalist impulse to rescue nature from its status as inert and passive by attributing agency to all its constituents is especially appealing. In theory, this approach could help reenchant nature, foster a holistic worldview and reposition the human being as one among other agential subjects. However, it is one thing to recognize the dynamism and activity of the natural world, but it is quite another to suggest that every single entity from atom to single-celled organism to elephant is an agent. By spreading the concept of agency so thinly, the concept loses its ethico-political potency. The posthumanist impulse to emphasize animals' agency qua resistance in sites of violence is also important to follow because it protects animals from being reified as victims. However, if it is taken too far, it can obfuscate the reality of animals' systemic victimization.

The fourth approach of redefining agency outside the anthropocentric Kantian model while limiting its conscious and sentient subjects, I argue here, makes the strongest contribution to animals' emancipation from human tyranny. It paints a much more accurate and honest picture of what human and nonhuman animal agency actually constitutes, and it underscores the vital importance of promoting animals' rights to self-determination as an integral component of the emancipatory project. However, following Donaldson and Kymlicka's argument, I emphasize that more work needs to be done to mobilize animal agency politically— that is, to develop political structures that promote and protect it. Donaldson and Kymlicka provide a fruitful example of how to move in this direction by proposing that we attribute citizenship, sovereignty or denizenship to other animals depending on the kind of agency they exhibit. Their political theory of animal agency is especially attractive because of its nuanced analysis of how agency manifests itself among different species, individuals and different interspecies communities. But I argue that it is also limited by its attachment to a specifically liberal understanding of political membership, which, among other things, fails to account for the grave injustices perpetuated by global capitalism. The task therefore remains to politicize animal agency along the lines Donaldson and Kymlicka propose, but without remaining beholden to a liberal political framework. This may or may not involve abandoning the concept of citizenship altogether and introducing alternative categories of political agency and belonging that capture the spirit, if not the letter, of the most compelling dimensions of citizenship theory.

THE FIRST APPROACH: ELIDING ANIMAL AGENCY

Tom Regan carves out a path for animals into the moral community by diminishing the importance of (a Kantian understanding of) agency in determining a subject's moral worth altogether. What counts, Regan argues, is whether a being constitutes a subject-of-a-life. On his definition, subjects-of-a-life experience "physical pleasure and pain" and also "fear and contentment, anger and loneliness, frustration and satisfaction, cunning and imprudence".[3] They also "possess a variety of sensory, cognitive, conative, and volitional capacities", "exhibit preference and welfare interests", and care about what happens to them.[4] In short, they are emotionally, psychologically and socially complex beings. Subjects-of-a-life possess inherent value, and it is on this basis that they should be treated as ends in themselves, not means to others' ends. Though they may not be moral agents, other subjects-of-life are moral patients. In Regan's words, "The rights view recognizes the equal inherent value of all subjects-of-a-life, including those who lack the necessary capacities for agency. These moral patients . . . have the same equal right to respectful treatment as moral agents".[5] Once a being is deemed a moral patient, it is owed direct duties, not simply indirect duties, as Kant would have it.[6]

Regan's emphasis on moral patienthood is one way out of the problem that Kant's moral philosophy presents vis-à-vis other animals. However, this approach is problematic because it ignores what are obvious instantiations of animals' moral agency, albeit not as Kant defines it. Ethologists Marc Bekoff and Jessica Pierce enumerate several examples in which animals go to great lengths to offer aid and assistance to other animals in need:

> Eleven elephants rescue a group of captive antelope in KwaZula-Natal; the matriarch undoes all of the latches on the gates of the enclosure with her trunk and lets the gate swing open so the antelope can escape. A rat in a cage refuses to push a lever for food when it sees that another rat receives an electric shock as a result. A male diana monkey who has learned to insert a token into a slot to obtain food helps a female who can't get the hang of a trick, inserting the token for her and allow her to eat the food reward.[7]

I have seen video footage of a crow caring for, feeding, playing with, and protecting a stray kitten for months; a piglet jumping into a river to help usher a terrified, drowning goat to safety; and a dog nurturing and protecting orphaned goslings.[8] Jennifer S. Holland tells the story of a macaque who adopted a stray kitten in Indonesia, a papillon dog who adopted a squirrel into her litter and pitbulls and a bulldog who consoled and cared for a grieving ferret, among many other touching stories.[9] These examples are important, not because they somehow lend further justification to including animals into a Kantian moral universe, but rather because they illuminate the contextual specificity of their self-development and expression, and what we might call a kind of existential freedom, loosely defined, that enables animals to make choices and engage in actions that do not necessarily conform to their species-specific behaviours. They also challenge the validity of Kant's rigid criterion (viz., the capacity to universalize maxims and norms) for moral agency. By sidestepping the question of agency, Regan is missing a potentially fruitful opportunity to reconceptualize agency (both moral agency and agency as such) outside the narrow anthropocentric confines in which Kant embedded it.

It is also crucial to establish that animals are agents inasmuch as the commission of systemic atrocities against animals revolves around deliberately denying and/or curtailing animal agency. In the animal industrial complex, animals have no authority whatsoever over their own lives and deaths. Rather, human beings claim an *authoritarian* control over both. This serves a psychological and a practical purpose. Psychologically, even hinting at animal agency would give the perpetrators of violence cause to reconsider their brutality and would thereby threaten the stability of the system that depends upon animals' radical objectification. Practically, paying heed to animal agency would require dismantling the animal industrial complex, which by its very nature must subject animals to unspeakably cruel ontological predetermination as barely living commodities. Animals' personal preferences are deliberately ignored, they have no opportunity to make meaningful choices, to pursue their own ends, to interact meaningfully with their environment and with the other subjects and objects in it. They are physically confined and mutilated to prevent the expression of agency. They are bred and genetically altered to curb agency from within, as it were. They not only are made more docile but also suffer debilitating injuries and illness as a result of monstrous modifications they undergo. Their mobility, a vital vehicle for agency, is therefore severely impeded. Since denying animal agency has serious practical ethical implications for animals, animal scholars ought to reconsider the meaning(s) of animal agency, rather than abandon the concept to its human exceptionalist articulations.

Debra Durham and Debra Merskin have shown that discourses in animal industries are specifically tailored to suppress what seems to be an otherwise obvious intuitive recognition of animal subjectivity/agency. This enables egregious violence and cruelty to take place with little objection, even from those assigned with protecting animals' basic welfare interests, such as members of so-called animal "care" committees. Animals used in experiments are systematically stripped of agency and

autonomy in how they are represented in discussions at animal care committee meetings: "In the case of animals used in experiments, individual
agency is lost not only in the physical sense because of captivity, but also
symbolically when animals are reduced to numbers, not names, and to
protocols rather than personalities".[10] Durham and Merskin illustrate
this by pointing to one animal care committee's discussion about whether
to approve a particularly heinous experiment on mice that involved shav-
ing off the mice's fur and immersing them in scalding water at a tempera-
ture of 140 degrees for eighteen seconds, followed by "debraiding" or
scrubbing "the skin". Durham and Merskin argue that the committee
members—including the member who demonstrated his discomfort at
the nature of the experiment—consciously or unconsciously used language that erased the mice's subjectivity and agency (qua their objection
to being tortured). For example, "most verbs" the committee members
used "describe what was done to the skin, not to an animal or to an
animal's skin, and the violent act of burning the mice is stated in a passive voice and reframed as exposure".[11] The use of seemingly neutral or
"cold", "hard", detached scientific language is widespread across animal
industries and serves the purpose of legitimating brutality against animals—brutality that would otherwise be considered unconscionable if
the animals' agency were respected.

THE SECOND APPROACH: MISREPRESENTING
AND MISATTRIBUTING AGENCY

A number of posthumanist theorists take the converse approach to Regan
and suggest that every being and every thing—including bacteria, miner-
als, garbage and computers, among other things—is an agent. It is without question crucial to resuscitate the natural world and its constituents
from its centuries-long relegation to the status of organic machinery. The
view that nothing but the human exhibits agency has had devastating
consequences for the earth and the beings that live and exist in and on it.
But recognizing the awesome power and vitality of nature, rejecting its
commodification, and seeking to establish robust ethical (and political)
norms to protect it from the excesses of human exceptionalism and late
capitalism do not require indiscriminately attributing agency to everything, as though there are no ontologically—or ethically and politically—
meaningful differences between air particles and dogs.

    As I have argued in detail elsewhere, Myra Hird's microontology of-
fers a good example of the ontological and ethical quagmire the misattri-
bution of the concept of agency can lead to.[12] In her article, "Meeting
with the Microcosmos", Hird claims that bacteria are given too short
shrift in our understanding of the universe. First of all, she argues, human and nonhuman subjects are not subjects per se, but clusters of bacte-

ria.[13] Secondly, she insists, bacteria are agents—moreover, they are agents with a world-historical role. She claims that they "invented" a number of historically significant objects such as the wheel and initiated important sociocultural shifts in the area of reproduction and community organization.[14] They also "sustain the chemical elements crucial to life on earth" and "invented symbiogenesis".[15] Not only do bacteria displace/ replace human agents in these momentous historical events, but, she implies, they also displace/replace human and nonhuman subjects altogether. This ontological shift leads to a troubling ethical shift. Veganism, or the refusal to consume or use any products made up of animal parts or to engage in any activities involving animal exploitation, may not, Hird concludes, be the appropriate ethical response after all, since it is not necessarily animals we ought to be concerned about, but the bacteria of which they are composed.[16] To be sure, Hird does not make a definitive claim about whether or not to abandon veganism one way or the other, but to even question the ethical and political importance of boycotting violence against animals on the grounds that they are made up of bacteria is outrageous.

To be sure, every being has its own *telos* to fulfill.[17] But this does not mean that it is an agent, or that it makes ethical claims on us. Microorganisms make no ethical claims on us because they are neither conscious nor sentient. By its very nature, the *telos* of bacteria can never be undermined, for bacteria simply self-perpetuate ad infinitum. Though flora, such as trees and plants, are also neither conscious nor sentient, they do make strong ethical claims on us because they are living beings whose *telos* can be obstructed and is under threat. But the ethical claims they make on us as nonagents are substantively and qualitatively different from the ethical claims made on us by conscious, sentient beings such as birds, fish and mammals. Collapsing these distinctions does a disservice to both animal and nonanimal beings by obscuring specific responsibilities we have to different beings depending on their needs. It is vital to keep the distinction between conscious and unconscious beings in mind. As Helen Steward remarks, this distinction is intuitive.

> The results of the primitive and unreflective categorization of animals as agents are phenomenologically tangible to those open to its influence—watching a bird pecking around for food or a cat stalking a mouse is just utterly unlike watching, say, trees blow in the wind or a car drive down a road.[18]

Unfortunately, under the growing influence of posthumanist thought, this distinction is being blurred so that cars and cats and trees are effectively placed on the same ontological plane.

THE THIRD APPROACH: CONFLATING ISOLATED ACTS OF RESISTANCE WITH FULL-FLEDGED AGENCY

Another worrying tendency emerging in animal studies literature is to glorify animals' isolated acts of resistance in the animal industrial complex to the point of obscuring the reality of their systemic victimization. There is no question that other animals express and assert agency qua autonomous action in contexts of violence. There are numerous anecdotal accounts of animals mobilizing their agency to express opposition to their exploitation and to pursue their own freedom by, say, biting or attacking their tormentors. For example, in February 2013 a tiger killed his trainer during a performance in Sonora, Mexico.[19] The popular 2013 documentary *Blackfish* featured the story of Tilikum, an orca whale who resisted the horrifying circumstances of his incarceration and exploitation as a performing whale by killing three people during his long period in captivity. His most recent fatal attack was against his trainer, Dawn Brancheau, in front of a packed audience during a performance at Sea World in Orlando, Florida. Brancheau was rubbing his side when he pulled her into the water and thrashed her around. It is unclear as to whether she died from trauma or drowning.[20] Either way, Tilikum clearly set out to harm her and most likely also intended to kill her. Though she treated him "well" by industry standards, Tilikum was apparently disgruntled by the fact that she was his master, ordering him to do the same tricks over and over, day after day, and punishing him by denying him good rewards when he made an error. We can never know what Tilikum was thinking, but it is clear that no degree of gentleness on the part of his oppressors would pacify him into accepting his brutal kidnapping from the ocean and his pod and his decades-long confinement in barren enclosures barely larger than his twelve-thousand-pound body. Animals also engage in nonviolent acts of resistance. pattrice jones, cofounder of VINE (Veganism Is the Next Evolution) sanctuary, relayed that a pregnant cow now residing happily at VINE with her young calf had managed to jump a fence on the dairy farm in which she was formerly confined and had run into the forest to have her baby without risk of interference or of the calf being taken from her.[21] Other examples of this nature abound.

One might even go so far as to suggest that animals are demonstrating a kind of *political* agency, with existentialist and phenomenological overtones, when they resist their enslavement. Jean-Paul Sartre famously contended that consciousness is born of the tension between "being" and "nothingness" — that is, between what is and what has not yet come into being, and also between immanence and transcendence. To become truly conscious, in Sartre's view, is to take a "negative" or critical position vis-à-vis the present state of things. Consciousness "withdraws itself from the full world of which it is consciousness" and "leave[s] the level of being in order frankly to approach that of non-being", which is to say that it recedes from the immanence of the everyday, of the present, into a realm of reflection about what ought to be. That latter is as yet nonexistence, it is nothing, but recognizing it as such is the first step into making it something.[22] Only those who develop their consciousness in this way can act, in the true sense of the word, and only those who act are agents, world-historical and otherwise.[23] As an example, Sartre points to a worker becoming conscious of his exploitation through this process of reflection and struggling against it as a form of conscious action. Conversely, without being able to "conceive of a social state in which these sufferings would not exist", the worker "does not act".[24] Sartre explains that

> [t]o act is to modify the shape of the world; it is to arrange means in view of an end; it is to produce an organized instrumental complex such that by a series of concatenations and connections the modification effected on one of the links causes modifications throughout the whole series and finally produces an anticipated result.[25]

Of course, for Sartre this kind of action is specific to human beings. And he is not entirely wrong. Nonhuman animals do not universalize their struggle and therefore do not engage in world-historical action per se.

But that does not mean that they are entirely incapable of agency as Sartre defines it here. Animals in the animal industrial complex are clearly conscious of their exploitation on some level. Such consciousness inevitably accompanies suffering. Suffering, especially as a result of torture, is, in its essence, the negation of what should be. As such, animals can be said to have at least an intuitive sense of the tension between the Is and the Ought, even if they do not articulate it through language. Indeed, perhaps *because* they don't use verbal language, their experience of this tension is even greater than it is for human beings. Whatever the case, it is clear that inasmuch as many animals resist the conditions of their oppression in a variety of ways, they are conscious that what is happening to them is wrong.

The existential freedom of animals may not emerge out of the dialectic between being and nothingness and the action that ensues, at least not as Sartre construes this tension. But it does, I think it is fair to say, express itself in their refusal to accept the existing conditions of their subjugation. These refusals suggest that the tension between being and nothingness may be both beyond or within the domain of language or reason. Perhaps this tension is equally if not more fundamentally grounded in an embodied (which is to say, felt) sense of the vast chasm between the Is and the Ought (that is, between the horror that is and the well-being that ought to be) that a system of violence produces.

Acts of resistance also involve an assertion of a certain kind of phenomenological freedom qua agency. As an example of this, Traci Wartenkin points to bottlenose dolphins trapped in Dolphin Cove at Sea World. Part of the exhibit's main attraction was that visitors could feed the dolphins.

The dolphins figured out how to avoid being touched while stealing the fish from the white trays visitors were using to feed them from. According to Wartenkin, this is important because it belies evolutionary or behaviourist explanations that deny agency and instead attribute animals' actions to "instinct" or genetic or behavioural coding. She suggests that the white trays were "perceptually significant" to the dolphins and that they "learn[ed] through interacting with other social agents and their environments" how to outwit the human beings who were clearly bothering them.[26] By way of perception, then, the dolphins transformed an object of their humiliation into an object of empowerment.

Because human beings, too, engage in perceptual intersubjectivity, the dolphins' change in physical comportment towards the spectators would have also changed how the humans perceived them. The seemingly permanent smiles etched onto the dolphin's faces, their movements towards the visitors, for example, may no longer have indicated docility and unquestioning friendliness, but may have come to indicate cleverness and perhaps even despair. Thus, by reclaiming these objects, the dolphins transformed the world they inhabited and the worlds of those who came to gawk and handle them, if only subtly.

Whatever angle from which we choose to analyse animals' acts of resistance, it is clear that these acts, no matter how subtle or symbolic, constitute meaningful expressions of agency. It is also important to highlight these and other examples of agency qua resistance to prevent the reification of animals as permanent victims. Asserting agency obviates the extinctionist perspective advanced by Gary Francione. According to Francione, all domesticated animals are condemned to slavery by virtue of their human-constructed ontologies and therefore are better off not existing at all. He is not wrong to point out that they have been selectively bred and genetically engineered to serve human ends, often to horrifying ends. Francione does not condone killing existing animals, but rather enjoins phasing them out by preventing their reproduction.[27] While one can understand his impulse, not only given the suffering modified animals are inflicted with *by their own bodies*, to suggest that their subjectivity is irredeemable is to confirm the dominant attitude towards them—that they are nothing more and nothing less than barely living commodities. It is true that many animals have been so invasively manipulated that they can barely move, let alone resist or assert agency meaningfully. However, to deny them the potential of developing agency should circumstances change only concedes defeat.

That said, it is equally if not more important to recognize that acts of resistance and other expressions of agency within the context of systemic violence are always already attenuated and cannot be conflated with a fully developed agency. This is the mistake many contemporary theorists of agency make. Elsewhere I point to Donna Haraway as one of the most well-known posthumanist scholars who commits this blunder. Haraway,

I argue, manipulates the language of agency to level the proverbial playing field between animals and their abusers. She distorts the meaning of
agency by claiming that animals in laboratories (and by implication other
sites of violence) are not only agents but also "partners" in their own
destruction—in other words, she implies that they are willing participants in their own destruction. Agency, as we have been defining it here,
is antithetical to such suicidal participation. Existential agency, by definition, entails resistance against the conditions of oppression. Yet, while
animals are agents in this distorted sense, and also workers, Haraway
maintains, they are not slaves. Slavery is reserved for human beings
whose nature is such that their exploitation is inevitably more ethically
problematic than that of animals.[28] Haraway's perversion of the concept
of agency and her misrepresentation of acts of resistance as equal to the
power that condemns animals to servitude derails the emancipatory project by obfuscating the reality of their victimization.

THE FOURTH APPROACH: REDEFINING HUMAN
AND NONHUMAN ANIMAL AGENCY AS CONSCIOUS
AND INTENTIONAL ACTION

A fourth strand of animal studies scholars seeks to redefine agency so
that it applies to both human and nonhuman animals, without broadening its scope so widely that it applies to every entity. Although there is
great variation among these scholars as to what constitutes agency, there
appears to be consensus that reason is not a prerequisite for agency, and
that conscious beings can be considered agents. From this perspective,
agency is roughly defined as the capacity to act in, on and through the
world, to express preferences, to make choices—from the mundane to the
life altering—and to orchestrate meaningful experiences for oneself.[29] As
Steward points out, traditional philosophical denials of animal agency
tend to belie our intuitive appreciation of it. As noted above, when unen-
cumbered with anthropocentric claims to the contrary, we intuitively recognize that animals are conscious, aware and engage in intentional and
meaningful actions and relationships. We witness "animals do such
things as build nests and burrows, seek food, attempt to elude predators". We observe them communicate in intricate ways, play, fight, and
problem solve, and we often do many of these things with them.[30] We
know from these and other observations that animals engage in self-
motivating action.

Of course, action is, like agency, a complicated concept with many
definitions attached to it, some of which are exclusive to humans. Ralf
Stoecker argues, for example, that although it is obvious that "many animals do act on various reasons", nevertheless, "strictly speaking—animals don't act. Strictly speaking, there is no animal action, only behavi-

our".[31] This is because actions, he claims, are the products of reason and its correlate, verbal language. "Actions . . . are just those of our doings that are due to our ability to align whatever we do to the call of reason, materialized in the call of the social practice".[32] Because animals do not engage in "practices of public deliberation", the proper manifestation of action, they cannot and do not act.[33]

But Stoecker's anthropocentric definition of action is by no means the only one. Maria Alvarez, for example, argues that agents act either intentionally or "for a reason", but not in the sense that the latter phrase is traditionally understood. With regard to the former, to act intentionally simply means that an agent "has some awareness of what [it] is doing, and some degree of control over it", while acting for a reason simply means that an agent consciously pursues a specific goal, or acts "in light of some fact that she is aware of, and in pursuit of a goal".[34] Other animals clearly engage in both kinds of action. Intention is a precondition for agency itself. It is also a precondition for what we understand to be "animal" in the context of ethics. Birds, fish, and mammals clearly act with awareness of what they are doing and exercise control over their actions. Awareness is concomitant with control in some sense, for awareness enables the agent to orient herself towards the fulfilment of the activity in which she is engaged. Agency in the second sense outlined by Alvarez refers to instrumental actions, with a specific goal in mind, such as, say, sheltering one's young from the cold and/or predators or seeking affection from one's companions. One acts for a reason, in other words, if one has a specific goal in mind one sets out to accomplish, but one does not need reason (in the way it is traditionally defined) to act for a reason. On this reading, if we take reason to refer to the optimization of outcomes, rather than as practical, reflective, or deliberative reasoning, most animals qualify as agents. Of course, the point is not to *expand* our definition of reason so as to include as many animals as possible in an otherwise human-centric conception of agency. The point, rather, is to define agency according to how animals actually exhibit it. They do so in part by acting for a variety of reasons, from seeking out food to initiating and engaging in complex patterns of play, to making demands on us and on each other, to indulging in the many indulgences a good life can and ought to afford them.

Phenomenology offers further insight into what animal agency constitutes. From a phenomenological perspective, agency is embodied and is manifested in animals' perceptual interactions with other subjects and objects. Animals are agents in a phenomenological sense via their capacity, as embodied subjects, to construct their own phenomenological worlds or *Umwelten*. The *Umwelt* is the perceptual "field" or environment that each human and nonhuman animal subject inhabits. "The *Umwelt* is not the world as such", but "the world of a living being. . . . It is the aspect of the world in itself to which the animal addresses itself".[35] The *Umwelt* is not the geographical or physical environment in which a subject is situated, in other words, but the *world of meaning* the subject constructs by way of intentionality.

Jacob von Uexküll explains that each subject relates to other subjects and objects as "carriers of meaning". Uexküll insists that while different subjects engage with carriers of meaning differently, no one experience is more valid than another, whether human or nonhuman. If one imagines the same living room, for example, with the same furniture in it (e.g., a dining table and a set of chairs, a sofa, a bookshelf, a cabinet, a stool, a lamp hanging from the centre of the ceiling), and imagines three different body subjects (human, dog and fly) inhabiting the space, one must imagine three different sets of perceptual experiences taking place. For the human subect from a Westernized cultural milieu, the floor will have a walking effect tone, the bookshelf will have a reading effect tone, and the desk will have a writing effect tone. For the dog, on the other hand, the table is likely to take on an eating effect tone (it may have food on it), while the floor and couch will take on a sitting effect tone. The other objects in the room will either blend into the background or take on an obstacle tone. Meanwhile, for the fly, everything will have a "running tone" — that is, it will be something the fly simply passes over, except for cutlery and dishes on the table that may have food on them, and also the lamp to which it is drawn for its heat and light.[36] Uexküll insists that while different subjects engage with carriers of meaning differently, no one experience is more valid than another, whether human or nonhuman. What is important for our purposes is Uexküll's emphasis on each subject's active participation in constructing a meaningful world for itself. As Traci Wartenkin points out, however, while subjects construct their own world, they are by no means atomized. Instead, subjects' "worlds are formed through [their] interactions with other beings and things, which are distinctively meaningful for them".[37] Each animal shapes how it engages in and with its own *Umwelt* and that of other subjects, which, in turn, shape its own perceptual experiences.

Thus, phenomenology teaches us that agency is *productive* and *creative*. In contrast to the objectivist position, which regards the world as passive and inert, the phenomenological position insists that both perceiver and perceived are actively involved in an intentional co-constitutive exchange. This is not to attribute false agency to inanimate objects, but rather to emphasize that perception mediates the subject's meaning-making. The subject does not impose meaning on objects but constructs meaning and makes worlds with those objects (and subjects). In the words of ecophenomenologist David Abram, "Perception always involves, at its most intimate level, the experience of active interplay, or coupling, between the perceiving body and that which it perceives".[38] It is in these participatory, productive, and creative elements of agency that phenomenological freedom lies, the freedom to produce and transform one's own world, albeit not without the active engagement of others.

These are just some examples of what animal agency constitutes. Even on these definitions alone, agency is an ethically and politically important concept, not least because it suggests that animals are entitled to playing an active role in determining how their lives unfold, that they are not just passive recipients of justice but also active members in determining what justice constitutes. But more than just revised definitions of agency are necessary for animals' agency to be mobilized in this way. For animal agency to truly come to life, as it were, a political structure must be implemented with this as one of its chief aims.

THE FOURTH APPROACH, PLUS: POLITICIZING ANIMAL AGENCY

In their 2011 book *Zoopolis: A Political Theory of Animal Rights*, Donaldson and Kymlicka make a compelling proposal for how to politicize animal agency. They suggest that we ascribe one of three categories of political membership to animals depending on what kind of agency they exhibit and what kinds of communities they do or could thrive in. Domesticated animals, they argue, ought to be considered co-citizens. This is because they are "dependent agents"—which is to say, they have come to depend on human beings to "play an active role in interpreting" and enabling their "subjective good".[39] Citizenship provides a formal institutional framework for carrying out these tasks.[40] As dependent agents, domesticated animals are not incompetent. To the contrary, they have a variety of competencies which it is our responsibility to recognize and promote. As they explain,

> First we must recognize that animals are trying to communicate, then we need to observe carefully to interpret individual repertoires [of gestures, vocalizations, and so on], and finally we need to respond appropriately—confirming for the animal that attempts to communicate with us are not a wasted effort.[41]

Rather than simply reducing animals to completely dependent moral patients, this approach actually seeks to promote more independence. At present, "a paternalistic frame reigns". Although in the paradigm of citizenship, "some paternalism is inevitable, we exercise far more control over animals' lives than is necessary for their safety".[42] The goal is to balance providing them the care they have come to rely on us for (e.g., providing shelter and food) with opening up channels for them to express their individual competencies and talents. Although domesticated animals are not deliberative agents, they do have political voices. Pointing to France's relaxed attitude towards the presence of dogs in public

places, for example, Donaldson and Kymlicka explain, "The dogs themselves, by their presence, are agents of change. They are not deliberate
agents. But they are agents—leading their lives, doing the things they
do—and because agency is exercised in the public realm it serves as a
catalyst for political deliberation".[43] What is important, then, is to translate animals' expressions of nondeliberative agency into practical
changes that promote the myriad forms of agency they do exhibit.

Wild animals, on the other hand, are "competent" agents who thrive
on distance from human beings and are fully capable of sustaining themselves. They live in their own communities, sometimes mixed with other
animals, but not with humans. As such, respecting their agency requires
that we accord them "legitimate sovereign authority" over their own
territory and communities and an absolute and irreversible claim to self-
determination and self-governance.[44] By conceptualizing wild animals as
members of sovereign communities, Donaldson and Kymlicka provide a
"secure normative and conceptual basis" for defending wild animal
agency, which a simple ethic of noninterference as advocated by traditional animal rights theorists fails to provide.[45] To be sure, sovereignty
requires that we let wild animals be, so to speak. But not without engaging in limited interventions that promote rather than undermine their
sovereignty, such as rescuing injured animals in the wake of natural disasters.[46] Sovereignty places very specific demands and limits on both its
members and those outside the sovereign community, demands and limits that are designed to protect the sovereign community against inva-
sion, usurpation, and destruction by outside forces. As political subjects
with political claims, entitlements, and rights, sovereign wild animals are
in a much stronger position to defend against human encroachment and
destruction of their territory and lives than they would otherwise be. In
Donaldson and Kymlicka's words,

> Sovereignty is a form of protection against external threats of annihila-
> tion, exploitation, or assimilation. It provides the space for commu-
> nities to develop along their own self-determining paths, under con-
> trolled conditions of interaction with outsiders, rather than being sub-
> jected to the unchecked forces of powerful outsiders (regardless of the
> good intentions of those outsiders).[47]

Sovereignty, in other words, offers a firm political structure by which to
formally protect and promote wild animals' agency in a meaningful way.

Finally, liminal animals, Donaldson and Kymlicka argue, ought to be
accorded denizenship. Liminal animals are "neither wilderness animals
nor domesticated animals", but "in-between" animals "who live amongst
us, even in the heart of the city: squirrels, raccoons, rats, starlings, spar-
rows, gulls, peregrine falcons, and mice, just to name a few".[48] Most
liminal animals avoid direct human contact, and some have suffered
from the impact of human encroachment on their territory, but others

have come to benefit from living in human settlements because of the "greater food sources, shelter, and protection" they offer.[49] Most liminal animals, therefore, live in mixed communities with humans, albeit in a different way than domesticated animals. They are spatially intermixed with us in an interspecies community, but not interpersonally or socially intermixed, at least not to the same extent as domesticated animals. As members of a mixed community, the principle of noninterference advocated by most traditional animal rights theorists does not apply.[50] According them denizenship is more appropriate, Donaldson and Kymlicak maintain, because it would protect their entitlement to living in and among urban settlements while preserving their relative independence. For example, as denizens they would be entitled to "secure residency", "fair terms of reciprocity", and "anti-stigma".[51] Their agency would be promoted through these entitlements in a number of ways. The first and the last entitlement would ensure that they would have the right to move about freely without being considered pests and being targeted for elimination. At present, their agency qua mobility and residency is consistently undermined because they are constantly under threat of violent intervention from human beings who can effectively injure and kill them with impunity through "pest control" initiatives.

Were Donaldson and Kymlicka's theory of animal agency to be implemented, it would clearly reap enormous benefits for other animals. Citizenship, sovereignty and denizenship as they have defined them here offer much more substantive positive rights to animals than any other approach posited thus far. While attributing personhood to animals, as a number of scholars and advocates such as Gary Francione, Peter Singer and Paola Cavalieri have proposed, would signal an important symbolic change, and may have significant legal repercussions, it does not capture what is most at stake in political and ethical recognition of animals—that they are not just passive bearers of negative rights but also agents who are entitled to play an active role in determining the shape their lives take.[52] However, while Donaldson and Kymlicka's theory of citizenship promises to make great gains for animals within the context of a liberal democracy, the spirit of their project—to promote animal agency and flourishing and the development of dynamic interspecies communities— if not the latter, might be realized to even greater success in a different political structure. It is outside the scope of this chapter to engage in a detailed critique of liberal citizenship theory, or to propose a substantive alternative in all its detail, but in brief, the main problem with citizenship theory is that, as a specifically liberal theory, it leaves the problem of capitalism relatively untouched. It fails to acknowledge and remedy the vast social and economic injustices perpetuated by the prevailing capitalist socioeconomic order, which, by its very nature, systematically undermines meaningful agency and democratic participation for the vast majority of citizens, especially among marginalized communities. Moving forward, perhaps we might try to formally promote and enable animal agency within the context of an explicitly anticapitalist socioeconomic and political system, one based loosely on socialist, communist, and/or anarchist principles. How this would take shape remains to be explored.

CONCLUSION

Of the four general approaches to determining who/what are agents and what this means ethically and politically that I have identified here, the last, which is to redefine agency according to how it actually manifests itself in conscious, sentient nonhuman animals, is the most promising and poses the fewest ethical and political risks. Remaining attached to the Kantian conception of agency only perpetuates anthropocentrism, and is, in a sense, dishonest. Claiming that everything, animate and inanimate, is an agent or conflating individual acts of resistance with full-fledged agency purges the concept of agency of its ethical and political salience and threatens to obscure the urgency of the task at hand to protect animals from the atrocities we casually inflict on them as a matter of course. Asserting that agency is present in every conscious, sentient human and nonhuman animal, and that it manifests itself in a variety of equally important ways, is imperative if we are to see the project of liberation through. But in order to do this successfully, we need to do more than simply redefine agency. We need to politicize it.

NOTES

1. Immanuel Kant, "Grounding for the Metaphysics of Morals", in *Grounding for the Metaphysics of Morals with On a Supposed Right to Lie Because of Philanthropic Concerns*, 3rd ed., trans. James W. Ellington (Indianapolis and Cambridge: Hackett, 1993), 53f.

2. Gilles Deleuze and Félix Guattari, *A Thousand Plateaus: Capitalism and Schizophrenia*, trans. Brian Massumi (Minneapolis: University of Minnesota Press, 1987); Bruno Latour, *We Have Never Been Modern*, trans. Catherine Porter (Cambridge, MA: Harvard University Press, 1993); N. Katherine Hayles, *How We Became Posthuman: Virtual Bodies in Cybernetics, Literature, and Informatics* (Chicago; London: University of Chicago Press, 1999). See also Diana Coole and Samantha Frost, ed., *New Materialisms: Ontology, Agency, and Politics* (Durham: Duke University Press, 2010); Jane Bennett, *Vibrant Matter: A Political Ecology of Things* (Durham: Duke University Press, 2010); Myra Hird, "Meeting with the Microcosmos", *Environment and Planning: Society and Space* 28 (2010): 36–37, doi: 10.1068/d2706ws; Ian Bogost, *Alien Phenomenology or What It's Like to Be a Thing* (Minneapolis: University of Minnesota Press, 2012).

3. Tom Regan, *The Case for Animal Rights* (Berkeley; Los Angeles: University of California Press, 2004), xvi.

4. Regan, *The Case for Animal Rights*, 243.

5. Regan, *The Case for Animal Rights*, xvii.

6. Paola Cavalieri, *The Animal Question: Why Nonhuman Animals Deserve Human Rights* (Oxford; New York: Oxford University Press, 2001), 29.

7. Marc Bekoff and Jessica Pierce, *Wild Justice: The Moral Lives of Animals* (Chicago; London: University of Chicago Press, 2009), ix.

8. "Miracle Pets", http://www.youtube.com/watch?v=1JiJzqXxgxo, accessed 22 December 2012; "'Hero' Pig Rescues Baby Goat from Drowning", http://www.youtube.com/watch?v=yLV5Lr5pauc, accessed 22 December 2012; "Dog Adopts Orphaned Goslings", http://www.youtube.com/watch?v=E70kQHvacNU, accessed 22 December 2012.

9. Jennifer S. Holland, *Unlikely Friendships: 47 Remarkable Stories from the Animal Kingdom* (New York: Workman Publishing, 2011), 91; 131; 47.

10. Debra Durham and Debra Merskin, "Animals, Agency, and Absence: A Discourse Analysis of Institutional Animal Care and Use Committee Meetings", in *Animals and Agency: An Interdisciplinary Exploration*, ed. Sarah E. McFarland and Ryan Hediger, *Human Animal Studies*, vol. 8, series ed. Kenneth Shapiro (Leiden and Boston: Brill, 2009), 229.

11. Durham and Merskin, "Animals, Agency, and Absence", 239.

12. For a detailed critique of this and other passages in Myra Hird's article, see Zipporah Weisberg, "The Trouble with Posthumanism: Bacteria Are People Too", in *Thinking the Unthinkable: New Readings in Critical Animal Studies*, ed. John Sorenson (Toronto: Canadian Scholar's Press, 2014), 108.

13. Hird, "Meeting with the Microcosmos", 36–37.

14. Hird, "Meeting with the Microcosmos", 36f.

15. Hird, "Meeting with the Microcosmos", 37.

16. Hird, "Meeting with the Microcosmos", 38.

17. Paul W. Taylor cited in Sarah E. McFarland and Ryan Hediger, "Approaching the Agency of Other Animals: An Introduction", in *Animals and Agency*, 2.

18. Helen Steward, "Animal Agency", in *Inquiry* 52, no. 3 (2009): 229, doi: 10.1080/00201740902917119.

19. Carolino Moreno, "Tiger Kills Trainer During Circus Performance for Circo Suarez in Senora, Mexico", Huffington Post, 4 February 2013, http://www.huffingtonpost.com/2013/02/04/tiger-kills-trainer-mexico_n_2617478.html.

20. Gabriela Cowperthwaite, *Blackfish*, Magnolia Pictures, 2013.

21. Conversation with pattrice jones at VINE Sanctuary in Springfield, Vermont, on 9 July 2014.

22. Jean-Paul Sartre, *Being and Nothingness*, trans. Hazel E. Barnes (New York; London: Washington Square Press, 1984), 560.

23. Sartre, *Being and Nothingness*, 559.

24. Sartre, *Being and Nothingness*, 560.

25. Sartre, *Being and Nothingness*, 559.

26. Traci Wartenkin, "Whale Agency: Affordances and Acts of Resistance in Captive Environments", in *Animals and Agency*, 34f.

27. Gary Francione, *Introduction to Animal Rights: Your Child or Your Dog* (Philadelphia: Temple University Press, 2000); "Animal Rights and Domesticated Nonhumans", *Abolitionistapproach.com Blog*, 10 January 2007, http://www.abolitionistapproach.com/?s=Animal+Rights+and+Domesticated+Nonhumans.

28. Zipporah Weisberg, "The Broken Promises of Monsters: Haraway, Animals, and the Humanist Legacy", *Journal for Critical Animal Studies* 2, no. 2 (2009): 37f.

29. McFarland and Hediger, "Approaching the Agency of Other Animals", 2. It should be noted Regan insists that adult mammals possess these capacities, and yet he does not associate them with agency per se.

30. Steward, "Animal Agency", 217.

31. Ralf Stoecker, "Why Animals Can't Act", *Inquiry* 52, no. 3 (2009): 256.

32. Stoecker, "Why Animals Can't Act", 267.

33. Stoecker, "Why Animals Can't Act", 268.

34. Maria Alvarez, "Acting Intentionally and Acting for a Reason", *Inquiry* 52, no. 3 (2009): 29, 296.

35. Maurice Merleau-Ponty, *Nature: Course Notes from the Collège de France*, comp. Dominique Séglard, trans. Dominique Séglard, *Northwestern University Studies in Phenomenology and Existential Philosophy*, series eds. James M. Edie, Anthony J. Steinbock, and John McCumber (Evanston: Northwestern University Press, 2003), 167.

36. Jacob von Uexküll, *A Foray into the Worlds of Animals and Humans with A Theory of Meaning*, trans. Joseph D. O'Neil, *Posthumanities*, vol. 12, series ed. Cary Wolfe (Minneapolis; London: University of Minnesota Press, 2010), 97.

37. Wartenkin, "Whale Agency", 23.

38. David Abram, *The Spell of the Sensuous: Perception and Language in a More-Than-Human World* (New York: Vintage, 1996), 57.

39. Donaldson and Kymlicka, *Zoopolis*, 175.

40. Donaldson and Kymlicka, *Zoopolis*, 107.

41. Donaldson and Kymlicka, *Zoopolis*, 109.

42. Donaldson and Kymlicka, *Zoopolis*, 109.

43. Donaldson and Kymlicka, *Zoopolis*, 114.

44. Donaldson and Kymlicka, *Zoopolis*, 177.

45. Donaldson and Kymlicka, *Zoopolis*, 177.

46. Donaldson and Kymlicka, *Zoopolis*, 182.

47. Donaldson and Kymlicka, *Zoopolis*, 180.

48. Donaldson and Kymlicka, *Zoopolis*, 210.

49. Donaldson and Kymlicka, *Zoopolis*, 210.

50. Donaldson and Kymlicka, *Zoopolis*, 213.

51. Donaldson and Kymlicka, *Zoopolis*, 241–48.

52. See, for example, Gary Francione, *Animals as Persons: Essays on the Abolition of Animal Exploitation* (New York: Columbia University Press, 2008); Paola Cavalieri and Peter Singer, ed., *The Great Ape Project* (New York: St. Martin's Griffin, 1993).

Part II

Epistemology: Knowing and Speaking for Nonhuman Animals

FIVE

Enchanted Worlds and Animal Others

Wayne Williams

Papers in animal ethics typically focus on applied and normative issues. They tend to concentrate, that is, on questions about how we ought to behave towards nonhuman animals (hereafter "animals") and on systems of ethics that best provide answers to such questions. In environmental ethics, by contrast, it is much more common to see a focus on metaethical and axiological issues—that is, on questions concerning the nature of value and on such second-order matters as the meaning of moral terms. This difference is understandable, at least up to a point. That humans and animals are, for the most part, sentient provides a seemingly obvious hook from which to hang moral considerability, whereas nonsentient entities, what will be referred to here for the sake of simplicity as natural entities, do not have a perspective on, and so cannot plausibly be said to care about, their own good or well-being.

The temptation, then, is to conceive of the value of natural entities as being only instrumental, to see them as having value only insofar as they hold value for sentient beings. For many environmental ethicists this is a diminished account of the value of natural entities, of things such as trees and other plants, of ecosystems and even of populations and species of sentient beings, and so, as noted, it is not surprising that axiological and metaethical questions feature more heavily in environmental ethics and environmental philosophy papers. It would be difficult to deal adequately with related first-order questions until these second-order matters are addressed.

In animal ethics, meanwhile, questions about value and the ontology or epistemology of ethical concepts might seem an unwelcome and unhelpful distraction if, as is commonly thought, sentience does indeed provide a sufficient explanation for why animals matter morally, and all the more so when animals continue to be slaughtered for their flesh, used as vivisection subjects, hunted for their skins or for human pleasure and so on. Better to focus on real issues rather than waste time on abstract theorizing and philosophical navel-gazing.

My overarching contention here, however, is that these second-order questions are not only illuminating but also foundational in any analysis of the moral relationship between humans and animals, so much so that consideration of such questions challenges any easy distinction between, on the one hand, the inherent value of humans and animals and, on the other, the merely instrumental value of nonsentient natural entities; it also makes such a distinction incompatible with any proper recognition of the moral worth of animals. In other words, I will argue that in order to viably account for the moral considerability of animals as well as humans, at the same time one needs to account for the noninstrumental value of natural entities.

To explore this, I will take as my starting point Tom Regan's thesis in "Does Environmental Ethics Rest on a Mistake?"[1] Given his rights-based, individualistic animal ethics, this might seem an odd choice, one that is antithetical to any holistic or noninstrumental account of environmental value and ethics, but I believe, and will try to argue here, that Regan's wider theory is in fact better suited than many to bridge what are often perceived as gaps between environmental and animal concerns. To make this argument I will offer a particular metaethical reading of some of the underlying principles, and although this reading might diverge from that suggested by Regan himself, I will nonetheless try to demonstrate its merits.

INHERENT WORTH AND INTRINSIC VALUE

Regan's theory of animal rights hardly needs introduction, and so I will not go into any lengthy exposition here. It is worthwhile reiterating some key points, however, first to clarify why it might seem out of keeping with many environmental ethics and, secondly, to contrast it with other dominant approaches to animal ethics.

Regan's theory is deontological. Like Kant, he rejects any normative system that treats morally considerable individuals as mere contributors to an aggregate good or mere means to a greater or collective end. He moves away, therefore, from the utilitarian normative principles that underpin theories of animal ethics such as that most famously espoused by Peter Singer, where what matters is that the best possible outcome be achieved for the greatest possible number.[2] Regan instead insists that each morally considerable individual has equal and categorical inherent value, "categorical" in the sense that it cannot be weighed favourably or unfavourably against that of another and cannot be traded off against another. Unlike Kant, he does not restrict this set of categorically inherently valuable individuals to those who can exercise full rational autonomy. Instead he includes all "subjects-of-a-life", by which he means any being that can "have a psychophysical identity over time and thus have an experiential welfare". He cites this as a sufficient rather than necessary condition of moral considerability, although as we will see there are few, if any, alternatives offered or thought plausible.

Subjects-of-a-life, then, have inherent moral value, and this is a value not based merely on sentience or the capacity to feel pain and pleasure, although this capacity is still central.[3] Regan rarely uses the term *sentience* in descriptions of his own position, presumably to mark a difference between his position and theories such as Singer's. It is not that he is denying that sentient experiences have their own intrinsic value, contrasted in this sense with mere instrumental value, although, as we can see below in his analysis of theories of value that might ground duties to nature, he questions whether sentient experiences in themselves can have direct moral relevance, and thus whether sentience on its own can be enough. Varner clarifies Regan's (and also Feinberg's) further requirements: "According to Regan and Feinberg . . . something more [than mere sentience] is required: the capacity to consciously desire things in one's future—it is in terms of one's desires for the future, rather than bare consciousness of pain, that Feinberg and Regan unpack the notion of harm".[4] Instead, for Regan, it is being a "subject-of-a-life" that matters. To be a subject-of-a-life a being must

> have beliefs and desires; perception, memory, and a sense of the future, including their own future; an emotional life together with feelings of pleasure and pain; preference- and welfare-interests; the ability to initiate action in pursuit of their desires and goals; a psychophysical identity over time; and an individual welfare in the sense that their experiential life fares well or ill for them, logically independently of their utility for others and logically independently of their being the object of anyone else's interests.[5]

For Regan, inherent moral worth is not the same as intrinsic value. As suggested above, he defines the latter quite broadly to include anything valued for its own sake and so contrasts it directly with instrumental value.[6] Inherent moral worth, on the other hand, is something that he characterizes as commanding moral respect and, as already noted, does so categorically.[7] It is having such inherent moral worth that makes the individual morally important in a manner not reducible to their experiences, and that therefore makes them deserving of rights and protections against the demands of a greater, aggregated good, and that makes each and every subject-of-a-life morally equal. It is, as Goodpaster clarifies, a criterion of moral considerability rather than one of moral significance; it establishes a categorical moral equality rather than a means of measuring moral worth against that of another.[8]

What does it mean to say, as Regan does in the quoted passage above, that having an experiential life that "fares well or ill" for a subject matters or is of value in a manner which is logically independent of the interests or values of others and thus categorical? His response to Carl Cohen's critique is illuminating in this regard.[9] Regan corrects Cohen's assertion that his (Regan's) distinction between moral patients and moral agents maps exactly onto the distinction between animals and humans.[10] Regan is clear that not all animals, or for that matter humans, qualify as moral *patients*, and that not all humans are moral *agents*.[11]

Cohen is right, however, to identify those holding inherent moral worth (though not merely or indeed always humans) as being thought of by Regan as morally valuable in an irreducible way, valuable in themselves rather than merely as the vessel or container of valuable experiences. This irreducibility of the subject is crucial for Regan and grounds their categorical worth *as individuals*, not to be merely weighed as a collection of interests against a greater aggregate of interests. The individual carries inherent worth as the *sine qua non* of value. As Korsgaard puts it, in her parallel argument for a (small *k*) kantian theory of animal rights, "[t]he reason there is such a thing as value in the world is that there are in the world beings who matter to themselves: who experience and pursue their own good. Were there no such beings, there would be no such thing as value. Were there no such beings, nothing would matter".[12]

If my thesis here, however, is that the theory of value underpinning Regan's animal ethics must at the same time be compatible with an extension of moral considerability to at least some natural entities, how does this fit with what looks to be an essential subjectivity and mindedness in Regan's conception of inherent moral worth?

THE ONTOLOGY OF VALUE

Regan distinguishes, following Rolston and others, between an ethic *of* the environment and an "ethic *for its use*".[13] The latter is an environmental ethic that gives importance only to the resources the environment provides to humans and perhaps to other sentient beings. The former, by contrast, looks to recognize what Rolston describes as an environmental value that is primary, rather than secondary, to human interests.[14] Regan argues that any attempt to develop an environmental ethic "that attempts to illuminate, account for or ground appropriate respect for and duty to natural entities by appealing to their intrinsic value" will fail.[15] Regan's thesis is, as one would expect, detailed and philosophically dense, and there is no way that I could hope to do it justice here. What I will attempt to do instead is to pick up on what I think are the points most relevant to the argument I am presenting.

Why, then, does Regan think that accounts of intrinsic value could not ground the sort of environmental ethic Rolston and other theorists seem to be seeking? Comparing a number of differing theories of value, he asks "what types or kinds of object [can be] deemed to have intrinsic value" and from here attempts to determine whether these could provide a basis for extending moral worth to natural entities and beyond subjects-of-a-life.[16] He does not deny that environmental objects or systems can have intrinsic value but rejects claims that any such intrinsic value could, in itself, ground either moral respect or moral duties. He aims to reject, in other words, any "ethic that attempts to illuminate, account for or ground appropriate respect for and duty towards natural entities by appealing to their 'intrinsic value' . . . [as] there is no theory of intrinsic value that can do the philosophical work that this conception imposes on it".[17]

Regan begins by asking whether the intrinsic value of mental states could generate the sort of inherent moral worth needed to ground an ethics of the environment, noting that any mental states theory of value is immediately unsuitable because the sort of natural entities one is seeking to provide a morally relevant axiological account for are exactly those that lack mental states.[18]

Natural entities to one side, he accepts, at least in general and for the sake of argument, that mental states such as pleasure can be intrinsically good, and that most people would see pleasure as being of positive value most of the time. What he objects to is the idea that it could be the *only* intrinsic good, citing various other mental states that are valuable in their own right in a manner that could not feasibly be reduced to pleasure. He gives the examples of "the experiences of awe and mystery, moments of uncommon appreciation and nostalgia, times when we have a deepened sense of our embeddness [*sic*] in our familiar history", and so on.[19] This multitude of intrinsically valuable and incommensurable mental states, then, make it impossible to weigh one against the other or to determine which would take priority over others, and so this theory of intrinsic value is incapable of grounding an account of our duties.

My focus here, however, is on his third claim against the mental state theory of intrinsic value, and his similar reason for rejecting theories of value based on states of affairs. A state of affairs theory of value can include the intrinsic value of mental states, but importantly, as Regan notes, need not be restricted to or dependent upon mental states. He cites G. E. Moore as an example of a proponent of such a view, one in which the beauty of a sunset could have intrinsic value not only insofar as the mental state of someone perceiving it could have intrinsic value but also in a manner not requiring mental states at all.[20] In other words, the value of a beautiful sunset could, according to this view as Regan describes it, not need conscious valuers in order to exist. Such value would be a realist property independent of the need to be perceived, and thus, Regan suggests, might appear to provide a better basis for an ethics of the environment than one dependent on mental states. This appearance is deceptive, however, or so he claims, because even if we look past the metaphysical questions such realist value properties give rise to, the fact would remain that the intrinsic value of something like a beautiful sunset is no better suited to grounding moral worth than the mental states Regan has already considered. He asks what it can mean "'to respect a beautiful sunset', or 'to respect a beautiful rendition of 'O Danny Boy'? We can, of course, respect the skill or ingenuity of an artist or performer who, let us agree, creates a beautiful painting or gives a beautiful performance. . . . But none of this is the same as 'showing respect for beauty'".[21]

Thus the intrinsic value of states of affairs (or, for that matter, mental states) is not adequate to ground moral rights or duties not only because of the incommensurability of the values involved but also because it lacks any moral imperative. Sure, a sunset might be beautiful, and so command aesthetic respect, but that is not enough in itself to command moral respect, and the same is true of any other example of intrinsic value one might draw from mental states or states of affairs. It is in large part this aspect of Regan's thesis that I am seeking to challenge here—not that a sunset should command moral respect, per se, but his presumption that there is not a clearer link between what is intrinsically valuable and what is morally considerable, or at least relevant.

AUTONOMY AND THE MORAL PATIENT

As noted earlier, Regan goes on to explore other possible theories of intrinsic value on which an ethic of the environment could be based. I want to stick with his reasons for rejecting mental states and states of affairs theories though, not because I think they are any more useful than he suggests, but because I believe his reasons for rejecting them point to something of a metaethical tension in the axiology that informs his own theory of animal rights. To see this, let me return to some of the basic aspects of this theory.

Remember that Regan, although offering a theory that is Kantian up to a point, extends moral consideration to moral patients as well as moral agents. He distinguishes between Kantian autonomy and preference autonomy. The former is the kind of fully rational autonomy that characterizes moral agents and, for Kant, was required for a being to be morally considerable and to be considered as an "end-in-themselves". Kant says:

> Beings whose existence depends, not on our will, but on nature, have none the less, if they are non-rational beings, only a relative value as means, and are consequently called *things*. Rational beings, on the other hand, are called *persons* because their nature already marks them out as

ends in themselves—that is, as something which ought not to be used merely as a means—and consequently imposes to that extent a limit on all arbitrary treatment of them (and is an object of reverence). [22]

Regan's theory, however, extends inherent moral worth to moral patients as well as moral agents and so characterizes both moral agents and patients as categorically morally equal, thus requiring that they be treated as ends in themselves. It does seem here that Regan's theory is left in something of a strange position, and to my mind this is made the more so because of his rejection of the two theories of value considered in the previous section. In extending moral consideration beyond the Kantian moral agent to moral patients, and in dropping the requirement that those who are to be considered worthy of moral regard must themselves be capable of acting morally and being responsible for so doing, the grounds for extending categorical inherent worth to a nonmorally autonomous valuer is left somewhat opaque.

If Regan retains the Kantian requirement of full rational autonomy, then this would involve pinning moral worth not merely on a subject being capable of valuing, or having ends, but on moral agency and the capacity for moral responsibility. A moral agent's own values are thus due moral respect, whether that takes the form of commendation or censure, because they are the considered views of someone who is herself capable of deciding what is appropriately to be valued and who is therefore the appropriate bearer of responsibility for such judgements. Thus it is their will as moral agents, not mere valuers, that warrants their categorical moral status as ends-in-themselves. Regan doesn't advance this theory of value because if he did he would be unable to extend moral worth to moral patients, thus excluding many humans and most, if not all, animals.

The difficulty for Regan given his rejection of intrinsic value as a basis for inherent moral worth is how his own theory of value is to ground such an extension of categorical moral worth to moral patients, and it seems there is an unexplained gap here. Something being intrinsically valuable, Regan argued, is not enough to make it worthy of moral respect or appropriate as a basis for moral duties. Merely being of intrinsic value is not, according to this view, prescriptive or action guiding. That a subject-of-a-life is worthy of moral respect and generates moral duties is grounded in such a subject having a life that fares well or ill for them, having an identity over time and the other conditions that Regan describes. Essentially, it is the fact that such a being values and that these values matter to the individual as a persisting subject that seems to do the work for Regan's theory, but why does being a valuer, in this sense, matter morally in a way that merely being of intrinsic value does not?

What such subjects value matters to them, of course, but it is no longer clear whether it *should* matter *or be respected simply because it matters to them.* They differ to the Kantian autonomous agent whose will is respected on the grounds that they bear the responsibility for that judgement. If the mere fact that something has intrinsic value cannot be sufficient to explain why it should command moral respect, then Regan's own argument for extending categorical moral worth to moral patients begins to look incomplete.

ENCHANTED WORLDS, EMBODIED SUBJECTS

Perhaps, then, if Regan is to argue that moral patients as well as moral agents are due categorical moral regard, his rejection of the prescriptiveness or action-guidingness of intrinsic value should be reexamined. To do that, further axiological and then metaethical questions need to be addressed.

In the relationship between valuer and world, where does value reside? One might *initially* wonder, somewhat too simplistically as we will see, whether value is subjective and projected by valuers onto a valueless, disenchanted world or whether value somehow exists in the world objectively and independent of valuers. In earlier papers Regan proposes an explicitly realist view, that a thing has value because of certain real properties of that thing.[23] At times in "Does Environmental Ethics Rest on a Mistake?" his position seems still to be in accordance with this, such as when he allows, albeit somewhat sceptically, the possibility that natural entities can have their own intrinsic value; value, that is, in their own right and not just insofar as they serve other valued ends.[24]

Two things should be noted here, however, that at the very least prevent us reading Regan as offering an *objectivist* account of value. The first is that intrinsic value need not be the same thing as objective value, or value that could exist independent of valuers. To say that something is intrinsically valuable need only mean that it is valued for itself, still compatible with the ineliminable role of the valuer.

Secondly, even if Regan were offering an account of value that was not only realist but also objectivist, it is not at all clear that he is offering a similar account of *moral* value. In fact, his allowing of the possibility that natural entities might have intrinsic value is coupled with an explicit denial that such value could carry any prescriptivity.[25] What it is for something to have value as well as moral value warrants further examination.

Taking as a starting point that moral agents have moral worth, or *inherent value* as Regan uses this term, he then argues that because moral agents share with moral patients the characteristic of having a subjective life that can fare well or ill for them, in a manner that matters to them, and because this similarity is relevant to what it is to have inherent value, both moral agents and moral patients have this value equally. Now, one way to interpret this is to see it as a broadly projectivist conception of moral value, according to which what is valued by a morally considerable subject is *for that reason* of moral worth—the subject projects moral value onto objects, states of affairs or the natural entities that are otherwise absent moral weight. This might seem to be an attractive way of making sense of Regan's extension of moral worth from moral agents (including most, but not all, humans) to human and animal moral patients. Moral agents and patients have equal inherent value simply because they have a subjective existence that can fare well or ill for them and that it does so matters *to them*. However, there are at least two reasons for not accepting this too readily.

If value is projected by a subject, rather than being required of the subject in some way in response to the properties of the valued object, then some sort of story is required to explain whether and when evaluations are correct or incorrect, warranted or unwarranted. One could bite the bullet here and stick to a fully subjectivist account of value, and indeed moral value, according to which it is simply sufficient that a subject finds something to be of value. Aside from any other philosophical challenges that such simple subjectivism would face, it does not seem adequate to the task of underpinning Regan's deontological theory of animal ethics and the constraints on human behaviour that go with it.

Alternatively, one could try to make sense of the commitments that would make coherent any moral "truths" derived from a projectivist axiology, as is attempted by Blackburn or Gibbard, for example.[26] Regan, however, does not offer any sort of in-depth metaethical account along these lines, nor does it seem from his comments on the possible intrinsic value of natural entities that he would wish to.

Perhaps, then, something in between an objectivist value realism independent of subjects and a projectivist account of value would be more amenable to Regan's animal ethics, something like the theory of value outlined by McDowell—one that is realist but that seeks to retain the irreducible subjectivity of values. In "Values and Secondary Qualities" McDowell challenges the conception of objectivity in Mackie's error theory and according to which moral discourse is systematically in error because it depends for its meaning on objective moral facts or properties, when such objective facts or properties do not exist.[27] McDowell's thesis is that the kind of objectivity Mackie demands of moral qualities, one independent of perception, is inappropriate. He suggests, however, that there is another sense in which moral value could be said to be objective, without dissolving the essential subjectivity or phenomenal character of morality; that it can be a perception or awareness of "properties genuinely possessed by elements in a not exclusively phenomenal reality".[28] In other words, our values can be appropriately grounded in or merited by realist conditions of the world with which we engage.

McDowell compares value perception with that of colour, but only up to a point. There is a similarly secondary-quality nature to these perceptions, in that both are subjective and experienced responses to realist properties of the world, while at the same time having necessarily phenomenal aspects. Thus we see an object as red, and our perception of redness, or our phenomenal experience of redness, cannot simply be reduced to the physical properties that cause a perception of redness to occur but are essentially and inextricably a result, in part, of those physical properties. However, if something is red and I, as a subject with a capacity for normal colour vision, perceive it in normal lighting conditions, then it will appear to me as red and I will have a visual experience of redness. The object and conditions combine with my visual capacities to elicit the phenomenal response—the response is not subject to any judgement on my part. McDowell argues that what happens in the case of value is that the perceived qualities of the object *merit an appropriate response* by the perceiver.[29] To value, then, is to perceive that the response is merited.

McDowell seeks here to avoid a merely intuitionist account of moral values in which our moral judgements are determined for us by realist facts and we are inexplicably "simply helping ourselves to truth", and in which "external" or realist reality takes priority over our engagement with it, but he does not accept that our attitudes or sentiments take such priority.[30] He quotes Blackburn, who distinguishes between a realist view, according to which "moral features of things are the parents of our sentiments", and a Humean projectivist view that holds instead that moral features are the "children" of our sentiments.[31] McDowell's view, by contrast, is what he describes as a "no priority" account in which values arise from our subjective sensibilities to a realist world and are a product of both simultaneously, and in a manner that does not allow the two to be separated.[32] They arise, that is, from a "space of reasons".[33]

A theory of value construed broadly along these lines suggests the following points. First is an acceptance that value only exists in its *full* sense so long as there are valuers. However, this does not mean that the value of something like a redwood tree can only *come from* valuers or be projected by valuers; rather, it means that the intrinsic value of the tree, if it has intrinsic value, is a response merited from valuers by properties of the tree.

Second is that these sorts of judgements or merited responses do not come from "outside" or some wholly objective perspective (a contradiction in terms in any case). Rather, the judgement is informed precisely by being made from within a practice or even a "form of life". This has implications in keeping with Regan's wider theory, particularly in relation to how we conceive of "subjects", or "subjects-of-a-life", as Regan would have it, and their moral relevance.

Rather than conceiving of the subject as meriting moral regard for being an end-in-itself, with all of the Kantian connotations that suggests (notably the requirement that the subject be morally autonomous), or, on the other hand, being forced to choose between projectivist and objectivist accounts of value, I suggest that one instead sees both moral agents and patients as embodied subjects, encountering a world imbued with values. Valuing, then, including moral valuing, becomes a mode of engagement with the world, further implying that moral respect becomes something warranted not by moral patients (as well as moral agents) simply through their nature as valuers or through the intrinsic value of natural entities, but required of moral agents *qua* moral agents wherever and whenever appropriate evaluative responses are merited. In other words, we are looking in the wrong place and from the wrong direction if we expect prescriptivity to come from the natural properties of a valuable object on its own, or from the uncritical evaluative responses of a moral patient on their own. Instead, prescriptivity comes from the nature of a moral agent's evaluative engagement with the world, including their engagement with natural entities and with both moral patients and other moral agents.

This alternative conception of the subject, suggested by Burwood, Lennon and Gilbert, retains an irreducibly first-person perspective but places it firmly in the physical world rather than having it abstracted or removed as some sort of separate, Cartesian entity.[34] The subject is conceived of as embodied, with the body being not merely an object to which the self, or person, is attached or in which it resides. The body *is* the self, *is* the person. However, the subject is not conceived of as being reducible to mere physical responses. The subject has a first-personal conscious perspective and reacts and responds to a world that presents itself not as mere cold, disenchanted facts but as suffused with value and meriting appropriate responses.

> Moral values are real features of the world, but are detectable only to creatures like ourselves equipped to respond to them in a characteristic way. But this way is precisely to find them as calling for action that brings about the good and eliminates the bad. The response required to recognise value is that of pursuing it, so that recognition of value and motivation go hand in hand. . . .
>
> To find something desirable, however, is not to judge that it has some objective property in virtue of which it should be desired. For one could make that judgement without being moved by the desirability it imputes. Rather, to find something desirable is already to be moved to an appropriate response. . . . Yet it would be a mistake to think that the notion of desirability could be reduced to a disposition to bring about such a response . . . [f]or that would be to miss out the key feature here. The desirability of the object is what makes the response reasonable or appropriate. It brings it within the scope of reasons which on reflection

can be modified, for in the light of such reflection I can judge my response to be misguided. It is this feature that allows such desirability to be counted as a real feature of the world, albeit a perspectival one.[35]

The embodied subject, then, engages with a world imbued with value and requiring evaluative responses. Note the distinction, above, between something being "desired" and "desirable".[36] The former is not sufficient to entail the latter, which further requires critically informed judgement. Thus, evaluative responses themselves are not enough to make something of value; they can be mistaken and can rightly be revised or corrected upon reflection ("I was wrong to positively value X and would not so value it again . . ."), particularly by those with more developed critical faculties and evaluative sensibilities.

For moral agents there are further facets to this engagement. That animals, like humans, are embodied subjects is prima facie cause to see their individual existence as one permeated with valued engagement. The prescriptivity one attaches to this, however, comes not merely from the fact that such valued engagement matters to the subject, but that moral agents can have a morally evaluative response, appropriate or inappropriate, proper or improper, to the fact that it matters to the subject. The evaluative engagement of the moral patient or agent, animal or human, requires and thus prescribes an appropriate response from moral agents. By the same logic, however, the intrinsic and indeed instrumental value of nonsubjects such as natural, nonsentient entities also demands appropriate responses. Regan is wrong, then, to think that the intrinsic value of natural entities cannot ground moral respect for such entities. Consider Routley's "last man" example:

> *The Last Man.* You are the last human being. You shall soon die. When you are gone, the only life remaining will be plants, microbes, invertebrates. The following thought runs through your head: Before I die, it sure would be nice to destroy the last remaining Redwood. Just for fun. What, if anything, would be wrong with destroying that Redwood? Destroying it will not hurt anyone.[37]

The intuitive response to the "last man" example is that it would be wrong to fell the redwood tree, but these intuitions are difficult to account for in terms of sentience or ends-in-themselves theories of value, including any theory based on Regan's subject-of-a-life criterion. Of course, one could, to borrow from and paraphrase J. J. C. Smart, simply say "so much the worse for our intuitions".[38] Clearly, however, I am suggesting that there are other options. The example is set up so that the felling of the tree has no sentient-interests or subject-of-a-life-affecting results precisely so as to close off such accounts while still involving the role of an agent in choosing to fell the tree. Consider, by way of comparison, a slightly different example where we are asked to contemplate the felling of the last redwood tree by some natural event, say, lightning or a naturally occurring wildfire, subsequent to the extinction, and therefore absent the existence, of all sentient beings. While not intuitively carrying the moral-agent-related import of the first example, we might nonetheless imagine such an event with some sense of regret, not because any agent is responsible but simply because we attach intrinsic value to the imagined redwood tree, and perhaps particularly so as it is the last of its kind. Of course, the regret itself, even if presenting as phenomenologically real, is not grounded in a response to real properties. Nonetheless, one imagines it as the appropriate response had it been or if one imagines that such real properties were to obtain.

Jamieson is correct in pointing out that part of the problem with such examples, and thus much of the explanation for our intuitive response to them, stems from the fact that by imagining the effects we put ourselves into the example.[39] We cannot, so to speak, imagine the scenario from nowhere, and thus the example of the felling of the tree cannot be contemplated from the agent-free perspective that its setup requires. Nonetheless, this points to something further and illuminating about the relation between the "last man" as agent and the intrinsic value of the tree in both the "last man" and the lightning/wildfire examples.

Because the world presents to the moral agent laden with moral demands, imperatives, cares and rewards, we cannot imagine these examples without imagining the intuitive regret at the loss of the redwood tree because we cannot imagine such a world without the value it presents itself with. What makes this value morally significant, in this case, is partly the fact that it is the actions of this last person that fells the redwood tree. However, even in the different example, where we imagine the final redwood tree being felled by natural events, an intuitive response of regret is still an appropriate one. If the last redwood tree has value because of its natural properties, one of them perhaps being that it is the last of its kind and thus it is appropriate to value it, then it would be appropriate to regret its loss (or to imagine regret in the imagined instance of its loss). It would therefore not be to one's credit to fail to have such a response. Of course, the same would not be said of moral patients precisely because they are not considered culpable for inappropriate responses.

According to this account so far, then, there is a difference between moral agents and other beings and entities in that only moral agents can be culpable for their evaluative responses. Moral patients and natural entities can be of value, including intrinsic value, and can command moral respect but cannot be expected to behave morally. Regan, however, says that moral agents and patients do not just command moral respect but also do so categorically.

In the case of the embodied subject, the same principle applies. It is not the moral autonomy of the individual that affords the embodied subject categorical moral worth—it is the fact that its individuality is irreducible. A wholly objectivist account of value would not need the existence of subjects, and so value could be abstracted entirely from them, whereas according to this account value depends for its full sense on the existence of such valuing subjects. Valuing is a mode of engagement between subject and world. For the moral agent, however, this means that an appropriate response to value requires an understanding from within the practice of valuing (or at least with sufficient insight), not from outside.

Here, then, is the problem. Animals, like humans, are clearly embodied subjects; they are "others" whose engagement with the world clearly matters to them. This is not to say that I infer this from their bodily existence, as analogous to mine. It's not that I see another in pain, for example, and infer that this is something that matters: *I see it as something that matters*. But if I am to respond appropriately to it, then I need to have some understanding of how it matters. Regan counsels against seeing individual interests as mere parts of an aggregate because he is wary of the perfectionism that that would entail.[40] He is wary, that is, of ranking some goods ahead of others in a manner that ranks the individuals whose goods they are ahead of others. Given the account of value being offered here, one where value derives from engagement between a subject and the world and thus has no wholly objective truth, while also being denied the anything-goes freedom of simple subjectivism, Regan's wariness is even more appropriate. Without the deontological prohibitions that protect a subject from being treated as a mere vessel for positive or negative value, the moral agent is tasked with weighing up competing interests and indulging in the kind of pursuit of aggregate good that Regan is rightly wary of and that is inevitably prone to a "similar minds" or "similar interests" bias. Animals inevitably suffer from such attempts at value calculus, insofar as any human judgement of good or bad is necessarily a step removed from nonhuman perspectives by the otherness of species difference. It is inevitable, of course, that there are scenarios in which the overriding of deontological prohibitions will be required, but here I would suggest that Regan and others, notably Francione,[41] are broadly correct in emphasizing strict limits and means for considering these and in protecting the animal from anthropogenic or anthropocentric bias in our value judgements by affording them the protection of deontological or abolitionist constraints on human freedoms.[42]

What it is to be an embodied subject and of categorical inherent moral worth is precisely to be the kind of subject who engages with a world imbued with values, values that *merit* appropriate responses and constitute according reasons. That the inherent worth of moral patients, as well as moral agents, is categorical remains as crucial for my conception as it is for Regan's precisely because it is only moral agents who have the capacity to reflect *morally* on values, and yet they are necessarily confined to their own subjective and imperfect understanding of what such values are.

That the world is imbued with values, and that my engagement with it and the engagement with it by other subjects is inherently evaluative, implies not only that there is intrinsic value in the world (the kind that merits awe, fear, aesthetic wonder and so on), and that it is importantly but not wholly independent of the evaluative responses of valuers, but also that there is no gap in explaining the fact of such values and their reason-givingness in the manner that Regan supposed. It is the conception of the appropriate mental state, as an embodied one rather than one that is removed from reality or merely a brute effect of it, that underpins the difference between my account and Regan's, but it is with humbled regard for how much of his account Regan got right, and importantly right, that I have attempted to outline this difference.

NOTES

1. Tom Regan, "Does Environmental Ethics Rest on a Mistake?", *The Monist* 75 (1992): 161–82.

2. Peter Singer, *Animal Liberation*, 2nd ed. (London: Pimlico, 1995), 8–9.

3. Tom Regan, *The Case for Animal Rights*, 2nd ed. (Berkeley and Los Angeles, CA: University of California Press, 2004), 242–43.

4. Gary Varner, "Sentientism", in *A Companion to Environmental Philosophy*, ed. Dale Jamieson (Oxford: Blackwell, 2003), 195.

5. Regan, *The Case*, 242–43.

6. Regan, "Does Environmental Ethics . . . ?", 163.

7. Regan, *The Case*, 243–48.

8. Kenneth E. Goodpaster, "On Being Morally Considerable", in *Environmental Philosophy: From Animal Rights to Radical Ecology*, ed. Michael E. Zimmerman, J. Baird Callicott, George Sessions, Karen J. Warren and John Clark (Upper Saddle River, NJ: Prentice Hall, 2001), 59.

9. Regan, *The Case*, xxiii–xxvi.

10. Regan, *The Case*, xxv.

11. Regan, *The Case*, 244.

12. Christine Korsgaard, "Fellow Creatures: Kantian Ethics and Our Duties to Animals" (paper presented as *The Tanner Lecture on Human Values* at the University of Michigan, 6 February 2004), 36, http://www.people.fas.harvard.edu/~korsgaar/CMK. FellowCreatures.pdf (accessed 12 November 2013).

13. Regan, "Does Environmental Ethics . . . ?", 162.

14. Holmes Rolston III, *Environmental Ethics: Duties to and Values in the Natural World*, quoted in Regan, "Does Environmental Ethics . . . ?", 161.

15. Regan, "Does Environmental Ethics . . . ?", 162. This is the third of four sequential characterizations of an ethic of the environment that Regan lists, and the fourth adds the further requirement, from Callicott, that a differentiation be established between the intrinsic value of wild and domestic species. There is room for debate about how Callicott intends this, but it would take more space than I have here and it is not, in any case, relevant to the argument I am presenting. For that reason I have quoted the third of the characterizations Regan lists.

16. Regan, "Does Environmental Ethics . . . ?", 163.

17. Regan, "Does Environmental Ethics . . . ?", 162.

18. Regan, "Does Environmental Ethics . . . ?", 164–67.

19. Regan, "Does Environmental Ethics . . . ?", 165.
20. Regan, "Does Environmental Ethics . . . ?", 168.
21. Regan, "Does Environmental Ethics . . . ?", 169.
22. Immanuel Kant, *The Moral Law: Groundwork of the Metaphysics of Morals*, trans. Herbert James Paton (London: Hutchinson, 1947), 96.
23. Tom Regan, "On the Nature and Possibility of an Environmental Ethic", *Environmental Ethics* 3 (1981): 19–34.
24. Regan, "Does Environmental Ethics . . . ?", 169.
25. Regan, "Does Environmental Ethics . . . ?", 169–71.
26. Simon Blackburn, *Essays on Quasi-Realism* (Oxford: Oxford University Press, 1993); Allan Gibbard, *Wise Choices, Apt Feelings* (Oxford: Clarendon Press, 1990).
27. John McDowell, "Values and Secondary Qualities", in *Mind, Value and Reality* (Cambridge, MA: Harvard University Press, 1998), 131–50; John Mackie, *Ethics: Inventing Right and Wrong* (London: Penguin, 1977), 15–49.
28. McDowell, "Values and Secondary Qualities", 141.
29. McDowell, "Values and Secondary Qualities", 144.
30. McDowell, "Values and Secondary Qualities", 162.
31. McDowell, "Values and Secondary Qualities", 159.
32. McDowell, "Values and Secondary Qualities", 162.
33. McDowell, "Values and Secondary Qualities", 163.
34. Stephen Burwood, Kathleen Lennon and Paul Gilbert, *Philosophy of Mind* (London: University College London Press, 1998), 64–65.
35. Burwood, Lennon and Gilbert, *Philosophy of Mind*, 64–65.
36. This distinction has, of course, been noted by many others. For a clear and succinct example, see Alexander Sesonske, *Value and Obligation: The Foundations of an Empiricist Ethical Theory* (New York: Galaxy/Oxford University Press, 1964), 43.
37. Richard Routley's thought experiment as described by D. Schmidtz and E. Willott in their introduction to their edited volume *Environmental Ethics: What Really Matters, What Really Works*, quoted in Raffaele Rodogno, "Sentientism, Wellbeing and Environmentalism", *Journal of Applied Philosophy* 27 (2010): 84.
38. J. J. C. Smart and Bernard Williams, *Utilitarianism: For and Against* (Cambridge: Cambridge University Press, 1973), 68.
39. Dale Jamieson, *Ethics and the Environment* (Cambridge: Cambridge University Press, 2008), 74–75.
40. Regan, *The Case*, 233–35.
41. Gary L. Francione, *Animals as Persons: Essays on the Abolition of Animal Exploitation* (New York: Columbia University Press, 2008).
42. Regan, *The Case*, 286–97.

SIX

"The Flesh of My Flesh"

Animality, Difference, and "Radical Community" in Merleau-Ponty's Philosophy

Jonathan D. Singer

I was not present when Sammy—my family's silky terrier—passed away, and part of me is glad that distance and timing spared me what my father has described as the "most traumatic day" of his life. Sammy's health had slowly declined during the last two years of his life, and so his death was not entirely unexpected when, on 8 April 2011, two veterinarians reported that his organs were failing and that not much more could be done for him. Around a week prior to what my father describes as a "life-changing" decision, my parents had brought Sammy to the vet to be fed food and medicine intravenously. On 8 April, my father met my mother at the vet's office on his way home from work. The instant my father stepped into the area where Sammy was being kept, he perked up, and our vet remarked, "He knows who loves him". My parents were told that not much more could be done for him, and the decision was made. They knew that they were about to "lose an important member of the family". My dad even referred to Sammy as his "second son"—indeed, they would frequently call me Sammy's "brother". They said their goodbyes and cried inconsolably throughout the hours and days that followed. My father had initially resisted getting a dog; however, according to my mother, Sammy's death was the first time that she ever saw my father cry. Sammy was buried in a pet cemetery near our home, and to this day my father visits his grave every weekend and talks to him (as he always did), claiming that Sammy "had more humanity in him than most people".

Most humans who have lived with dogs know what it is like to enjoy such a bond with an animal; they know what it is like to be recognized and affirmed in the eyes—or in the bark, or in the wag of a tail—of an *other* Other. But are such experiences merely sentimental, anthropomorphic "projections"? As Merleau-Ponty argues, such an interpretation or dismissal of such experiences overlooks (and indeed begs) the very question that needs to be answered: What is it that prompts such a supposed projection in the first place? How are we to account for why this body—or for why any-body—emerges for us as an Other? If it is possible for us to project ourselves into animals, we must have certain experiences with animals that motivate such projections in the first place, but these experiences cannot themselves be explained—or explained away—as mere "projections", for such an explanation begs the question or issues in an infinite regress. Merleau-Ponty argues that "every theory of projection . . . presupposes what it tries to explain, since we could not project our feelings into the visible behavior of an animal if something in this behavior itself did not suggest the inference".[1] In other words, the sceptical charge that any attribution of mindedness to animals is a mere projection invites the question: What occasioned such a "projection" in the first place? The possibility of such a projection actually renders the sceptic's position incoherent. A "projection" of human features into animal behaviour could only be occasioned by an experience that evokes the presence of these features in the first place, but then such a projection is, indeed, no longer a mere "projection" at all. "Projectionism" begs the question, for it presupposes the very experiences that it is supposed to explain (or explain away): an experience of animal behaviour is explained (or explained away) as an instance of anthropomorphic projection, but this anthropomorphic projection is itself only possible on the basis of an experience of behaviour that "invites us to anthropomorphism",[2] an experience of a form of behaviour that is precisely *anthropomorphic* in certain ways, which is precisely what projectionism is supposed to explain in the first place. Thus, sceptical "projectionism" is circular (and self-defeating) insofar as "projections" are only possible on the basis of those very kinds of experiences they are supposed to explain away.

And if we attempt to rescue projectionism from circularity, we confront an infinite regress. I say that my dog is "sad", and a sceptic says that this apparent sadness is a projection on my part. What, then, occasioned this projection of sadness on my part? Such a "projection" of sadness can only follow upon an experience of my dog that suggests "sadness", but this experience that "suggests sadness" must *ex hypothesi* be another projection on my part, and *this* projection will have to follow from a prior experience that suggests *it*, and this prior experience will also have to be a projection, and so on ad infinitum. Thus, in order to account for why we "project" familiar human features into nonhuman animals, we cannot appeal to prior experiences that would be reducible to mere projections, and so there must be some primary layer of lived experience that informs them, a relatedness with nonhuman others *as others* that is prior to, and the foundation of, veridical and erroneous interpretations of behaviour alike.

So, did Sammy really love any of us? When I lived at home and would arrive from school, Sammy would race in a figure eight around the living room and dining room, climb on top of me, and lick my face so furiously that his tongue would burn my cheeks, and he would often tighten his grip on my shoulders as I struggled to pry him away and settle him down. Did he love my parents and me? I'm sure that he did, but is my certitude warranted? Do the outward appearances in this case really reflect the inward reality — the particular (nonhuman) mindedness or *otherness* — that they irresistibly suggested to us? Or do they merely reflect the "inward reality" of us, the human spectators, to whom they appear? Was Sammy merely a body through which we ventriloquized our own familiar sentiments and manner of being? As Merleau-Ponty suggests, my confidence in (or putative knowledge of) the loving regard of others is grounded in my prereflective engagements with them, in the imbrications of our bodily intentionalities through which we learn what love is and through which subjectivity in general is constituted, enacted, and known as such prior to reflective predication. The projective, expressive intentions or gestures that others address to me are immediately, irreducibly intelligible as such. Behaviour is an irreducible modality of meaning in the world; it is the vehicle of selfhood and otherness. "Other persons . . . are not there as minds, or even as 'psychisms', but such for example as we face them in anger or love — faces, gestures, spoken words to which our own respond without thoughts intervening".[3]

Of course, interpretations of behaviour may be mistaken, but — as Merleau-Ponty argues — this does not cast doubt on the *primary* evidence we have of existing with others, the primary evidence we have of being seen and touched by others, of being loved or hated or simply recognized or even ignored by others; indeed, such mistakes presuppose this evidence. Some of these others greet us with a handshake and a smile, and others do so with paws and a tongue. Only a dualistic notion of "subjectivity" — that is to say, only the notion that subjectivity is ontologically divorced from, or "hidden" within, the living, behaving body — could motivate or licence me to doubt a priori that a dog can express or evidence love and affection just as much as a human Other can, or that I can simply share my life with a canine or nonhuman Other just as genuinely as I share my life with human Others; in all cases, it is behaviour — it is a living body — that immediately *means* the love and affection or, in general, the *otherness*.

Scepticism concerning nonhuman minds depends upon the same (false) ontological commitments as ordinary scepticism concerning other human minds: in both cases the claim that we can never know whether a body is "minded" depends upon the assumption that mindedness is essentially disembodied. In order to dismantle such scepticism, it is necessary and sufficient to dismantle the dualistic commitments upon which it is based. If subjectivity is necessarily embodied, then the living, behaving body of the Other is not an impregnable barrier to his or her subjectivity or otherness; it is not something that I need to "get beyond" or "behind"—indeed, not something into which I must analogically transport myself—in order to apprehend the Other *qua Other*; it is not an exterior that somehow contains or conceals an entirely separable and private interior, for the living body is neither a pure subject nor a brute object, but rather *both* subject and object, which is to say, something that is prior to, and the foundation of, the very distinction between the two. The lived body is precisely that from out of which the poles of subject and object, interiority and exteriority, inward consciousness and outward behaviour are abstracted and later reified as opposed. If we begin from an opposition between subject and object, we will never be able to explain how I (as a subject) can ever know or even perceive that a body (human or nonhuman) is minded. If consciousness is pure interiority, then it is by definition inaccessible from the outside. If interiority and exteriority were mutually exclusive orders of reality, the *inter* in *intersubjectivity* would be inconceivable.

Merleau-Ponty's solution is not to begin from a dualistic subject/object standpoint in the first place, but rather to begin with what is actually primary: the lived body and its constitutive involvements with other living bodies. If we "reject the age-old assumptions that put the body in the world and the seer in the body, or, conversely, the world and the body in the seer as in a box",[4] then we must realize that "interiority" is not quite as "interior" as it has traditionally been conceived, and that we do not need to *infer* the presence of an Other "behind" behaviour or a living body any more than we need to infer the presence of an animating thought "behind" an instance of language: mindedness and behaviour—just like thought and language—are immediately cogiven, yet not reductively equivalent. The reflexivity or auto affection that defines a living body—that is, the self-differentiating or self-signifying sense that a living body has of itself precisely by virtue of its exposure to, or contact with, what is other than itself—just is perception, intentionality or "interiority" at the foundational level.

It may be replied that this definition of subjectivity is too broad, for while one may grant that every subject must be an embodied subject or a living body, one may nevertheless doubt the converse claim that every living body must be a "subject", for this would require us to accord "subjecthood" to a number of forms of life that may not seem to count as such, like termites, clams, amoebas, paramecia and even plants. My reply to this concern is that, were we to agree that not all living bodies are "subjects", we would need to develop a set of a criteria to differentiate those living bodies that are subjects from those that are not, and I think that any attempt to do so would be beset by a number of philosophical problems that would be just as difficult and worrisome, and perhaps even more so, than the one that such a set of criteria is supposed to solve in the first place. It is difficult to conceive of how one could mark such a distinction in a non-question-begging or nonchauvinistic way.

The main point, however, is that Merleau-Ponty attempts to break us free from any paradigm that takes subjectivity to be disjunct from a manner of bodily being-in-the-world, and for him this means that the typical being of the human (i.e., "personhood") can no longer be privileged as the locus of all meaning and value in the world. As Merleau-Ponty puts it, "The concern is to grasp humanity first as another manner of being a body".[5] If we truly reject Cartesian dualism (along with its reductionist counterparts), then we must accept that consciousness is essentially incarnate: it is not "in" a body, but is a manner of animate, responsive bodily existence itself. Incarnate consciousness *just is* a living body, which is to say that all living bodies are by definition "consciousnesses", and that there are as many different consciousnesses in the world as there are living bodies. If being a subject simply means having subjectivity, then we cannot conceive of a living body that is not in some sense "a subject" unless we somehow separate subjectivity from animate bodily being-in-the-world. Of course, from the premise that mind and body are necessarily intertwined, it follows that all minds are embodied but not all bodies are minded. However, it *does* follow that all *living* bodies are "minded", for a living body *just is* an embodied mind. Is, then, a paramecium "a subject"? Yes, because it is a living body and because all living bodies are by definition modes or expressions of subjectivity, but it should be emphasized that this means that "subjectivity" is precisely not a monolithic phenomenon, or that there are as many different subjectivities as there are forms of embodied life. If subjectivity is embodied life, then every living body is a form of subjectivity, and we thus cannot deny subjectivity to, say, a paramecium without denying it a living body. This is the only conclusion one may consistently draw if one rejects a Cartesian opposition between mind (subject) and body (object).

But is it not the case that we can be wrong about what behaviour seems to reveal to us? Of course, we can be wrong. As Merleau-Ponty argues, the behaviour and consciousness of another—the exteriority and interiority of a living body—are intertwined and yet *not* reductively equivalent to one another. To reject dualism is also to reject its reductive (usually materialistic or positivistic) counterparts, and thus Merleau-Ponty is not a "behaviourist" in the traditional sense of the term. If dualism is false, then "we no longer see where behavior begins and where mind ends", [6] which is to say that interiority and behaviour are inseparable yet noncoincident, and this is precisely how it is paradoxically possible to have contact with Others in a way that does not dissolve or negate their otherness; it is how we may access the inner life of another in a way that preserves the requisite inaccessibility of that life. This nondisjunctive distance between consciousness and behaviour—which is also precisely the distance between self and Other—is also the very distance that at once makes communication and miscommunication possible. The lived body does not belong entirely to either side of the classical subject-object divide, and this ambiguity of the lived body grounds intersubjectivity and thus the second-order intersubjective phenomena of correct and incorrect judgements of others.

So while behaviour always inherently *means* the presence of an interior and intentional existence, we can always be wrong about what is behaviourally meant—about what is lived or intended on the "other side" of a body—in specific instances and circumstances. Timothy Treadwell (the subject of Werner Herzog's documentary *Grizzly Man*) thought that the bears with whom he interacted in the Alaskan wilderness loved him, and eventually they ate him. But perhaps the bears really did love him at some point. All of us, after all, have or will hurt the ones we love. And rather than focus on the fact that the bears had Timothy for lunch one day, why should we not also pause to appreciate the fact that they did not harm him for such a long time up to that point? However, it probably was the case that Timothy drastically misread his bear companions. The bears probably did not love Timothy, but Timothy was nevertheless in community with them, as we all are. Ursine subjectivity—like human subjectivity—is, after all, a form of lived embodiment, or a site of that reflexivity or directedness toward an outside that defines life or what we call interiority and intentionality. Subjectivity is primordially flesh in touch with itself through the circuit of a carnal world in which it is thus implicated along with all other subjectivities. This common carnal inherence in the world sets bears, humans, and indeed all living beings in contact—in community—with one another.

This is not, of course, to deny that there are distinct and often deeply divergent communities of living beings in the world. A bear community is deeply different from a human community, and yet—if dualism is false, if to be a subject is to be a living body, or if consciousness is necessarily doubled by an "outside"—they must overlap or "encroach upon" one another. Yes, human beings are in community with bears, but being in community does not always entail intimacy or reciprocity: I am not at all close to anyone in Africa or the Middle East, and I am perhaps just as far away from the people driving on Lakeshore Drive right outside my apartment window as I type this. And sometimes the best way to be in community with Others is to *let them be*. By this, I do not mean to suggest a kind of libertarianism: indeed, libertarianism (or the atomistic individualism to which it is committed) represses community. Selves (hence goods) are never isolated. I simply mean that sometimes the most authentic or appropriate manner for us to coexist with one another is for us to recognize and honour the distance that is really there between us.

So it is clear that Timothy probably should have left the bears alone; he did not belong with them in that manner. Timothy thought otherwise and was tragically wrong; his empathetic overtures were misplaced. Sometimes animals disappoint our expectations; sometimes human beings do as well. Such, then, is the lot—the ambiguity and indeed the risk—of lived, embodied, intersubjectively constituted experience.

It is clear that my father's relationship with Sammy constituted and transformed his being-in-the-world. The fact that my father could refer to Sammy as his "second son"—and the fact that my parents could refer to me as Sammy's "brother"—reveals to us the fact that the family is constructed without essential species boundaries, that community is not (or need not be) rigidly demarcated intraspecifically: as Merleau-Ponty puts it, kinship is indeed always "strange",[7] always open and fluid, always a "cohesion of extreme divergencies".[8] My father can make sense of the idea that he has both a canine son and a Homo sapiens son, and thus living with Sammy brought my father to think about his own humanity differently. Yet the categories of canine and human are fluid as well, as is evidenced by my father's insistence that Sammy "had more humanity in him than most people" he had ever known.

The speaker of such a claim no doubt means that what we think of as the finest human qualities are also to be found in a dog, and that we find such qualities in dogs more often than we actually find them in humans. But it is not necessarily naïve or crude anthropomorphism to say that Sammy really did possess "humanity": dogs (and other animals) really are human in certain ways; indeed, what it means to be human is to be dog as well, and vice versa. That is to say, human beings and other animals are defined by a limit between them that is never quite clear or decidable; their distinct identities are achieved by precisely a bidirectional, antepredicative transference of sense, or by an overlapping of bodily intentions and comportments prior to reflective categorization and ascription. My father recognizes his own humanity in Sammy, and this means that he also recognizes Sammy's dogness in himself. To recognize "humanity" in a dog is at once to recognize our own "dogness". It is not so much the case that my father "projected" human qualities into Sammy but rather that, in their dealings with one another, my father and Sammy taught one another more about what it is to be human and dog, and above all more about what it is to love and to be loved.

I hasten to underscore that this notion does not negate alterity, but rather affirms it. Indeed, alterity is constitutive of identity or selfhood, and it would be impossible for me to recognize or affirm an Other if there were no continuity or "kinship" between us. And yet the Other—in order, precisely, to *be* Other—must also be irremediably distant from me. That is the aporia of intersubjectivity. My relations with others are possible only if I am indeed a distinct or individualized self, but at the same time I am the distinct or individualized self that I am only if I am differentiated from, hence situated in and amid, relations with others:

> The solitude from which we emerge to intersubjective life is not that of the monad. . . . What "precedes" intersubjective life cannot be numerically distinguished from it, precisely because at this level there is neither individuation nor numerical distinction. The constitution of others does not come after that of the body; others and my body are born together from the original ecstasy.[9]

In short, there is no self without the other and no other without the self, and this is what Husserl means when he says that self and other are primordially paired, or co-constituting. The self may be differentiated as such only in and through contact with otherness. Auto-affection is always hetero-affection. Thus, the self can never be atomistically individuated and can never enjoy a pure, internally translucent, unmediated contact with itself: the contact of the self with itself is always at the same time dependent upon and suffused with its paradoxical contact with what is not itself, its contact with a world and with others.

And so, to recognize "humanity" or an affect such as love in a nonhuman animal (like a dog) is not necessarily a "mere" projection, nor is it necessarily a totalizing or reductive gesture. It is not to collapse, say, humanity into dogness or dogness into humanity, but to recognize the ambiguity, or what Merleau-Ponty calls the "strange proximity"—the distance as well as the continuity—between them that inflates them to meaning. If anthropomorphism is problematic, it is not primarily so because it may be a naïve psychological bias, but rather because it may presuppose or inscribe an anthropo*centric* standpoint that would deny nonhuman alterity just as surely and violently as ordinary scepticism. The only responsible manner for us to relate to our nonhuman cohabitants is one that does not negate their alterity either by assimilating them to familiar human categories and features or by denying them any kinship at all with our manner of being and refusing to recognize familiar human features in them when those features are really there to be recognized. Thus, Derrida writes of his "avowed desire to escape the alternative of a projection that appropriates and an interruption that excludes".[10] On the one hand, it is important that we honor the *alterities* of animals; this means that we should carefully attend to the significant differences between human and nonhuman forms of life and that we should not think that the conscious lives of animals are meaningful or real only insofar as they are *akin* to ours. On the other hand, if we push the alterities of animals *too far*, then no meaningful relationships with them are possible. This would be to exile them entirely from the scope of possible human understanding and community, and such an extreme othering of animals amounts to the very ontological "human-animal" dualism—which is ultimately a repetition of Cartesian mind/body dualism—that Merleau-Ponty repudiates. We need to navigate between a kind of anthropomorphism that would fail to honour the alterities of animals and a wholesale repudiation of anthropomorphism that would encourage us to refuse them alterity altogether.

My parents and I are certain that Sammy loved us, but Sammy was a dog, and so the sceptic may yet reply that we surely do not see the living body of, say, a lizard or an earthworm as suggestive of love quite so readily, nor do we have the same grounds to do so. But why not? It seems that the problem here has less to do with lizards and earthworms and more to do with our notion of love. Perhaps we need to rethink our notion of love so that we can see it already at work in all forms of embodied life. It is easy to see love in dogs because they express it in ways that are similar to how we humans tend to express it. However, there are many different forms of love in the world. Does the fleshy, cold-blooded lizard not enjoy the fact that his body is warming against a hot rock in the sun? Because he is a body, does this fleshy being not include the fact that he is passionately connected to the world, entwined with other subjects and objects in complex webs of affects and desires? This is indeed just what it means to be a living body. When we see earthworms squirming in mud, does it not make the most sense to see in their squirming a form of joy, a love of the earth, a kind of passion? To do so would not be to impose a projection on them. The ascription of such love would not be the *addition* of something to their behaviour. To see love in a lizard basking in the sun or in the frenzied, ecstatic squirming of a worm in mud would not be to see the comportment of the lizard or the squirming of the worm and *then* think that there must also be a component of love there, but rather it would be to see the submission to the sun and the squirming in the mud *as* love; it would be to see that what it means to be a living body is to be invested in parts of the world and in various activities with love. This is what Merleau-Ponty means when he claims that behaviour is not a mere *sign* or indication of mindedness—not the external signifier of an internal, homuncular signified—but rather its immediate, irreducible expression as such. Of course, we cannot always be sure about the interior lives of nonhuman beings, but all living things express a *telos*, which is to say a directedness toward a good that compels us to realize that "love" is a category broad enough to include many different types of love and loving-beings, and indeed I do not really understand or experience love without already being enmeshed in a world that is full of it. It is not necessarily the case that I "project" love into, say, dogs or lizards or earthworms, but rather that their ways of being and my attachments to them teach me more about what love and life is, and without them my life and the love in it would be impoverished, if not altogether unintelligible.

To be sure, a point that Merleau-Ponty insists upon in his later writings is that we are essentially—we might even say transcendentally—in community with animal (nonhuman) Others: "humanity" and "animality" and all embodied beings are foundationally, intercorporeally intertwined. The human, for Merleau-Ponty, is fundamentally continuous with the animal, but the human does not fundamentally "arise" from the animal, for the human and the animal primordially arise in sense *together*, as neither is intelligible as such without the other: they are neither opposed nor reductively identical to one another, and they are neither "higher" nor "lower" than one another; at the most basic level, they are *laterally* related, or co-constituting—coupled and interdependent by virtue of a constitutive difference between them, or by what Merleau-Ponty calls a shared Flesh.

Again, this is not, of course, to deny that there are distinct and often deeply divergent communities of living beings in the world. But all communities or lifeworlds are never absolutely divorced from one another, for they precisely acquire their distinct identities or styles of being from their mutual differentiation from one another, and hence also from their mutual involvement or copresence with one another; they are all but variations of the same world, irreducibly different styles of corporeity that are for that very reason intercorporeally implicated in one another. The world is "a pell-mell ensemble of bodies and minds", a "promiscuity of visages, words, actions, with, between them all, that cohesion which cannot be denied them since they are all differences, extreme divergencies of one same something".[11] This is one definition of what Merleau-Ponty later calls "the flesh of the world".

What is ontologically (and epistemically) foundational is coexistence or overlapping-through-difference, which is neither synthesis nor antithesis, neither monistic unity nor dualistic nonidentity. This is what Merleau-Ponty (in his later writings) calls "reversibility" or the "chiasm" or simply "Flesh". The "Flesh", for Merleau-Ponty, is surely intended to evoke, but is not at all reducible to, the flesh of the sentient body. As Merleau-Ponty emphasizes, "The flesh is not matter, is not mind, is not substance".[12] That is to say, the Flesh is not *a* thing or a *kind* of thing, but rather the relational medium or mediation *of* things; it *is* the differentiation—the space or interval—that constitutes any relation and that thus constitutes the meaning and being of any-thing. An irreducible divergence between the relata of a relationship is necessarily constitutive of relationality as such (indeed, it simply is the very "between-ness" of any relationship *between* things), but at the same time this divergence between relata cannot be the negation of any continuity between them, for this would dissolve their relationship just as surely as would the total absorption of one in, or the total reduction of one to, the other. Thus, a relationship requires both proximity and distance, both conjunction and separation, which is to say a kind of divergence between terms that is *not* an impassable divide but is precisely that which brings them into touch with one another. The reflective inflection and reification of this coupling-through-divergence as a binary opposition is precisely what engenders a mind/body problem and consequently a problem of other minds (whether human or nonhuman).

However, Merleau-Ponty suggests that there is an analogy between the living body and what he later calls the "flesh of the world". Merleau-Ponty's concept of "Flesh" is an extension of his earlier insights into the incarnation of (inter)subjectivity. If subjectivity is essentially incarnate, and if (as Husserl argued) subjectivity is always already intersubjectivity, then intersubjectivity is essentially inter*corporeity*. As the living body is a kind of "middle term" ("a third genus of being"[13]) between subject and object, so is the flesh of the world a kind of "middle term"—a metaxic, differentiating and conjunctive spacing (*écart*)—between all things (between consciousness and behaviour, between consciousness and the world, and between consciousness and other consciousnesses):

> Our glances are not "acts of consciousness", each of which claims an invariable priority, but *openings of our flesh which are immediately filled by the universal flesh of the world*. All depends, in short, upon the fact that it is the lot of living bodies to close upon the world and become seeing, touching bodies which . . . are *a fortiori* perceptible to themselves. The whole enigma lies in the perceptible world, in that tele-vision which makes us *simultaneous with others and the world in the most private aspects of our life.*[14]

As a living body is at once the dehiscence and contact between perceiver and perceived—as perception is the folding back of flesh upon itself—so is the flesh of the world the dehiscence and consequent encroachment of all perceivers or embodied perspectives; as my right hand and my left hand can reversibly touch one another because they both belong to the same living, self-sensing body, so can my living, self-sensing body sense not only things but also other living, self-sensing bodies, for all living bodies are nodes or folds of reflexivity cleaved in the same Flesh; they all belong to the same carnal world, the same differentiating and connective tissue or field of Being or, in a sense, the same "Body". "My two hands 'coexist' or are 'compresent' because they are one single body's hands. The other person appears through an extension of that compresence; he and I are like organs of one single intercorporeality".[15] All embodied beings—no matter how deeply divergent their styles of bodily being may in fact be—intercorporeally constitute a community, and thus what Merleau-Ponty says of the parts of an individual living body may equally well be said of all living bodies in their relationships with one another and with the world that differentiates and grounds them in common: that they are "'inter-related' in a peculiar way . . . not spread out side by side, but enveloped in each other".[16] All things are in community; they encroach upon one another, and their encroachment entails a distance or hiatus between them. For Merleau-Ponty, this "paradox" of our relations with others—this paradox of a "distance that is consonant or synonymous with proximity"[17]—discloses the nature of Being itself.

The intercorporeal constitution of subjectivity has profound implications for how we think about and draw the boundaries of identity and community. It reveals to us our embeddedness in what I would like to call a "radical community", a community that is "radical" in the original sense of that term: a community that is the *radix*—the originary, generative and differentiating field, the "dehiscence" and attendant overlapping—of every specific community and lifeworld. It is just such a community that Merleau-Ponty refers to as the "Flesh", as a lattice of internal and affective relations, or as that "formative medium of the object and the subject"[18] that renders all living bodies receptive to a common world, perceptible to themselves and perceptible to one another as such: no matter how different they may be from my own style of being, all living bodies truly are, as Merleau-Ponty says, "the flesh of my flesh",[19] for all embodied beings, hence all communities of embodied beings, are differentiated articulations of a common sensible world, different styles of a shared embodiment, variations or deviations of the world in which I too participate, the world of which my sensing body is also a variant.

We are all caught up in the same "circuit", the same skein of phenomena, and at the most fundamental level we must understand this "we" to embrace all living bodies. All living bodies—human and nonhuman alike—are fundamentally in-corporated in the world they interrogate, and they are therefore fundamentally in-corporated in one another. My body is "in a circuit with the world, an *Einfuhlung* with the world, with the things, with animals, with other bodies . . ."[20] All carnalities are implicated in one another. If subjectivity is incarnate, then we cannot maintain a rigidly "speciesist" account of subjectivity, nor can we maintain a rigidly speciesist account of community. All living bodies are "subjectivities", and living bodies simply cannot be dualistically (or essentialistically) opposed to one another. As M. C. Dillon puts it, "The bifurcation of body and soul is the essential presupposition of humanism".[21] Thus, animals, Merleau-Ponty says, are (like nonsentient things and "madmen") our "quasi-companions", "thorns in our flesh".[22] Is it, then, the case that animal others constitute who "we" are just as much as human others, and that we reciprocally constitute animal others as such? Might it be the case that, as the self is to the Other, so is "humanity" to "animality"? This is, indeed, the conclusion to which Merleau-Ponty was led.

Thus, Merleau-Ponty's insights into intersubjectivity lead him to rethink what it means to be that specific kind of embodied being that we call human. Merleau-Ponty is led to understand the relationship between "humanity" and "animality" in the same way that he, following Husserl, understands the relationship between self and Other: not as oppositional or hierarchical or reductively identical, but as primordially "paired" (or "lateral"). Thus, in the *Nature* lectures Merleau-Ponty claims that "animality and human being are given only together".[23]

Merleau-Ponty seems to suggest that humanity and animality are co-constituting in just the same way as self and Other: the sense and being of each are instituted *at the same time*; they come into meaning and being together, as distinct yet inseparable, which is to say as coupled through reciprocal differentiation. This coupling or overlapping through differentiation is, of course, chiasmatic be(com)ing: the human and the animal are internally and *laterally* entwined in and through a constitutive fission between them. Merleau-Ponty's reference to the "laterality" of the human-animal relationship is clearly intended to evoke the bilateral constitution of self and Other, and in general it is clearly intended to displace any hierarchical or oppositional understanding of this relationship. "The relation of the human to animality is not a hierarchical relation, but lateral, an overcoming that does not abolish kinship".[24] Human-being and animal-being are distinct yet never opposed or hierarchically subordinated to one another, for each is constituted by a reciprocal, differentiating transference of sense,[25] or by what Merleau-Ponty elsewhere explains as an exchange of corporeal schemata. Merleau-Ponty simply understands the relationship between the human and the animal in the same way that he understands all relationships: as sites of pure difference, or as intertwinings, for these, indeed, are the only relationships "worthy of the name". The relationship between humanity and animality—just like the relationship between self and Other—does not conform to a classical, dualistic logic of identity and negation.

To say that humanity and animality are related "laterally" (non-oppositionally and non-hierarchically) is to say that they are related *chiasmatically*, that the institution of the distinction between "humanity" and "animality" is just one instance—though an exemplary instance—among others of dehiscence in Nature, and like all such instances it entails a kind of "strange kinship" or "encroachment". Since this dehiscence or opening between "the human" and "the animal" is not an opposition or ontological vacuum but is subtended or enveloped by a common carnality and carnal world, it entails (or simply *is*) their intertwining and compresence, and thus it indeed compels us to rethink the signifiers "human" and "animal", for they no longer signify anything like clearly demarcated and disjunct essences; yet, even if we conceive of "the human" and "the animal" as continuous with one another, we can no longer conceive of the former as "emergent" from the latter, for they can only arise in sense—

they can only ever be(come)—*together*. This, again, is what Merleau-Ponty means when he speaks of a "lateral relationship" between the human
and the animal, and here it is what I mean by a "radical community"; it is
precisely the coupling-through-differentiation or the "identity-within-
difference"[26] constitutive of life and identity.

The dehiscence and consequent overlapping of living bodies in Nature—the differentiation and overlapping of different bodily styles of
being—is no different from the dehiscence and attendant overlapping of
subject and object, interior and exterior, touching and touched, self and
world, self and Other. In short, a bodily style of being acquires the sense
of being "human" only at the very same time that other styles acquire the
sense of being "nonhuman" (and vice versa). Thus, Merleau-Ponty writes
that "it is humanity that grounds the animal as animal and animality that
grounds man as man".[27] "Humanity" and "animality" are irreducibly
different, yet co-originary (constituted and given through reciprocal differentiation) and thus (like self and Other) are laterally coupled.

Of course, it is clearly the case we cannot achieve full human subjectivity without the attention or affirmation of human others. Feral children
attest to this fact: infants who develop outside of a human community—
infants who only "pair" with animals—do not become fully human, and
Merleau-Ponty acknowledges this.[28] We only achieve full human subjectivity by pairing with other human beings, and while the very existence
of feral children demonstrates the fluidity or instability of our borders
and categories, it is still the case that "human" infants possess a potentiality for "human subjectivity" that rocks, trees and dogs do not. Is this,
then, in tension with the claim that we are constituted as human by our
relationships with other animals?

To answer this objection, we need to recognize that Merleau-Ponty's
claim is deeper than a claim about psychosocial development: it is an
ontological and conceptual claim. Merleau-Ponty's implicit question is
this: How is it that anything comes to mean "human" in the first place?
That is to say, what does it mean to be human—how does any being
acquire the sense of being human—such that we can make any observations concerning the psychological development of human beings in the
first place? Yes, human infants require the attention of human Others in
order to achieve full human subjectivity, but how does such a claim or
observation "make sense"? How are we to account for the sense of the
term *human* that we are using here? We only become human in a community of humans, but how does such a community itself become "human"?
If we say that such a community becomes a human community by "pairing" with other human communities—in just the same way that a human
infant becomes fully human by pairing with a human adult—then we
have only pushed the question farther back, and we confront an infinite
regress. Merleau-Ponty's answer, of course, is that there is an *ineinander*
(intertwining) of "the human" and "the animal" that constitutes the hu-

man as such and that therefore subtends the constitution of any distinct human self or community. The dehiscence between "the human" and "the animal" is what enables any specific being or community of beings to appear as human or nonhuman. We only become human in community with other humans, but a human community only becomes human in a larger, "radical" community with other-than-human others and communities. Our sense of ourselves as human is necessarily—perhaps, again, we might even say "transcendentally"—informed by our relationships with nonhuman forms of life. *Pace* Heidegger, there is no "ontological abyss" between human beings and other animals, or, if we say that there is an abyss between them, then we must also recognize, along with Merleau-Ponty, that "an abyss is not nothing", for it has its "environs and edges".[29]

At the beginning of *The Visible and the Invisible*, Merleau-Ponty discusses the inherently paradoxical task of phenomenology, and elaborates the various difficulties or paradoxes with which it must contend. "We see the things themselves, the world is what we see . . . but what is strange about this faith is that if we seek to articulate it into theses or statements, if we ask ourselves what is this *we*, what *seeing* is, and what *thing* or *world* is, we enter into a labyrinth of difficulties and contradictions".[30] The effort to bring unreflective life to reflective clarity—the effort to understand thematically the prethematic sources of thematic knowledge—is inherently aporetic. Indeed, for Merleau-Ponty the world is an ensemble of "figured enigmas" and "incompossible details".[31] Throughout all of his works and before the introduction of deconstruction, Merleau-Ponty laboured to show that any binary, either/or logic or conceptual scheme is grounded in, and is disrupted or displaced by, the both/and "logic" (the ambiguities or "teeming incompossibilities") of lived experience.

What I wish to underscore here is that one of these "figured enigmas" is precisely our relations with others, or precisely the nature of the very community in which life is always already embedded. Merleau-Ponty registers the nature and constitution of the "we" to be just as paradoxical or question worthy as the nature of perception and worldhood. This is why Merleau-Ponty becomes occupied with the question of the relationship—the "strange kinship" or the "radical community"—between the human and the animal: the question of human-animal *difference* (which is at the same time the question of human-animal *togetherness*). Such a question is an extension of Merleau-Ponty's earlier insights into intersubjectivity; it is a question that addresses the ambiguity that constitutes and attends—and that decentres and defers—the meaning of any identity, and principally the meaning of "the human".

Thus, in the final working note published in *The Visible and the Invisible*, Merleau-Ponty indicates that he was planning to give "a description of the man-animality *intertwining*".[32] As I hope to have shown, it is clear that Merleau-Ponty came to see that "the human" and "the animal" are intertwined in precisely his technical understanding of that term, and that an account of this intertwining has a significant place in his larger ontological project. The human and the animal are two moments of a particular dehiscence in Nature. Simply put, "dehiscence" is generative differentiation; it is the opening or spacing through which specific relations, affects, identities and meanings are engendered; it is precisely that differentiation that weaves together the skein of perceptual life and perceptible Being, that commingling or encroachment through divergence that Merleau-Ponty also calls the Flesh, the chiasmatic institution and imbrication of all things. "Infinite distance or absolute proximity, negation or identification: our relationship with Being is ignored in the same way in both cases".[33] Neither identity nor negation, neither synthesis nor opposition, but rather *overlapping through differentiation*—or, in a word, genuine *community*—constitutes life, identity and meaning. As the living body is the dehiscence (and thus the site of an intertwining or "strange proximity") between subject and object, so is the "flesh of the world" the dehiscence, or relational openness, between all beings and phenomena; it is that "intermundane space"[34] or "interbeing"[35]—that element or medium—that, like the literal flesh or skin of a body, joins or conjugates the very terms it separates, or which is at once a limit and a site of passage. The "Flesh" or "the chiasm" names Being not as a monistic substance, unitary identity, simple origin or subsumptive totality, but rather as *reflexivity*, which is to say as the mediation of identity through differentiation, of which the reflexivity or auto-affection of the sentient body is but a particular though remarkable exemplar.[36]

In closing, human beings and nonhuman animals often demonstrate very different styles of existence, but these styles nevertheless envelop and implicate one another. On Merleau-Ponty's account, we are just as radically embedded in relations with other-than-human Others as we are with human Others. Indeed, conspecific relatedness and community—the constitution of a human "we"—necessarily announces and depends upon a larger, deeper, "radical" cross-specific community, "an open and indefinite multiplicity of relationships which are of reciprocal implication",[37] an ensemble of overlapping lifeworlds, horizons, and styles of being, a place where borders are trespassed—or where "avenues are crossed"[38]—the very moment they materialize. The intercorporeal differentiation and communalization of all living bodies subtends any binary logic of inclusion/exclusion that suppresses it. Such a radical community is not established through either the dualistic expulsion or the totalizing, reductive appropriation of what is "Other". And it is thus that Merleau-Ponty would say—along with my father—not only that I have been a brother to a dog, but also that I continue to belong to a radical community, to a carnal world that "even in my most strictly private life, summons up within that life *all other corporeities*",[39] "quasi-companions" and "strange kin" who are also, as such, the "flesh of my flesh".

* This chapter has benefitted significantly from discussions with H. Peter Steeves (DePaul University) and from anonymous reader comments. I also would like to acknowledge my parents, Stewart and Ellin Singer, and my late brother, Sammy, whose love inspired this chapter.

NOTES

1. Maurice Merleau-Ponty, *The Structure of Behavior*, trans. A. L. Fisher (Boston: Beacon Press, 1963), 156. See also 125.

2. Merleau-Ponty, *The Structure of Behavior*, 125.

3. Maurice Merleau-Ponty, *Signs*, trans. Richard C. McCleary (Evanston, IL: Northwestern University Press, 1964), 181.

4. Maurice Merleau-Ponty, *The Visible and the Invisible*, ed. Claude Lefort, trans. Alphonso Lingis (Evanston, IL: Northwestern University Press, 1968), 138.

5. Maurice Merleau-Ponty, *Nature: Course Notes from the Collège De France*, comp. Dominique Séglard, trans. Robert Vallier (Evanston, IL: Northwestern University Press, 2003), 208.

6. Merleau-Ponty, *Nature*, 178.

7. Merleau-Ponty, *Nature*, 217.

8. Merleau-Ponty, *The Visible and the Invisible*, 84.

9. Merleau-Ponty, *Signs*, 174.

10. Jacques Derrida, *The Animal That Therefore I Am*, trans. Marie-Louise Mallet (New York: Fordham University Press, 2008), 106.

11. Merleau-Ponty, *The Visible and the Invisible*, 84.

12. Merleau-Ponty, *The Visible and the Invisible*, 139.

13. Maurice Merleau-Ponty, *Phenomenology of Perception*, trans. Colin Smith (New York: Routledge, 1989), 350.

14. Merleau-Ponty, *Signs*, 16.

15. Merleau-Ponty, *Phenomenology of Perception*, 168.

16. Merleau-Ponty, *Phenomenology of Perception*, 98.

17. Merleau-Ponty, *The Visible and the Invisible*, 135.

18. Merleau-Ponty, *Phenomenology of Perception*, 147.

19. Merleau-Ponty, *Signs*, 15.

20. Merleau-Ponty, *Nature*, 209.

21. M. C. Dillon, *The Ontology of Becoming and The Ethics of Particularity*, ed. Lawrence Hass (Athens: Ohio University Press, 2012), 105.

22. Merleau-Ponty, *The Visible and the Invisible*, 181.

23. Merleau-Ponty, *Nature*, 271.

24. Merleau-Ponty, *Nature*, 268.

25. See Merleau-Ponty, *Nature*, 214.

26. Merleau-Ponty, *The Visible and the Invisible*, 225.

27. Merleau-Ponty, *Nature*, 307.

28. See *The Merleau-Ponty Reader*, ed. Ted Toadvine and Leonard Lawlor (Evanston, IL: Northwestern University Press, 2007), 423–24.

29. Merleau-Ponty, *Signs*, 14.

30. Merleau-Ponty, *The Visible and the Invisible*, 3.

31. Merleau-Ponty, *The Visible and the Invisible*, 4.

32. Merleau-Ponty, *The Visible and the Invisible*, 274.

33. Merleau-Ponty, *The Visible and the Invisible*, 127.

34. Merleau-Ponty, *The Visible and the Invisible*, 48, 84, 62.

35. Merleau-Ponty, *Nature*, 208, 230.

36. Thus, Merleau-Ponty refers to the Flesh as a "mirror phenomenon". See *The Visible and the Invisible*, 255.

37. Merleau-Ponty, *Phenomenology of Perception*, 61.

38. Merleau-Ponty, *The Visible and the Invisible*, 160.
39. Merleau-Ponty, *Signs*, 171. Italics added.

SEVEN

The Problem of Speaking for Animals

Jason Wyckoff

Nonhuman animals are among a very small number of oppressed individuals who cannot (as far as we now know) at any point in their lives employ arguments to raise objections to their own oppression. Using Edward Said's *Orientalism*[1] as a model, I argue that animal advocates face a special case of "the problem of speaking for others".[2] I adopt the term *dominionism* to refer to a human knowledge system that takes animals as its objects, and argue that dominionism is similar to Orientalism in its key features. The problems for animal advocates are epistemological as well as ethical. Epistemologically, we are faced with the problematic fact that knowledge of animals is constructed using concepts that serve to minimize or erase animals' interests in human discourse about animals. Ethically, there is a framing problem (with respect to whether and how issues in animal ethics can be articulated within the dominant discourse about animals) as well as a problem of efficacy (with respect to our ability to advocate effectively for changes in human practice for the benefit of animals).

I argue that dominionism is a knowledge system structurally similar to Orientalism—animals are regarded not as subjects to whom equal moral consideration is due, but as resources and objects of study. (I refer to this orientation as the *resource paradigm,* and explain it more fully in the second section below.) In the spirit of postcolonial theoretical work on which I draw here, I intend the analysis to be limited to the problem of speaking for animals in the contemporary North American and European contexts, since thick conceptions of animality will be heavily dependent on time, place and local practice. The problem, therefore, manifests itself differently in different social contexts, and any detailed treatment of it should be mindful of the limitations imposed by these variations.

PROBLEMS IN SPEAKING TO, FOR AND ABOUT OTHERS

Though the present concern is speaking for nonhuman animals, there are at least two distinct but related problems we need to acknowledge. The first is the problem of representing animals and their interests, which is an instance of the more general problem of representing others. The second is the problem of speaking *to* humans, many of them marginalized and oppressed themselves, *about* animals and their interests. Human advocates for animals tend to occupy otherwise privileged social locations, or at least enact social identities that enjoy privilege along some dimensions.[3]

Linda Martín Alcoff suggests that we understand the problem of speaking for others in terms of two features of socially situated knowledge and discourse. The first of these is that "where one speaks from affects both the meaning and truth of what one says, and thus one cannot assume an ability to transcend one's location . . . In other words, a speaker's [social] location . . . has an epistemically significant impact on that speaker's claims and can serve either to authorize or de-authorize one's speech".[4] The second is that "not only is location epistemically salient, but certain privileged locations are discursively dangerous. In particular, the practice of privileged persons speaking for or on behalf of less privileged persons has actually resulted (in many cases) in increasing or reinforcing the oppression of the group spoken for".[5] In speaking for (and about) others, "I am engaging in the act of representing the other's needs, goals, situation, and in fact, *who they are*".[6] In speaking for or about someone, one engages in the construction of that individual's social position. The problem of speaking for others is therefore a specific instance of the more general "problem of representation", about which I will have more to say in the next section. In the case of speaking for animals, the problem is especially pronounced since vis-à-vis animals nearly *all* human beings occupy a position of privilege and so nearly all speakers and their audiences will be situated in "discursively dangerous" positions.

So the general problem of representation generates a problem of speaking for others, and one special instance of that problem is the problem of speaking for animals. Catharine MacKinnon concisely sums up the problem of speaking for animals as follows:

> This recognition [that those who are oppressed rarely benefit from solutions offered by their oppressors] places at the core of the problem of animal rights a specific "speaking for the other" problem. What is called "animal law" has been human law: the laws of humans on or for or about animals. These are laws about humans' relations to animals.

Who asked the animals? References to what animals might have to say are few and far between. Do animals dissent from human hegemony? I think they often do. They vote with their feet by running away. They bite back, scream in alarm, withhold affection, approach warily, fly and swim off. But this is interpretation. How to avoid reducing animal rights to the rights of some people to speak for animals against the rights of other people to speak for the same animals needs further thought.[7]

The problem, as MacKinnon sees it, is that social institutions (such as bodies of law) are constructed from the perspective of human beings, and predictably serve (powerful) humans' interests. Within such an institutional structure, there is simply no room for the perspective of animals.

DOMINIONIST KNOWLEDGE: KNOWLEDGE SYSTEMS

I will speak of dominionism as a *knowledge system*, an expression that might strike some readers as involving a commitment to an unacceptable relativism about truth and knowledge. I should take a moment to dispel this worry.

I am referring here to knowledge that is socially contextual; since the propositions in question contain content that depends crucially on the social context, any knowledge claims relating to these propositions will be only evaluable by reference to the social context. Such propositions are not at all unusual; in fact, they pervade our thought and speech. Consider a claim as mundane as "The Toronto Maple Leafs are a North American ice hockey team". At the time of this writing, the claim is clearly true. Consider, though, how deeply socially contextualized the claim is; it depends for its truth on the meanings and connections between such expressions as "Toronto", "Maple Leafs", "North American", and "ice hockey (team)". At other times besides the present, each of these terms would have failed to refer at all. At present, their referents are contingent upon human social conventions through which the city of Toronto is constituted, a group of people (the membership of which is fluid) are collectively called the "Maple Leafs" in virtue of their joint participation in a certain activity, which convention has it is "ice hockey", and which is played in what we today call North America, among other places. To have all of this knowledge, and thus knowledge of the original proposition, one must have mastered the relevant components of the conceptual apparatus that is used to articulate the knowledge claim.

For present purposes, then, a knowledge system may be understood to comprise the social norms and conventions that give content to the expressions used to make knowledge claims among some group of persons whose speech and behaviour are informed by those norms and conventions. I am proceeding on the modest assumption that humans' knowledge of animals is embedded in social contexts that inform the interpretation and assessment of knowledge claims about animals. The norms and conventions of our speech and actions, the structured and unstructured social institutions that emerge from (and are constituted by) these norms and conventions, and the knowledge claims that are legitimated (or even more strongly, made true) by this entire context constitute a system of knowledge about animals that I am calling "dominionism". The central claim here is one familiar from postcolonial theory: that the linguistic and conceptual resources available to formulate and communicate claims about oppressed Others (or even ourselves, as Gayatri Spivak argues[8]) are themselves expressive of inequalities of power and status.

ORIENTALISM AND DOMINIONISM

Said cites two historical and cultural circumstances out of which Orientalism emerged. The first is the "culturally sanctioned habit of deploying generalizations by which reality is divided into various collectives: languages, races, types, colors, mentalities, each category being not so much a neutral designation as an evaluative interpretation".[9] The second is that the "fields" commanded by the White Man and the Other conveyed a sense of distance and differential power, so that only the White Man could speak of people of colour—as *an object of study*.[10] These two historical and cultural circumstances provided the context in which the Oriental was constructed as something to be known, mastered, controlled—in a word, subjected:

> The Oriental was linked thus to elements in Western society (delinquents, the insane, women, the poor) having in common an identity best described as lamentably alien. Orientals were rarely seen or looked at; they were seen through, analyzed not as citizens, or even people, but as problems to be solved or confined or—as the colonial powers openly coveted their territory—taken over . . . Since the Oriental was a member of a subject race, he had to be subjected: it was that simple.[11]

Orientalism, then, is a knowledge system in which socially contingent and normatively loaded binaries are deployed in such a way as to reinforce and naturalize power differentials, with those in a position of dominance having knowledge of those in a position of subordination. Said summarizes, "It is therefore correct to say of any European, in what he could say about the Orient, was consequently a racist, an imperialist, and almost totally ethnocentric".[12]

I argue that humans, in what they can say about nonhuman animals, are largely confined to a conceptual framework that is speciesist, dominionist and anthropocentric. Humans define themselves in opposition to animals, just as colonizers define themselves in opposition to the colonized, through the use of dubious binaries; the "natural" and the "human", the rational and the animal, us and them. Within this framework, to know animals is to dominate them, just as "knowledge" of the formerly colonized is domination of them, since this knowledge is expressed in a lexicon in which the power differential is pervasive. Indeed, Orientalism presupposes (or at least draws upon) dominionism, in that "reified notions of race and outsider subjects were part of national projects to shape human nature and who counted as human. As such, concepts of race and culture depended on ideas about animality and humanity".[13] The influence runs in the other direction as well, given that "Western ideas of 'man's dominion' over animals reflect a deeply gendered and imperial understanding of human relationships with animals".[14] As is the case when deconstructing Orientalist knowledge claims, the project of reinterpretation is unavoidable if we are to get at any kind of truth that is not anthropocentric.

It is worth spelling out in detail how inequalities of power are embedded in a knowledge system such as Orientalism. The problem, as I noted above, is at its base one of representation. As Spivak observes, "representation" in English is ambiguous between political representation (in the sense of substitution, in the way a senator is thought to represent her constituents) and representation in the sense of signification, in the way that a portrait represents the person of whom it is a portrait.[15] The problem of speaking for others (and for oneself) is, in part, a problem of (politically) representing a subject through speech that contains politically loaded signifiers. As such, the problem is quite pervasive in our discourse. If, for example, the poor are generally regarded as lazy or unworthy, and "poor" comes to be associated with laziness and unworthiness, then advocacy for the poor (whether or not one is among the poor) becomes conceptually problematic. The poor *cannot* be unjustly badly off, because to be poor is to be lazy and unworthy; only the lazy and unworthy find themselves living in poverty.

Orientalism and dominionism are both knowledge systems in which the conceptual framework available for the articulation of knowledge claims—including claims that certain groups are systematically wronged—undercuts the possibility of political representation, since in both cases the framework offers only conceptual resources that reflect and reinforce relations of domination and subordination. In the final section of the chapter, I argue that advocacy for nonhuman animals must simultaneously express and motivate a rejection of dominionism as the architecture of knowledge about nonhuman animals.

DOMINIONIST BINARIES AND DOMINIONIST KNOWLEDGE

Knowledge of animals and speech about animals is problematic in much the same way that Orientalism is problematic. To *be* an animal is to be a thing of inferior moral status, or to lack any moral status whatsoever. And more precisely, to be an animal of a certain kind (a "farm animal", a "pest", or even a chicken or a rat) is to be the sort of entity that cannot be the subject of serious moral claims. Farm animals exist to be raised on farms for human consumption; pests exist for no purpose and are to be eliminated; rats and chickens are pests and farm animals, respectively.

The complexity of the problem immediately becomes apparent once we recognize the fact that animal signifiers are numerous, diverse, multi-layered and morally ambiguous. The meanings that human beings ascribe to cows and their features are not those that we ascribe to dogs and their features, and the meanings that (many? most?) American Christians, say, ascribe to cows are not those that (many? most?) Indian Hindus or Jains ascribe to cows. In Anglo-American societies, it is apparent that most people can dismiss any cognitive dissonance that attends the performance of care work on behalf of dogs while consuming foods made from the bodies of cows.[16] One cannot advocate for cows in the same terms that one advocates for dogs. I will start, then, with the most general categories that we find in dominionism and then proceed to examine the complexities generated by the narrower ones.

Many theorists have noted that there is a homogenizing[17] and essentializing[18] effect of the word *animal*. Animals are defined by their difference (from humans) and categorized by the human purposes that they serve. Meanwhile, differences between nonhuman animals vanish insofar as they are irrelevant to the specification of animals' functions as humans' resources.[19] That is an important qualification: humans do differentiate among animals, but they generally do so in the service of human interests.[20] The dualism at work here is not value-neutral, and it cannot be when one considers that the human purposes at issue are not arbitrary but represent a valuation of some particular ends. As such, the categories are political ones.[21] They are shaped by purposes that are given by human valuation, and the categories then form part of the conceptual framework within which further determinations of value and disvalue are made.

It is crucially important to recognize that speciesism is an imposition of *cultural* or *social* norms, and so is instantiated as a culturally specific domination that bears striking similarities to imperialistic domination of other humans.[22] (Indeed, the (hu)man/nature binary that places the (hu)man on one side and the animal on the other has been deployed so as to exclude some human beings from full membership in the moral community, often by likening them to animals.[23]) For example, it is a matter of social convention that animals are defined as food sources for humans, since "food" refers not simply to any edible thing or source of nutrition, but to those edible things that we do, in a given social context, tend to eat. In some contexts it is true that dogs are food, while in others it is not; in some contexts it is true that pigs are food while in others it is not. In both contexts, a dominionist binary (food/nonfood) operates to distinguish some things in the world from others; the only question is which animals fall on which side.[24]

But the imposition of cultural norms extends beyond those animals that ordinarily live in close proximity to humans. Kay Anderson argues, for example, that "zoos are spaces where humans engage in cultural self-definition against a variably constructed and opposed nature".[25] Similarly, David Nibert argues that museums of natural history, which ostensibly exist to educate the public and especially children, produce much the same effect with displays that emphasize animal aggression and humans' use of animals for food and hunting.[26]

What we find in human-animal relations is a sort of anthropocentric—yet fragmented and not entirely coherent—Othering. There is at bottom an important and fundamental human/animal dichotomy by which humans are elevated above nonhumans in a moral hierarchy, but on the Other side of this boundary, there are further distinctions, the most morally and politically significant of which always reflect the interests of (powerful groups of) humans—domesticated versus wild, pet versus lab/farm animal, tame versus savage, game versus pests. The underlying logic of the dichotomies that constitute dominionism is fairly easy to identify, however: we can call it *the resource paradigm*. As Tom Regan,[27] Andrew Linzey,[28] Gary Francione,[29] Bob Torres,[30] Joan Schaffner[31] and Erika Cudworth[32] have argued, the general contours of human-animal relations are best illuminated by the thesis that animals are the resources of humans, and their value is purely instrumental.[33] Some animals are more valuable resources than others; some—designated "pests"—are regarded as having only disvalue.

The resource paradigm manifests itself, in the first instance, in the distinction between domesticates and wild animals. The latter are regarded as inhabiting a world apart from humans (where "apartness" does not connote distance so much as the fact that these nonhuman animals are not directly under human control), while the former exist in varying degrees of control, submission and subservience. The domesticate/wild binary erases the subjectivity of domesticated animals as well as the interdependence and entanglements of wild animals and human beings. It also erases completely a third category of animals, "liminal animals", such as squirrels, pigeons and raccoons, who live among human beings but whose breeding and feeding are not directly and fully controlled by humans.[34]

These categories set the parameters and ends of knowledge about the animals (or, more precisely, the types of animals) that are sorted into each category. Knowledge of wild animals has as its end the control and "management" of animal populations. Knowledge of domesticated animals serves to enable and ease the control of particular animals while maximizing their value to human beings—whether economic or otherwise. Liminal animals, because they live thoroughly among human beings, cannot be managed as wild animal populations and therefore become "pests" and "vermin".[35] No animal is simply a *rat*, as if "rat" connoted a purely natural kind, the instances of which lack socially or culturally defined features. What a rat *is* depends upon the meanings that humans ascribe to rathood—pestilence, vermin, filth. As Colin Jerolmack notes, "Animals that disgust us, such as rats, are often associated with the most undesirable urban interstices such as sewers".[36] Given this, one cannot speak for rats without speaking "for" pestilence and filth. But since speaking for pestilence and filth is, almost by definition, absurd, the attempt to speak for rats is absurd and usually treated as such.

The resource paradigm goes beyond categorization of animals themselves, however, for the content of other concepts employed in knowledge claims about animals is also inflected with dominionist normativity. Animal cruelty and animal welfare laws, for example, prohibit the infliction of "unnecessary" suffering on animals, but which instances and types of suffering are deemed "unnecessary" is deeply influenced by the dominant set of cultural practices.[37] As Francione and Schaffner both argue, "necessary" is not to be understood to mean "strictly unavoidable", but rather something closer to "what is ordinary and accepted in the course of a widely-recognized use of the type of animal in question".[38] The concept of "unnecessary suffering" is thus intimately bound up with the ways in which humans differentiate themselves from nonhumans and some nonhuman animals from others. The distinction between "necessary" and "unnecessary" suffering is an anthropocentric one, and nonhuman animal suffering that is instrumental to the ends served by particular animal property is routinely deemed "necessary" even when the human interests served are trivial and the suffering is intense and protracted.[39] "Pets" are afforded marginally more protection than other nonhuman animals by the prevailing moral and legal frameworks in North America and Europe, but they still have the legal status of property in most jurisdictions. While suffering that is "necessary" in the raising and slaughter of cattle for "meat" and "dairy" is widely regarded as unnecessary—indeed, gratuitous—when inflicted on, say, a dog or a cat, the animals that humans keep as "pets" may still be killed (though the euphemism *euthanized* is usually employed) by their owners, and legal remedies for harms that others cause to these animals are generally available only to their human owners, with compensation being limited in most jurisdictions to the market value of the animal (if killed), lost utility or earnings, and some veterinary expenses.[40] Our discourse on human-animal relations in such contexts is already shaped by culturally specific and speciesist understandings of terms such as *unnecessary*, and so arguments for the prevention of "unnecessary" suffering to animals will be interpreted (to the detriment of animals) in light of those understandings.

None of this should be construed as a suggestion, much less an assumption, that all human beings intend the violent domination of animals. Most of us are decent, if not always so virtuous. Domination of sentient beings cannot be seen plainly as domination if it is to persist; a certain degree of rationalization is necessary in order for the resource paradigm to sit easily in human consciousness, and, as Nibert observes, this involves an element of distancing:

> One way in which humans anthropocentrically distance themselves from others is in the "deanimalized" description of our bodies and our social activities. For example, humans have "hair" while others have "fur", humans have "skin" while others have "hide", and deceased humans are "corpses" while deceased others are "carcasses". Associated humans are called "groups", while associations of some other animals are "herds". Humans "have sex" while other animals "mate", "rut", or "reproduce".[41]

In the final section, I suggest that animal advocacy must bridge the distances created by the dominionist lexicon by challenging this kind of terminology, perhaps by jolting listeners with unconventional usage. But first, we should consider some of the ways in which dominionism has shaped animal advocacy for the worse.

DOMINIONISM AND SPECIESIST ANIMAL ADVOCACY

So far, I have focused on the ways in which animals' oppression is expressed in dominionism, but advocacy on behalf of animals also tends to be constrained by dominionist binaries. Advocacy for domesticated animals tends to presuppose their use by humans (in agriculture, sport, medical experimentation or pet ownership), and it aims at the conservative end of ridding systems of animal exploitation of the worst abuses. Advocacy for wild animals tends to focus on wild animal populations and species protection rather than on particular animals as claimants of justice or loci of moral value. And advocacy for liminal animals tends to presuppose their status as "pests" and focuses on "humane" management of the problems (to humans) presented by animals living in close proximity to human homes, workplaces and public spaces.

Given the binary—human on one side, nature (including animals) on the other—and the fact that the binary is taken to be morally salient—humans and their interests are intrinsically significant, animals' interests are at best derivatively significant—it is perhaps unsurprising that animal advocates frequently attempt to plead their case by arguing that animals are "like us" in various respects. The dichotomy is a given; the role of the advocate is to redraw its boundaries, or to transport some of the marginalized across the existing boundary. Some animals are enough "like us" to be afforded some measure of human privilege. Matthew Calarco articulates the problem in this way:

> The difficulty concerns the tacit anthropocentric constraints at work in political and legal institutions and how animal rights discourse ends up acceding to and reproducing the constraints that found and sustain these institutions. Thus [animal rights discourse is] subtly constrained to determine animality and animal identity according to anthropocentric norms and ideals. This problem can be seen clearly in various aspects of animal rights theory and activism. If one looks at the field of philosophy, for example, it is clear the dominant model of animal rights philosophy espoused by Tom Regan seeks to demonstrate that animals are, in many significant ways, the same as human beings.[42]

There are two respects in which such defences of animals are problematic. The first is that these defences assume that likeness to human beings is the basis of a nonhuman being's moral status, an assumption that fails to challenge the moral priority of the human.[43] One might think that this, in itself, is not an insurmountable difficulty as long we attempt to locate some basis of humans' moral status that is not species specific. But this takes us to the second problem, which is that the features to which we usually point are, at least implicitly, understood in anthropocentric terms. As Cudworth notes,

> Much time and effort . . . has been spent on the project of evaluating animal intelligence, but the organization of human power fundamentally shapes such attempts—we measure the extent to which animals do or do not approximate to human capabilities looking at the use of different kinds of human language (such as sign language) or the study of animal behaviours and sociality wherein for example with primatology, a "simian orientalism" shaped much of that which is found.[44]

In short, these defences of animals are presented as if they rely on species-neutral conceptions of the moral salience of certain features, but the features themselves are selected precisely because humans have them, and it is humanlike instantiation of the features that is then investigated in nonhuman animals.

Consider, for example, Donald VanDeVeer's "two-factor egalitarianism", which appeals to what he calls the Weighting Principle: "the interests of beings with more complex psychological capacities deserve greater weight than those with lesser capacities—up to a point".[45] VanDeVeer argues that the view he develops is not speciesist because it does not treat species membership per se as a morally relevant consideration. It does, however, treat such features, or "psychological capacities", as the capacity to dread an impending harm, or suffering caused by the memory of past misfortunes, as morally relevant. One question we must ask is this: How are such capacities to be detected and measured? How do we know when a nonhuman experiences dread or a painful memory? And a second, more fundamental, question is, what are the criteria for calling a state one of *dread*? Must the dread of a cow on its way to slaughter be expressed in the way that humans express dread? Must we have reason to think that the phenomenology of the cow's experience is similar to "the" human experience of dread? I have suggested that we tend to regard the answers to the second set of questions as affirmative, which is problematic enough, but it is even more deeply problematic that—if MacKinnon is right—*they are the wrong questions*. They presuppose that humans and humans' experiences are the measure of moral value and disvalue, and that likeness to humans is the ticket by which other creatures gain entry to the moral community.[46]

In addition to the constraints it imposes on theories of animal mentality, dominionism sets the parameters for animal advocacy in the political realm. Consider the remarks of the late U.S. senator Robert Byrd in 2001, approvingly quoted by Matthew Scully in a book-length defence of animals entitled *Dominion*: "Our inhumane treatment of livestock is becoming widespread and more and more barbaric. . . . These creatures feel; they know pain. They suffer pain just as we humans suffer pain. . . . God gave man dominion over the Earth . . . Let us strive to be good stewards and not defile God's creatures or ourselves by tolerating unnecessary, abhorrent, and repulsive cruelty".[47] As we have seen, what is "inhumane" turns crucially on the concept of "livestock" and the human use to which animals designated "livestock" are put, as does the meaning of such terms as *unnecessary* and *abhorrent*. Such an argument is situated squarely within the framework of dominionism, and as such it does not—and cannot—call into question the social meanings of "livestock" and "inhumane treatment".

There are endless examples of theory and advocacy such as these; space does not permit a fuller discussion of them here. But I hope that what I have said suffices to show that when we take on board the conceptual framework and corresponding lexicon of dominionism, we find ourselves in the position of advocating for animals in language that excludes them from the social domain or, when it locates them within human social norms and practices, relegates them to a position of subordination.

CONFRONTING THE PROBLEM: IDEOLOGY CRITIQUE

The problem of speaking for animals is a particularly vexing instance of the problem of representation. Given the difficulties canvassed in the previous section, one might begin to wonder whether the problem can ever be solved, and how we should proceed if we think, as some of us do, that human advocacy for animals is necessary. A beginning might be a rethinking of the ability of animals to speak for themselves, perhaps not linguistically but through nonlinguistic expressions of preference.[48] Such a suggestion is important because it is a direct challenge to the structure of dominionism, a refusal to recognize its categories as setting the parameters for moral dialogue. But "listening" to animals (whether or not their communication has the structure of a propositional language) is not all that is required of humans. Since it is difficult if not impossible to see how justice in human-animal relations could be achieved without human advocacy on behalf of animals, I should try to at least sketch the considerations that we should take into account when speaking for animals, or evaluating the speech of other advocates.

Dominionism produces a hegemonic discourse—meaning one that dominates the understanding of most people in a social context, to the point where it becomes "common sense"—that constrains both imaginative possibilities and outcomes.[49] Animal advocacy should challenge the legitimacy of this discourse, rejecting its constraints and premises; it should, to put it another way, be a form of ideology critique. This task is necessarily transformative and requires a new framework and a new lexicon. Speaking for others, especially from a position of privilege, always requires the speaker to put intense pressure on the conceptual framework with which s/he is familiar, since that structure is almost certainly not adequate to the task of articulating moral claims on behalf of those whose social position within that structure is one of subordination. Just as it is true that "[t]he liberal feminist vision of liberation does not challenge the underlying structure of patriarchy",[50] it is also true that animal advocacy within the parameters of dominionism does not challenge the underlying structure of speciesism.

The key point, which I have emphasized throughout this discussion, is that words *do* things in the world; they, and our utterances of them, have an ideological dimension.[51] One way in which to engage in ideology critique is to make explicit one's refusal of the standard categories. Two sentences, one containing the word *flesh* and the other containing the word *meat* instead, may, under strict interpretations, say more or less the same thing, but utterances of them will have different impacts nonetheless. A critical discourse should involve a conscious effort to disrupt the dominant social schemas that comprise the resource paradigm.[52]

Utterances like "meat is not food" or "animals are not livestock" may strike most audiences as odd, but strategically deployed they may have the effect of jolting the hearer, at least momentarily, out of the comfortable space of familiar classifications. But what the speaker really does, in uttering claims such as these, is to make vivid both the contingency and the normativity of the relevant classifications. It is obvious to most listeners that "meat" is food in that it is not only edible but also (depending on the animal in whom it originates) treated as food in the given social context. So the claim is obviously false as a description of the state of the social world, and both speaker and audience know this. The only way to interpret the utterance so as to make it interesting (and this may require a bit of nudging) is to regard it as an explicit refusal of the assumption that "meat" is properly regarded as food.[53] The listener, or the reader, is made to confront the usual assumptions about humans' position relative to animals: substitution of "farmed animals" for "farm animals", "flesh" for "meat", or "companion" for "pet" can disrupt the normative foundation of dominionism and create possibilities for reimagining humans' relationships to animals. As Iris Young observes, "[o]ne of the activist's goals is to make us *wonder* about what we are doing, to rupture a stream of thought, rather than to weave an argument".[54]

This is, however, a difficult thing to do for many reasons, not the least of which is that one must still speak in terms that resonate with one's audience—too radical a departure from familiar concepts results in confusion at best, hostility and mockery at worst. Utilitarian and rights-based arguments made within the confines of dominionism employ familiar moral idioms, but to the extent that they aim to establish a moral status for animals by demonstrating a likeness between animals' pain or consciousness and humans' pain or consciousness, they are at cross-purposes with radical critiques that call into question the moral centrality of the human features that standard arguments attempt to locate in (some) animals. The transformative liberatory project, though it requires us to navigate a narrow path between complacent adherence to familiar categories and a counterproductive abandonment of any familiar moral discourse, is nevertheless a necessary project. We have little choice but to grapple with these difficulties as best we can. Mistakes and setbacks are probably inevitable, and the best methods must be worked out in practice, on the ground.

Liberatory discourse does recommend one particularly clear but controversial principle, however: animal advocates should not engage with institutional animal exploiters on the latter's terms. No partnerships should be made with them, no agreements with them sought. We should, for example, refuse participation in campaigns to employ "humane slaughter" methods and withhold praise for measures—such as "enhanced cages" for hens—that may produce marginal welfare gains while leaving intact the resource paradigm. Most importantly, animal advocates should never concede to institutional animal exploiters the terms of the debate or the framing of any problems.[55] Animal liberation moves beyond Senator Byrd's criticism of "inhumane treatment of livestock" to a critical assessment of the concept of "livestock" itself.

I have argued here for a radical approach to speech on behalf of animals. Animal advocacy requires more than an attempt to persuade people to treat animals, as we currently understand them, differently or better; it requires a paradigm shift in the meaning and representation of animality itself. Advocating for animals means changing perceptions (beginning with one's own) of what animals are and can be. It is not simply the task of persuasion; it is the task of transformation.

NOTES

1. Edward Said, *Orientalism* (New York: Vintage Books, 1978).

2. See Linda Martín Alcoff, "The Problem of Speaking for Others", *Cultural Critique* 20 (1991): 5–32, for a thorough discussion, on which I rely heavily below.

3. For a commentary on the demographics of animal advocates, see David Nibert, *Animal Rights/Human Rights: Entanglements of Oppression and Liberation* (New York and Oxford: Rowman & Littlefield, 2002), 229.

4. Alcoff, "The Problem of Speaking for Others", 6–7.

5. Alcoff, "The Problem of Speaking for Others", 7.

6. Alcoff, "The Problem of Speaking for Others", 9.

7. Catharine MacKinnon, "Of Mice and Men: A Feminist Fragment on Animal Rights", in *Animal Rights: Current Debates and New Directions*, ed. Martha Nussbaum and Cass Sunstein (Oxford and New York: Oxford University Press, 2004), 269.

8. Gayatri Spivak, "Can the Subaltern Speak?", in *Marxism and the Interpretation of Culture*, ed. Cary Nelson and Lawrence Grossberg (Urbana and Chicago: University of Illinois Press, 1998), 271–313.

9. Said, *Orientalism*, 227.

10. Said, *Orientalism*, 228.

11. Said, *Orientalism*, 207.

12. Said, *Orientalism*, 204.

13. Maneesha Deckha, "Toward a Postcolonial, Posthumanist Feminist Theory: Centralizing Race and Culture in Feminist Work on Nonhuman Animals", *Hypatia* 27, no. 3 (2012): 538. See also Tim Ingold, "From Trust to Domination: An Alternative History of Human-Animal Relations", in *Animals and Human Society*, ed. Aubrey Manning and James Serpell (London and New York: Routledge, 1994), 4 (arguing that distinctions such as wild/domestic and collection/production, both used to rationalize the subjugation of indigenous peoples, rest upon a more fundamental Western distinction between humanity and nature).

14. Deckha, "Toward a Postcolonial, Posthumanist Feminist Theory", 537.

15. Spivak, "Can the Subaltern Speak?", 275.

16. See Brock Bastian, Steve Loughnan, Nick Haslam and Helena R. M. Radke, "Don't Mind Meat? The Denial of Mind to Animals Used for Human Consumption", *Personality and Social Psychology Bulletin* 38, no. 2 (2012): 247–56. (The studies involved students at Australian universities.) See also Boyka Bratanova, Steve Loughnan and Brock Bastian, "The Effect of Categorisation as Food on the Perceived Moral Standing of Animals", *Appetite* 57 (2011): 193–96.

17. Erika Cudworth, *Social Lives with Other Animals: Tales of Sex, Death, and Love* (New York: Palgrave Macmillan, 2011), 68.

18. Matthew Calarco, *Zoographies: The Question of the Animal from Heidegger to Derrida* (New York: Columbia University Press, 2008), 4–5. See also Jacques Derrida, "The Animal That Therefore I Am (More to Follow)", *Critical Inquiry* 28, no. 2 (2002): 369–418.

19. Kay Anderson, in "Culture and Nature at the Adelaide Zoo: At the Frontiers of 'Human' Geography", *Transactions of the Institute of British Geographers, New Series* 20, no. 3 (1995): 277, argues that this tendency, in the precise forms in which it manifests itself today, may have solidified around the fifteenth century as the reason/nature dichotomy began to gain traction and to imply a hierarchy with humans at the top. See also Lisa Johnson, *Power, Knowledge, Animals* (New York: Palgrave Macmillan, 2012); Esther Cohen, "Animals in Medieval Perceptions: The Image of the Ubiquitous Other", in *Animals and Human Society*, ed. Aubrey Manning and James Serpell (London and New York: Routledge, 1994).

20. Michael Allen Fox and Lesley McLean, "Animals in Moral Space", in *Animal Subjects: An Ethical Reader in a Posthuman World*, ed. Jodey Castricano (Waterloo: Wilfrid Laurier University Press, 2008).

21. See Cudworth, *Social Lives with Other Animals*, 68; see also Marti Kheel, "The Liberation of Nature: A Circular Affair", in *The Feminist Care Tradition in Animal Ethics: A Reader*, ed. Josephine Donovan and Carol J. Adams (New York: Columbia University Press, 1997).

22. See Fox and McLean, "Animals in Moral Space", 154; Cudworth, *Social Lives with Other Animals*, 68.

23. See, for example, Anderson, "Culture and Nature at the Adelaide Zoo", 276: "Historically, the nature/culture opposition has informed diverse and culturally variable practices of domination and subordination on the part of humans. The cultural sense of separation has implied no neutral relation between humans and the non-human world but rather entailed detailed and persistent disciplinary practices". See also Colin Jerolmack, "How Pigeons Became Rats: The Cultural-Spatial Logic of Problem Animals", *Social Problems* 55, no. 1 (2008): 73.

24. Cf. Calarco, *Zoographies*, 9. See also Sally Haslanger, "Ideology, Generics, and Common Ground", in *Feminist Metaphysics: Explorations in the Ontology of Sex, Gender and the Self*, ed. Charlotte Witt (Dordrecht and London: Springer, 2011).

25. Anderson, "Culture and Nature at the Adelaide Zoo", 276.

26. Nibert, *Animal Rights/Human Rights*, 216–17.

27. Tom Regan, *The Case for Animal Rights* (Oakland: University of California Press, 2004).

28. Andrew Linzey, *Animal Theology* (Urbana and Chicago: University of Illinois Press, 1994).

29. Gary L. Francione, *Introduction to Animal Rights: Your Child or the Dog?* (Philadelphia: Temple University Press, 2000); Gary L. Francione, *Animals, Property, and the Law* (Philadelphia: Temple University Press, 1995).

30. Bob Torres, *Making a Killing: The Political Economy of Animal Rights* (Oakland and Edinburgh: AK Press, 2007).

31. Joan E. Schaffner, *An Introduction to Animals and the Law* (New York: Palgrave Macmillan, 2011).

32. Cudworth, *Social Lives with Other Animals*.

33. See also Fox and McLean, "Animals in Moral Space", 154.

34. The expression is used by Donaldson and Kymlicka, who devote considerable attention to liminal animals in arguing that simply "leaving animals alone" is neither feasible nor morally defensible. As they use the term *wild*, its reference is determined in part (and maybe even mostly) by animals' choices to avoid areas of human settlement. Sue Donaldson and Will Kymlicka, *Zoopolis: A Political Theory of Animal Rights* (Oxford: Oxford University Press, 2011).

35. See generally Jerolmack, "How Pigeons Became Rats".

36. Jerolmack, "How Pigeons Became Rats", 74. See also Nibert, *Animal Rights/ Human Rights*, 219 (on the reconfiguration of wild animals as "pests" once their habitats become "developed").

37. Deckha, "Toward a Postcolonial, Posthumanist Feminist Theory", 538.

38. See Schaffner, *An Introduction to Animals and the Law*, 27, 117; Francione, *Introduction to Animal Rights*, 58–63.

39. Francione, *Introduction to Animal Rights*, xxv, 8–9, 81.

40. Schaffner, *An Introduction to Animals and the Law*, 162–67.

41. Nibert, *Animal Rights/Human Rights*, 219.

42. Calarco, *Zoographies*, 8.

43. See MacKinnon, "Of Mice and Men", 266.

44. Cudworth, *Social Lives with Other Animals*, 38.

45. Donald VanDeVeer, "Interspecific Justice", in *The Environmental Ethics and Policy Book*, ed. Donald VanDeVeer and Christine Pierce (Belmont: Thomson Wadsworth, 2003), 158.

46. For further discussion of the limits of traditional approaches to the question of moral status, see Morton Tønnessen and Jonathan Beever (this volume), and Wayne Williams (this volume).

47. Matthew Scully, *Dominion: The Power of Man, the Suffering of Animals, and the Call to Mercy* (New York: St. Martin's Griffin, 2002), 390.

48. Cathryn Bailey, "On the Backs of Animals: The Valorization of Reason in Contemporary Animal Ethics", in *The Feminist Care Tradition in Animal Ethics: A Reader*, ed. Josephine Donovan and Carol J. Adams (New York: Columbia University Press, 2007), 350; Carrie Packwood Freeman, Mark Bekoff and Sarah Bexell, "Giving Voice to the Voiceless: Incorporating Nonhuman Animal Perspectives as Journalistic Sources", *Journalism Studies* 12, no. 5 (2011): 590–607. See also Cudworth, *Social Lives with Other Animals*, 50–51 (on the erasure of animals' agency in animal rights theory), and Donaldson and Kymlicka, *Zoopolis*, 56–61, 108–16 (on animals and political agency).

49. Iris M. Young, "Activist Challenges to Deliberative Democracy", *Political Theory* 29, no. 5 (2001): 685.

50. Lori Gruen, "Dismantling Oppression: An Analysis of the Connection between Women and Animals", in *Ecofeminism: Women, Animals, Nature*, ed. Greta Gaard (Philadelphia: Temple University Press, 1993), 77.

51. Alcoff, "The Problem of Speaking for Others", 26.

52. Sally Haslanger, "'But Mom, Crop-Tops *Are* Cute!' Social Knowledge, Social Structure and Ideology Critique", *Philosophical Issues* 17 (2007): 89 (on the disruption of dominant social schemas).

53. See generally Haslanger, "Ideology, Generics, and Common Ground".

54. Young, "Activist Challenges to Deliberative Democracy", 687. Consider as well the sentimentalist position defended by Elisa Aaltola in this volume.

55. Cf. Carrie Packwood Freeman, "Framing Animal Rights in the 'Go Veg' Campaigns of U.S. Animal Rights Organizations", *Society and Animals* 18 (2010): 163–82.

EIGHT

Doing Without Moral Rights

Elizabeth Foreman

Those with ethical concerns regarding our treatment of nonhuman animals have sought (generally) to establish their moral status, the assumption being that our horrific treatment of nonhuman animals is an outgrowth of failing to recognize their moral status. However, there is disagreement concerning both the ground and the nature of that status. One way to establish the moral status of nonhuman animals is to assert that, like human animals, nonhuman animals have moral rights. Given the importance of rights in the political sphere, this makes sense; rights (both moral and legal) are politically weighty things, and appeals to rights are hard to ignore. One might lament that many people lack health care because it is bad for people not to have it, but if one claims that this lack is a violation of some moral right, one's objection seems stronger. One is not simply claiming that if people are suffering, a good person should care. One is claiming that those who are suffering have a *valid claim* against others that they do something about that suffering.[1]

The idea that rights are *valid claims* explains why an appeal to rights is so powerful; rights give individuals *standing*, and so rights seem to be the firmest possible ground for moral status. If I have a valid claim against you, then I undeniably have moral standing, and the treatment to which I lay claim is owed to me as one with the *status to demand it*. It is understandable that when animal rights activists look at the treatment of nonhuman animals in the world today, they see the solution in terms of giving nonhuman animals a "voice" so as to show potential abusers that those animals, too, can make demands on them.

However, whether there are such things as moral rights is contentious, and in this chapter I will discuss Tom Regan's rights theory in

133

particular, and the problems it faces as an ethical view, ultimately arguing that it is unsatisfactory as the ground of obligations to nonhuman and human animals alike (with some discussion of how this applies to rights views in general). Most notably, the idea that rights involve the activity of claiming seems to immediately rule out nonhuman animals (and some human beings) as possessors of rights, so I will begin by discussing Tom Regan's attempt to retain the force of rights as valid claims, while cutting this analysis away from the activity of claiming. However, even though the desire to ground obligations in rights seems to stem from an understandable desire to give one moral standing to protest given types of treatment (even if only by proxy), I will argue that this way of understanding our obligations fails to capture many of our moral judgements, and fails to capture the way in which we actually see those that have moral status. What's more, I will argue that thinking in terms of rights actually runs counter to the goals of the animal rightist, since the notion of rights is fundamentally anthropocentric. Though it is useful politically, I will argue that thinking about morality in terms of rights (in the case of both human and nonhuman animals) is a flawed way of understanding our obligations, in part because it prioritizes one very human moral concern and makes it the sole ground of obligations. More specifically, I will argue that some common views about *how bad* our bad treatment of nonhuman animals actually is (i.e., though bad, it is not as bad as the same sort of treatment of human animals), and about how seriously we should take concerns over nonhuman animal welfare, are unfortunate outgrowths of legislative views of morality that seek to evaluate and prohibit conduct on the basis of a creature's "standing to complain".

As a possible alternative to rights-based discussions of moral status, I will suggest that understanding our obligations in terms of appropriate attitudes, rather than rights-based prohibitions on/demands on conduct, helps us better understand what a failure to appreciate the moral status of an individual amounts to, and why the mistreatment of nonhuman animals is so pervasive. Understanding morality in terms of the attitudes of agents helps us to see that what our actions say about how *we* view the world is fundamentally morally important, and can help explain, and also undermine, the pervasive view that caring about nonhuman animal welfare is antihuman. I will argue that understanding morality in this alternative way can show us that what matters primarily is not how bad our treatment of an individual is, which is often thought of in terms of how much standing an individual has (this can cash out in rights, sentience, etc.). What matters is what that treatment says about how inappropriately one views the individual with which one is engaging.

REGAN'S RIGHTS VIEW

Tom Regan's *The Case for Animal Rights* laid the philosophical ground-work for the animal rights movement, and is a richly detailed argument for the claim that many of our modern interactions with nonhuman animals constitute rights violations. In the course of argument, Regan positions himself in opposition to (1) those who think that human beings have rights, but that nonhuman animals do not, and (2) those who eschew thinking of our obligations to human and nonhuman animals in terms of rights at all (his target here is Peter Singer's utilitarian argument, which appeals to "equal consideration of interests", rather than to rights). I will focus mainly on his debate with the first group, discussing the second once I have made my case as part of that group.

As already noted, one of the major philosophical hurdles to arguing for animal rights is their analysis as *valid claims*. If rights are closely tied to the activity of claiming, then they seem to be uniquely human, since such activity involves the kind of consciousness of self that most nonhuman animals seem not to have. In making his case, Tom Regan thus attempts to sever the idea of rights as valid claims from the requirement that such claims be made by those that possess them. Says Regan,

> To make a claim, we have said, is a performance, and no account of moral rights can be adequate that makes the existence of moral rights contingent upon the performance of this or that voluntary act. To have a valid claim, as distinct from making a claim, is to have a certain sort of moral status, and one can have this status without claiming it or even being able to do so. Whether one has this status depends not on whether one can claim one's rights but on whether one has them, and this depends on whether sound arguments can be given for the recognition of these rights *independently* of the ability on the part of the individual who possesses them to claim them.[2]

Here, in order to overcome the fact that some moral patients cannot make claims, Regan retains the idea that rights are valid claims, but denies that one must be able to *make a claim* in order to have a valid claim against another. That is, an individual has a claim so long as she has the moral status that grounds unacquired duties towards her. If she is unable to *make* that claim, that is all the more reason for others to work to make sure it is recognized. On Regan's view, the vulnerability that comes with being voiceless does not undermine one's claims, but generates a further duty on the part of others to mitigate the effects of vulnerability.

This is an interesting feature of animal rights views, and of the rhetorical use of rights in general. Asserting rights is often a way of trying to draw attention to injustice, and even Peter Singer talks loosely of rights when discussing liberation movements in *Animal Liberation*.[3] It is characteristic of the animal rights struggle, however, that those who are op-

pressed are unable (not temporarily, but by fact of nature) to draw attention to themselves and to the injustice they suffer. This has seemed to
some to show a significant asymmetry in the injustice suffered, but Regan's view is meant to show that this does not mean that there is an
asymmetry in the injustice itself, though this difference does make a difference with respect to what must be done to stop it.

However, it is one thing to use the language of rights rhetorically in
the course of activism, and another to ground one's ethical view on them.
For Regan, our ethical obligations to human and nonhuman animals are
best understood on the model of rights. On his view, anything that is a
subject-of-a-life has inherent value, and a requirement to recognize and
respond appropriately to that value is what rights amount to. That is, I
have rights because I have a value that must be responded to appropriately, and not because I can demand that you respond to it appropriately.
Says Regan,

> [The Respect Principle] *We are to treat those individuals who have inherent
> value in ways that respect their inherent value.* Now, the respect principle
> sets forth an egalitarian, nonperfectionist interpretation of formal jus-
> tice . . . It enjoins us to treat all those individuals having inherent value
> in ways that respect their value, and thus it requires respectful treat-
> ment of all who satisfy the subject-of-a-life criterion.[4]

And to complete the case for rights,

> Since what is being claimed as their right [justice] is something claimed
> as their due, since justice is due them, and since the duty of justice is an
> unacquired duty, there is nothing logically untoward in correlating a
> basic right to just treatment with the unacquired duty of justice. Sec-
> ond, if one's making a claim to just treatment is to be valid, then both
> the claim-to and claim-against aspects of such a claim must be valid.
> Demands for just treatment, when these are informed by the notion of
> respect central to the respect principle, can be validated on both
> counts.[5]

The idea here is that if we look at our considered judgements about
how we ought to treat other human beings, we can identify the Respect
Principle as a moral principle to which we are committed. Regan also
identifies something called the Harm Principle, which he argues is deriv-
able from the Respect Principle, according to which we have a prima
facie duty not to harm individuals. What's more, when we examine these
principles more closely, we see that they apply not just to our treatment
of human beings but also to anything that has the relevant value-conferring characteristic of being a subject-of-a-life (though there is not space to
go deeply into the argument here, Regan relies largely on the intuitive
force of the argument from marginal cases in order to make this move).[6]
The Respect Principle (and the Harm Principle derived from it), in turn,
generates rights, and morality is in large part a matter of navigating the

various rights claims that arise from the existence of inherently valuable beings.

It is notable that Regan's methodology here is a process of reflective equilibrium. That is, he starts with our considered judgements and endorses a test for moral principles that involves the kind of back-and-forth testing between theory and principles described by John Rawls in *A Theory of Justice*.[7] Regan devotes a good deal of space to defence of this methodology, and though one might have concerns about it (there is much debate within the animal rights literature with respect to how much weight we ought to give even considered intuitive judgements), I tend to agree with Regan that we must start somewhere when building a theory, and our considered ethical judgements are the only place we can start.[8] However, the rights view that Regan ends up defending seems to fail in this regard; though it is good that the view unequivocally asserts that it is an injustice to experiment on unwilling animal subjects, no matter the consequences, the idea that this is so because those subjects have a *right* against such treatment fails to capture what is wrong with doing this. And that is simply because the invocation of rights seems to be a gloss on the simpler, founding idea of respect, and this gloss attempts to reimagine the evaluation of an actor (it is wrong to see any subject-of-a-life as a mere means) as evaluation of an act (experimenting *is an injustice*, one has a right against *being experimented upon*). The evaluation of the actor, I will argue, is what really drives the judgement, and the attempt to apply it to acts is both unnecessary and unhelpful. In the end, Regan's process of reflective equilibrium fails to pinpoint what is driving moral evaluation in the human as well as the nonhuman case.

We can see the danger of emphasizing the act rather than the actor when we examine Regan's attempts to align the rights view more closely with our considered judgements. In considering various objections, Regan introduces additional moral principles concerning the scope and weight of various rights claims. These principles he calls the Miniride and the Worse-Off Principles. According to the Miniride Principle,

> Special considerations aside, when we must choose between overriding the rights of many who are innocent or the rights of few who are innocent, and when each affected individual will be harmed in a prima facie comparable way, then we ought to choose to override the rights of the few in preference to overriding the rights of the many.[9]

That is, when it comes to rights violations, we ought to prefer the situation in which we violate fewer rights. As a companion to this principle, we have the Worse-Off Principle:

> Special considerations aside, when we must decide to override the rights of the many or the rights of few who are innocent, and when the harm faced by the few would make them worse-off than any of the

many would be if any other option were chosen, then we ought to override the rights of the many.[10]

In introducing these principles, Regan is trying to meet various objections and questions that arise whenever one attempts to argue that one has a right not to be killed or harmed. Unless one wants to claim that these rights are absolute, one needs to explain when recognition of these rights can justifiably be overridden, or when it can accede to other considerations. Regan's introduction of the Miniride and Worse-Off Principles allows him to argue that if one is stranded on a lifeboat with three human beings and a dog, and it turns out that one of the creatures must be thrown overboard, one must throw the dog overboard (because it will be made less worse off in death than any of the human beings), and that this would be true even if one had to throw a hundred dogs overboard to save the three people.

Regan is trying to keep the deliverances of theory in line with considered judgements, and so he needs to explain how our settled intuitions about what to do in dog/human lifeboat cases are in keeping with the recognition that all involved have rights. In doing so, Regan recasts these objections, rather than giving in to the conclusions so often drawn when these cases are discussed. Because it is intuitive to so many that the dog(s) should be thrown overboard, it is often assumed that either dogs don't have rights or their rights don't matter as much. Regan attempts to save the idea that the dog has rights equivalent to those of the humans involved, while still explaining why it is permissible to do what seems to be the morally correct thing.

However, in introducing these moral principles, Regan focuses on what it is we are allowed to *do*, given that the individuals with whom we are engaged have rights. This is understandable, but it is here that his commitment to a legislative and anthropocentric understanding of morality is most clear. What Regan has to end up arguing is precisely what his view should avoid—that though all animals have valid claims on our conduct, some claims are stronger than others, and the strongest claims are held by the most sophisticated animals—that is, persons. Of course, this is not supposed to be the point of these principles; they are supposed to merely highlight, in a species-neutral way, that some harms make individuals worse off than others, and that fewer instances of bad action (rights violation) are better than more. Even so, these claims seem to tread dangerously close to the views that Regan wishes to reject. The former seems to rely on a scaled view of welfare, based on degrees of capacity to be harmed, and the latter seems to be grounded in an aggregative notion of better and worse states of affairs, with an added commitment to making it the case that the best states of affairs obtains. Both of these sound very utilitarian, which is not surprising. After all, Regan appeals to our considered judgements, and so many of these seem un-equivocally utilitarian.

Regan's view thus establishes duties to nonhuman animals by assert-ing that they, like human beings, have "standing to complain" about their treatment, and that this means they have rights that legitimately con-strain our conduct regarding them. But what is curious about Regan's view is that he starts with our considered judgements, systematizes them in terms of generally acceptable moral principles, and then argues that these principles are best understood as indicative of the presence of rights. Because of this, he employs a standard methodology in animal rights and animal welfare literature—starting with unchallenged as-sumptions about what human beings deserve from us, these assumptions are employed to show that there is no principle that could justify them that doesn't also commit us to extending our concern to nonhuman ani-mals. Peter Singer's arguments concerning equality run in a similar way; Singer's goal in *Animal Liberation* is to illustrate the ways in which our beliefs already commit us (as a matter of consistency) to caring about the welfare of nonhuman animals.[11] This, too, is a way of starting from our judgements about how we ought to treat people, and using them to show that we ought to evaluate our interactions with nonhuman animals in the same way.

The reason this is curious is that it preserves an anthropocentric way of viewing the world; it does not challenge human-centred moral judge-ments, but merely aims to show that "nonhuman animals are people too" (where "people" is a moral, not biological, category). While I do think we have to start from our considered judgements, and that any ethical theory needs to be able to capture those judgements, it would be better to cri-tique the nature of those judgements in the process, rather than trying to preserve them as they are. What is troublesome here is the idea that morality is a matter of responding to various demands made upon us by individuals with "rights" against us; what is causing the trouble is the idea that morality is a matter of doing or not doing things to individuals who either do or do not merit our consideration. This model of morality is legislative, focusing on *rules* that legitimately constrain our action. Be-cause of this, the model is very human-centred; on such a view, morality is the business of weighing various claims against our freedom to act as we wish, and our task is to navigate these claims. The question is not "What kind of people should we be?" but rather "What can we do?" This kind of view understands morality on the model of states implementing rules in order to constrain rational, and otherwise free, citizens (what are we not *allowed* to do, what can we be *required* to do), and so understands morality on the model of a uniquely human activity. That is, it sees our moral lives as extensions of our political lives; because of this, a concep-tion of morality as a system that regulates the activity of free and rational agents grounds the view, and the influence of that conception can be seen in various ways.

For example, it is because we view morality this way that we fall into various traps concerning lifeboat cases (in general, these kinds of cases test the adequacy of views that maintain an equivalency in moral status among individuals by asking what one ought to do in cases where someone's claims have to be overridden, such as in cases when some individual must be thrown from the lifeboat). That is, preserving a human-centred view of morality while trying to extend it to nonhuman animals also encourages the idea that, whatever we owe to other animals, our obligations to them can't be as strong as those we have to human beings. Regan's view, in the end, is about empowerment and freedom — one cannot experiment on a kitten because the kitten has standing to complain against treatment that violates her interests and/or her rights. And so the experimenter is not free to do what she wishes with the kitten, just as she is not free to do what she wishes with a human being; there are facts about the kitten that constrain that freedom.

However, by thinking of this in terms of the kitten as a possessor of something morally salient (rights), the question naturally becomes one of how empowered the kitten actually is. How *much* standing does she have? Surely not as much as a human being. How weighty are her claims? Surely not as weighty as counterclaims from human beings. If one denies there is a difference between the standing of a kitten and the standing of a human being, one is held to be "antihuman", because failure to acknowledge that the claims of fellow human beings are stronger than the claims of nonhuman beings is seen as a way of disempowering (that is, failing to recognize the unique and special claims of) our own species.[12] Thus, there is a strong temptation to temper arguments by acceding to the deeply held belief that the standing and claims of human persons are more robust than those of nonhuman beings. Regan does this through his discussion of the lifeboat cases and the introduction of the Miniride and Worse-Off Principles (interestingly, Singer does the same thing simply by holding to a utilitarian view of justification — what matters, in the end, is how the interests weigh out, and as a matter of fact, they often weigh out in favor of persons because of their capacities). This is a direct result of understanding morality in terms of "standing to object", where either (1) the ground of that standing comes in degrees (a utilitarian view) or (2) though the ground does not come in degrees (one is not more or less a subject-of-a-life), one's complaints can be more or less robust, and are to be counted and weighed against the robustness of the claims of others (Regan's view). On both kinds of views, the question is "How much does the thing with which I am engaging matter, morally?", and the theory gives us a way to answer that question.

REGAN'S VIEW, RE-THOUGHT

What does the theoretical work on Regan's view is arguably an appeal to proper attitudes, and yet he abandons this focus in favor of establishing strict prohibitions on conduct. The Respect Principle does the grounding work, in his view, but the Respect Principle is ultimately grounded in seeing individuals in ways that recognize their value as subjects-of-lives. In Regan's view, it is wrong to experiment on a kitten because she is the subject-of-a-life. Because she is such a subject, she has inherent value, and must be treated in ways that recognize that value. Treating her as a mere piece of "lab equipment" fails to treat her in ways consistent with recognition of her value, and so she has a *right* not to be treated in that way.

However, the appeal to rights is unnecessary once it has been established that the inherent value of a kitten sets limits on how we can treat her. If it is wrong to treat her in those ways, the appeal to rights simply adds rhetorical weight to an established duty. It is a way of saying that she has a card she can play against us; it is not *just* that we ought not treat her as a piece of lab equipment. She can *demand* that we not. But the idea of her having a *claim* is the source of resistance from those who are suspicious of nonhuman animal welfare as a moral concern, and of nonhuman animal rights as actual, existing things. Saying that she "can demand" that we not treat her in certain ways amounts to saying that we have to see her as theoretically, though not practically, in a position to demand that we not (as discussion of Regan's analysis of rights as *valid claims* shows). But that does seem different from the demand I could make in the same situation, and it is not unreasonable to think that, of course, my demands are different and need to be seen as such.

Beyond an appeal to rights being an unnecessary theoretical step, the focus on actions is also a red herring. The Respect Principle is formulated in terms of how we are allowed to *treat* any creature with which we are engaged. However, if I treat you in ways that fail to recognize your inherent value, that must mean that *doing* X is the sort of thing I simply cannot do, while at the same time recognizing your inherent value. But that must be because *acting* in that way is inconsistent with a *proper view* of *you*, the individual with inherent value. Focusing on the action is understandable, if one is starting from a legislative understanding of morality, according to which the goal is to determine which acts are prohibited or allowed. However, respect is an attitude, and when we dig to the theoretical bottom of what Regan is arguing, what's motivating the evaluation of certain acts is evaluation of the attitudes that they express. The evaluation of actions seems secondary, if that evaluation comes in terms of "treating a creature in ways that *recognize* their inherent value". The recognition, a cognized way of seeing, comes first here, and so the shift to actions as the objects of evaluation seems to be an unhelpful step away from the real theoretical ground. If Regan wishes to start from our considered judgements and systematize them into various moral principles, he needs to rethink how much those judgements really are, in the end, judgements about actions.

Why is it wrong to torture a kitten for fun? Regan's answer comes, ultimately, in terms of the failure to respect the inherent value of that kitten. Torturing her for fun fails to respect her value, because it treats her as a mere tool for my use. But the fact that I am treating her as a mere tool for my use is a function of the fact that I am *doing it for fun*; if for some reason I was performing the same action for her own good (for example, if I were pulling a tooth that is causing her pain, instead of pulling it *in order to cause her pain*), then it might not be the case that I am using her as a mere tool. Whether or not I am treating her in ways that fail to respect her value is a function of whether I see her in a way, and thus interact with her in a way, that stems from recognition of her value. The action doesn't get a negative moral valence unless the way in which I *view* the kitten is bad. Similarly, when we think about what is wrong with torturing *people* for fun, the salient point is that it is obscene to wish to overpower and destroy another person, just for the fun of it. It is wrong not to care about the suffering of others, or to want to inflict that suffering, and this is not *ultimately* because pain is bad, but rather because the fact that pain is bad for the one who suffers it is a reason why we should *care* about not inflicting pain. The fact that a person, or a kitten, will suffer if I torture her is the reason I ought not do it, but not because it is wrong to make it the case that suffering occurs, and not because it is wrong to violate one's right against being caused unnecessary suffering. It is wrong for me not to *care* that another suffers, and wrong for me to *like* that she does; that I do not care about, and in fact like, her suffering means that I do not see her or her suffering appropriately. The actions that express lack of care, or inappropriate proattitudes, are wrong because they exhibit this skewed way of seeing the one with whom I am interacting. It is this skewed way of seeing that differentiates torture from the identical actions performed for the medical benefit of the sufferer, and what makes the former, and not the latter, objectionable. It is not that causing suffering is justified when it is for the sufferer's benefit; it is that causing suffering in such situations does not involve a skewed way of seeing, so that what one does (in the sense of "makes happen"—that is, that suffering occurs) is not prima facie wrong to begin with.

Insisting on rights against certain treatment simply doesn't touch theoretical bottom, because the validity of the claim against the treatment has to rest in some moral principle. That moral principle (Regan's Respect Principle, for example) is what is doing the real theoretical work— establishing the wrongness of the treatment is antecedent to any valid claim I might have against it. We tend to focus on rights when we want to resist bad treatment, but this insistence can only be a way to more adamantly assert the badness of treatment. And because the badness of that treatment theoretically grounds the claim (and not the other way around), an appeal to rights is a gloss on a deeper idea. However, this deeper idea is not the utilitarian notion that people are better off if we recognize claims for protection in the possession of things necessary for survival.[13] This utilitarian reduction of rights to constructions for the betterment of society misses the important point that rights are about "looking another in the eye" and recognizing them as valid sources of claims.[14] But as the discussion of Regan was meant to show, this analysis doesn't capture the fundamental structure of our moral judgements; instead, it focuses on an activity that simply adds rhetorical weight to an independent theoretical structure. Trying to cast a discussion of moral status in terms of rights focuses on one very human concern (the wish, and demand, to be heard when one is vulnerable), and makes it the foundation of an entire moral system. But that means that the resulting theory doesn't capture the way in which we actually make moral judgements, or the way we actually see others when we see them as legitimate objects of moral concern. Those who have moral status are not simply those who can demand that we see them that way. Those who have moral status are those about whom some morally salient facts are true; it is wrong for *us* to ignore those facts, even if those about whom those facts are true are unable to explain to us that we are ignoring them.

One of the good features of a rights view is that it calls attention to the reasons moral agents have to act in certain ways, and it emphasizes the fact that those reasons are ultimately ones that others can demand we recognize. However, as the foregoing discussion was meant to show, that others can demand we recognize those reasons is not *why* they legitimately constrain our conduct, it is not primarily why they are important. Insisting that all of morality has, at bottom, the structure of claims and demands causes the view to be anthropocentric because *making* these demands is a human activity. This makes the struggle to change our treatment of nonhuman animals harder, because casting things in this way involves attempting to "empower" those incapable of engaging in this activity with some approximation of it. Though pushing for nonhuman animal rights might be useful politically and legally, it gets the moral situation wrong, and so, not surprisingly, the movement might strike some people as morally off target. But it is off target because rights are not really what are at issue for humans or nonhumans, not because nonhuman animals alone don't have rights.

EVALUATING ATTITUDES, NOT ACTIONS

My suggestion is that in the case of both nonhuman and human animals, what drives our moral evaluations, the ground of our considered moral judgements, is evaluation of the attitudes that certain actions express.

Where Regan systematizes our judgements in terms of various principles constraining action, from which rights are generated, I suggest that we need to systematize those judgements in a different way. Those judgements do not describe a sphere of prohibited and allowed action, but a range of appropriate and inappropriate attitudes. This way of understanding morality is less anthropocentric, because anything in the world can be seen appropriately or inappropriately; morality, then, is not just about navigating various interests or claims but also about seeing the world in the right way, which includes seeing those with interests or claims in appropriate ways.

If this is how our moral judgements work, it is obvious that caring about nonhuman animal welfare is not antihuman at all. The thought is that it is arises from thinking of morality as competing claims and interests, which must be weighed against each other. To those who are unconvinced, it may seem that to insist on the weightiness of nonhuman animal claims and interests is to fail to appreciate the ways in which their claims and interests are different from ours. But if we refocus the issue in terms of how we should *see* them, it should be clearer that what matters is not *how much* standing an individual has, nor *how much* they can legitimately demand of us. What matters is whether we see them in ways appropriate to the kinds of things that they are. There is a kernel of truth in both utilitarian and rights-based accounts—suffering is bad and we should have a certain kind of attitude towards it, and a laissez-faire attitude is appropriate towards those that are self-directed. But as in our interactions with people, neither of these is the sum total of all the morally salient facts, and the moral situation involves much more than ferreting out which actions can be done and which cannot, given that interests or rights exist. The moral landscape is defined by the more complex process of figuring out what kinds of attitudes are appropriate and which are not; it is from these that better or worse actions flow. Attitudes are the ground of the evaluation and the source of the problems; as with any social movement, what really needs to change is the attitudes that drive the actions that we wish to stop.[15]

One might worry that this sort of view is *more anthropocentric* than legislative views of morality, since the ground of moral evaluation is the agent and not the objects of her action. This might also raise the further worry that the view I am suggesting is indirect.[16] I will conclude with responses to these worries.

Though it may seem as if it is anthropocentric to locate wrongness in the attitudes of the actor and not in the actions performed, my argument is that the latter way of understanding morality structures it around largely human ways of understanding moral constraints. That is, if we focus on what we are allowed to do, given that certain things/facts/claims legitimately limit our actions, our concern is with the justification of our actions to those who would constrain us. This view of morality is a result of seeing moral constraints on the model of rules or laws that have authority. The idea of authority is inherent in the way these views structure moral evaluation and deliberation, whether what is appealed to is the authority of reasons, of rights, or even of the moral salience of suffering. My contention is not that these views are anthropocentric because they see morality as something that concerns only human beings; it is instead that they are anthropocentric because they structure theory around the sphere of morality closest to human concerns.

On the other hand, a view that is focused on the attitudes of the agent is anthropocentric in one way—it structures moral evaluation around the perspective of moral agents. However, since it is possible that moral demands are uniquely human preoccupations, this should not be too worrisome. Such a view is not anthropocentric in the way discussed above, for moral evaluation is not about what I can legitimately *do* (the perspective of one who navigates around moral demands) but about how it is right to see the world. This latter understanding of moral evaluation shows us that it is how we see the world, and it is how we see ourselves in it, that defines the moral landscape. Furthermore, the world is such that we do not get to choose how we see it. The world and all that it contains *just is* a certain way, and we need to see it as such—this involves getting past our own self-focus, our own bias, and our own group loyalties. Though both utilitarian and rights-based accounts seek to help us get past those things by showing us the ways in which nonhuman animals are "people too", my suggestion is that the better remedy is to emphasize the way in which the moral landscape is full of much more than people, and that it is as nonpeople that these other things are morally salient.

This view might also be thought to be indirect, since the claim being made is that the ground of the wrongness of torturing a kitten is a fact about the torturer (that she sees the kitten in the wrong way). This might sound very much like some of the views rightly rejected by nonhuman animal defenders, views that seek to explain our duties towards nonhuman animals by locating an ill effect in the moral agent. In particular, this may sound very close to the Kantian view that we can only have duties to rational creatures, and any duties we have with respect to nonrational creatures are only *actually* duties to rational creatures (i.e., we have a duty not to deaden our compassion by torturing kittens, because then we might be more likely to fail in our actual duty not to torture people).[17] However, the view I am suggesting is not indirect in this way, because ultimately, the attitude displayed in the torture of a kitten is an inappropriate way of viewing *this kitten*, not an inappropriate way of viewing something else. Torturing her is wrong because of the kind of thing that she is; what sort of thing *she* is drives the evaluation of the attitude, which in turn grounds the wrongness of the torture. One might still worry that this is indirect, because ultimately no action is wrong in itself, only attitudes are. However, if this means that obligations on such a view are indirect (though I do not think that they are, since they are still owed to the creatures involved), then any and all obligations would be indirect; so our obligations to nonhuman animals will be no different, in this regard, from our obligations to human animals.

CONCLUSION

In this chapter, I have attempted to explain that Regan's rights-based view is unsatisfactory as a general moral theory, and that this is partly due to the anthropocentrism underlying a concern with rights. I have briefly suggested an alternative way of understanding morality in terms of appropriate attitudes. Though appeals to rights can be politically and legally helpful, I have argued that it would be better to abandon them as the ground of moral argument for theoretical reasons. This would be better not only in the interest of offering the best theory of moral evaluation but also in the interest of progress in the struggle to improve the lives of the nonhuman animals among us.

NOTES

1. This understanding of moral rights is the dominant way of theorizing them, endorsed by thinkers as varied as Joel Feinberg, H. L. A. Hart, John Stuart Mill, and Tom Regan. [See Joel Feinberg, "The Nature and Value of Rights", *Journal of Value Inquiry* 4 (1970): 243–60; H. L. A. Hart, "Are There Any Natural Rights?", *Philosophical Review* 64 (1955): 175–91; John Stuart Mill, *Utilitarianism* (Indianapolis: Hackett Publishing Company, 2001); Tom Regan, *The Case for Animal Rights* (Berkeley: University of California Press, 2004)]. In what follows, I will focus on Tom Regan's discussion of rights, since it is the canonical discussion in the animal rights literature.

2. Regan, *The Case for Animal Rights*, 283.

3. Peter Singer, *Animal Liberation* (New York: HarperCollins, 2002), 1–9.

4. Regan, *The Case for Animal Rights*, 248.

5. Regan, *The Case for Animal Rights*, 277–78.

6. Regan, *The Case for Animal Rights*, 182–85, 192–93.

7. John Rawls, *A Theory of Justice* (Cambridge, MA: Harvard University Press, 1971).

8. Regan, *The Case for Animal Rights*, 140.

9. Regan, *The Case for Animal Rights*, 305.

10. Regan, *The Case for Animal Rights*, 308.

11. Singer, *Animal Liberation*, 4–8.

12. Objections against use of the Argument from Marginal Cases sometimes have this character. See, for example, Bonnie Steinbock, "Speciesism and the Idea of Equality", *Philosophy* 53 (1978): 247–56, and Elizabeth Anderson, "Animal Rights and the Values of Nonhuman Life", in *Animal Rights: Current Debates and New Directions*, ed. Cass R. Sunstein and Martha C. Nussbaum (Oxford: Oxford University Press, 2004), 277–98. Anderson's arguments draw attention to something for which I am arguing here—that trying to apply a conception of human rights to nonhuman animals fails to appreciate the way in which such rights are grounded in human-to-human relationships. However, she does not take this as a reason to reject appeals to rights altogether, as I will argue.

13. Mill, *Utilitarianism*, 54.

14. Feinberg, "The Nature and Value of Rights", 252.

15. There are similarities here with a diverse body of literature that focuses on attitudes, though I depart from views that ground moral evaluation in flourishing, or some other fact about the *agent* (the view suggested here is that facts about the object ground the rightness or wrongness of the attitude). For a virtue ethics view that emphasizes attitudes, see Rosalind Hursthouse, *Ethics, Humans, and Other Animals* (London: Routledge, 2000). For a very different understanding of the role that attitudes play in moral evaluation, see Cora Diamond, "Eating Meat and Eating People", *Philosophy* 53 (1978): 465–79, and "The Importance of Being Human", *The Royal Institute of Philosophy Supplement* 29 (1991): 35–62.

16. Regan devotes a whole chapter to showing that Indirect Duty Views cannot successfully explain our duties regarding nonhuman animals (Regan, *The Case for Animal Rights*, 150–94). One of his targets is Kant; I agree with Regan's critique of Kant and think that Regan is right in his analysis of the Respect Principle. However, I am suggesting that his analysis could have stopped there, with moral evaluation bottoming out in respect, because the appeal to rights that follows isn't necessary in order to establish the directness of the duty.

17. Immanuel Kant, *Lectures on Ethics*, trans. Louis Infield (New York: Harper and Row, 1963), 239–41.

Part III

Moral Psychology: Emotions and Metaethics

NINE

Disgust and the Collection of Bovine Foetal Blood

Robert William Fischer

To write *Every Twelve Seconds,* Timothy Pachirat spent almost six months working various jobs at a slaughterhouse in Nebraska: hanging livers in the freezer; driving cattle down the chute toward the "knocker" (the person who fires a steel bolt into their skulls); and handling food safety quality control on the kill floor. (The book's title refers to the rate at which they killed cows at his facility: one every twelve seconds, or 2,400 each day.) His time there allowed him to deliver exactly what he promises—namely, "a close account of what it means to participate in the massive, routinized slaughter of animals for consumption by a larger society from which that work is hidden".[1] To that end, he catalogues the nuances of butchering, explains the design and management of the slaughterhouse, and offers glimpses of how that environment affects the people who work within it. Here is a particularly memorable passage from the end of his overview of the butchering process:

> He stands on a raised webbed platform at another long metal table; this one has a vertical metal screen running down its length studded with sharp metal hooks, about fifteen in all. Sometimes out of the pipe in the wall an oblong gray mass shoots that is not a lung, kidney, windpipe, or liver. When that happens the white-helmeted worker walks over, picks up the object, and carries it back to his worktable, where he takes out a knife and cuts into the gray mass. There will be a foetus inside, with smooth, slick skin, and clearly marked hide patterns. Raising the foetus up by the neck and hind legs, the man swivels to the vertical metal screen and pushes the foetus's mouth onto one of the protruding hooks. Releasing the neck so that the body now hangs by the mouth, he

151

uses two hands to stick another hook into the foetus's anus. The foetus now hangs suspended by mouth and anus, and the worker makes an incision in the neck area, bringing a bottle with a straw cut at an incline up to the incision.

He then shakes and massages the body of the foetus, coaxing blood into the waiting bottle. The shaking becomes more vigorous as less and less blood remains in the body. Finally, when there is no more blood to be had, the man pulls the bottle from the incision, caps the straw, and nestles the bottle inside the chipped ice of a blue ice chest for later use in medical production. Once bled, the foetus is deposited in a gray circular barrel on top of other bled foetuses.[2]

Since discovering Pachirat's book, I've read this passage to my students when we've turned to animal ethics. If their faces are any guide, they find it disgusting. They know full well that, if you want steak, cows have to die. But most of them have never considered the grisly details of that process. When they do, they seem to be repulsed—and then troubled.

I'm inclined to think that, when my students are disgusted by this passage—or when people are sickened by video of piglets being slammed against a concrete floor, or by images of chickens right after debeaking—they thereby acquire a reason to believe that these practices are morally wrong.[3] Not everyone agrees. Daniel Kelly, for example, claims that disgust "is not wise about or acutely attuned to ethical considerations, and 'yuck' deserves no special moral credence; rather, repugnance is simply irrelevant to moral justification".[4] Kelly is one of several recent "disgust sceptics", all of whom have argued, on one basis or another, in favor of a view like the one summarized above.[5] Some of these philosophers are bothered by disgust's false positives, as when people are disgusted by gay sex or interracial marriage; others are bothered by its power to dehumanize, which is often marshalled by those engaged in genocidal campaigns (the Nazis, for example, promoted the view that Jewish people were vermin). A further worry concerns disgust's evolutionary pedigree: it seems to have evolved to help us avoid things that might make us sick, which seems not to have any significant connection with the moral status of actions.

Another batch of philosophers has replied to these arguments, showing that these debunking arguments either overgeneralize or are based on questionable empirical assumptions.[6] But while these replies may show that we shouldn't reject disgust's guidance out of hand, they fall short of showing that it in fact provides us with defeasible moral reasons. To work towards the latter position, it would help to have a theory of disgust's moral salience that fits with the empirical work that's been done on it. With that end in mind, I sketch such a theory and apply it to the case with which I began—the collection of bovine foetal blood. The payoff, I hope, is a plausible account of how disgust can guide our moral judgements, and particularly how it can be of value in animal ethics.

DISGUST: AN OVERVIEW

Before offering a theory, however, we need to be clear about the data that it ought to explain. We'll begin with the reaction itself; then we can ask about its causes ("elicitors", to use the jargon of the field) and effects.

Many psychologists judge disgust to be one of the "universal emotions", recognizably the same in expression and function across known cultures.[7] The experience of disgust is the experience of something being revolting. Thus, disgust has an object—one that the agent rejects as repugnant, offensive, or otherwise bad. This negative feeling tends to co-occur with nausea, a drop in blood pressure, increased salivation, and activation of the parasympathetic nervous system. It's typically expressed by "the gape face"—a wrinkled nose and raised upper lip; sometimes accompanied by an open mouth and protruding tongue. Disgust is, moreover, a withdrawal response: people tend to back away from, and subsequently avoid, things by which they're repulsed.

People are disgusted by many things: consumables; bodily waste and secretions; deformed, damaged, and dead bodies; sex acts (relative to an assumed norm); and some moral offences. But while there are similarities between the objects of disgust across cultures—*ceteris paribus*, people are more likely to be disgusted by foods that involve fermentation than those that don't—there are plenty of local differences. So, for example, Icelanders praise *hákarl*—shark meat that they bury in sand and allow to rot for a few months before further preparation—which has "a pungent, ammoniac, fishy odor which causes most newbies to gag or vomit. [It was] described by the globe-trekking celebrity chef Anthony Bourdain as 'the single worst, most disgusting, and terrible tasting thing' he had ever eaten".[8] Additionally, there is significant individual variation in terms of the degree to which a person is "disgustable". These individual differences in reaction strength are correlated with gender, age, and certain personality traits. We know, for example, that women are generally more disgusted by sex acts than men are (with at least one notable exception—namely, the strength of straight men's reactions to gay sex); that disgust sensitivity tends to wane with age; and that people who score high on the personality trait *neuroticism* tend to have greater disgust sensitivity than do those who score high on *openness to experience*.[9]

As I mentioned, disgust is a withdrawal emotion. Moreover, this aversion transfers. If x is disgusting, then people tend to avoid it. And if x touches the previously-not-disgusting y, then people tend to avoid y too. Paul Rozin and his colleagues found that people were disinclined to drink apple juice after it had been in contact with a sterilized dead cockroach, or stirred with a new and demonstrably clean flyswatter, or when offered to them in a perfectly clean bedpan. Likewise, people tend to avoid putting on a sweater that was once owned by someone who had his leg amputated or committed a morally atrocious act (e.g., murder).

This aversion doesn't depend on contact; conceptual association is enough. If you take a nondisgusting object (such as chocolate) and shape it like something disgusting (such as dog faeces), you can get the same effect.[10]

There are a number of theories about disgust's evolutionary history, its current function, and the physiological mechanisms behind it.[11] But despite these controversies, we can make some claims about disgust with a fair degree of confidence. The core disgust response seems to be directed towards objects that, for much of our evolutionary history, were often sources of poisons or parasites (or were regularly associated with such sources): for example, faeces, rotting flesh, blood, maggots, and more. So the experiential and behavioural aversion involved with disgust isn't surprising: we thereby avoid potential sources of harm. Moreover, the gape face and nausea aren't surprising: they aid in preventing the oral incorporation of such objects, enabling and encouraging disgusted individuals to spit them out immediately.

There is much more to say about "core disgust", but the above will suffice for present purposes. What about *moral* disgust—that is, core disgust coupled with moral condemnation?[12] Early on in *The Righteous Mind*, Jonathan Haidt tells a story in which a "man goes to the supermarket once a week and buys a chicken. But before cooking the chicken, he has sexual intercourse with it. Then he cooks it and eats it".[13] Many people are disgusted by this, and some are inclined to say that the man is doing something morally wrong.[14] How did we, as a species, come to be repulsed by actions of this variety? The details are controversial, but the outlines of the account are fairly straightforward. First, whatever the cognitive machinery behind the disgust reaction, it's teachable machinery. The cultural differences between the objects of disgust form part of the evidence for this. Perhaps evolution wrote a cognitive program with "if *slimy*, then *disgusting*" among its default settings, but the Japanese have restricted it so that it doesn't apply to *natto*—a slimy, fermented soybean product—and Westerners have restricted it so that it doesn't apply to soft cheeses (which many Japanese find revolting). The disgust response can be expanded as well: it's wildly implausible that natural selection could have written a cognitive program with "if *bedpan*, then *disgusting*" among its default settings, but it's plain that some people do indeed find bedpans repugnant. Why? Because they've learned to associate bedpans with human waste, they find human waste disgusting, and disgust transfers.

Second, if disgust can be redirected, then biological and/or cultural evolution can co-opt it for other purposes—for example, regulating human social interactions. Given that disgust is a withdrawal emotion, it would be particularly useful for drawing in-group/out-group boundaries and enforcing social norms: to be disgusting would be to risk exclusion from the in-group. And the research bears this out. It seems that disgust operates to enforce norms about, inter alia, diet generally, meat specifically, table manners, incest, homosexual sex, the "right" political commitments and smoking cigarettes.[15]

DISGUST AND WRONGNESS

Given what we know about disgust, how can we see disgust as providing moral guidance? How might it give us reason to think that something is morally wrong?

To answer these questions, let's consider the purpose of moral emotions (e.g., disgust, empathy, shame, guilt, anger, etc.). From an evolutionary perspective, such emotions are instances of fast thinking (to borrow a phrase from Daniel Kahneman): they are immediate responses that increase the odds that agents will navigate situations in certain ways. Some emotions—such as fear, which encourages avoiding high-risk situations—serve to benefit the organism directly. But moral emotions—like compassion—tend to be other-directed, benefiting in-group members. Insofar as the well-being of the group is in the interest of the individual, these emotions provide indirect benefits, and thus they contribute to fitness in a roundabout manner. As Joshua Greene puts it, moral emotions are "psychological adaptations that allow otherwise selfish individuals to reap the benefits of cooperation".[16] Of course, this isn't to suggest that evolution "defaults" to promoting selfishness, though it might be helpful to model some episodes in evolutionary history that way. Nor is it to suggest that people are *motivated* by self-interest (enlightened or otherwise) when they are inclined to cooperate. Rather, the idea is that evolution outfitted our ancestors with genuinely other-directed concerns for their offspring's good, since those concerns spared them from prisoners' dilemmas, the tragedy of the commons, and other non-zero-sum interactions where acting on self-interest is a poor long-term strategy. That is, our ancestors acquired emotional dispositions that made them less likely to seek the best for themselves at everyone else's expense—including their own—and more likely to act in ways that are mutually beneficial.

With this theory of the moral emotions in mind, which situations should we expect to prompt disgust? To answer this question, recall disgust's apparent social value: to draw in-group/out-group boundaries (recall the aversion/avoidance tendency) and to enforce certain social norms (since to be disgusting would be to risk exclusion from the in-group). Since sex (involving various bodily fluids) and eating (given the risk of contamination) were already triggers for disgust, it makes sense that communities would moralize these activities to create social boundaries. Moreover, since violations of especially important community norms raise questions about community membership—for example, someone using violence against an innocent in-group member—it makes sense that such violations would also be disgusting. In a modern context, this might explain why cheating at cards (usually) isn't disgusting, but cheating people out of their homes might well be.

Moral disgust emerges, then, as a moral heuristic. It's keyed to violations of community-defining norms as well as violations of especially important community norms. But are our community norms also *moral* norms? Sometimes, it's clear that they aren't: it certainly isn't morally wrong to drive on the left-hand side of the road, as odd as that may be to Americans. But in other cases, it's equally clear that they are. Our communities don't tolerate random acts of violence; such acts violate a shared norm. And there is a clear moral justification for that norm: such acts harm the victim (and the community generally, insofar as it creates a culture of fear), they fail to respect the victim (and again, perhaps the community in general), and more.

So we can refine the proposal: moral disgust is keyed to violations of community-defining norms as well as violations of especially important community norms *that are thought to be justified by moral reasons*. And if there *are* such reasons behind our norms, then disgust can lead us to fully justified judgements about moral matters; if there aren't, then it can't.[17]

In some cases, we can give adequate and relatively straightforward moral justifications of our norms—and hence our disgust—in terms of harm, unfairness, and the like. Consider, for example, experiencing disgust at the thought of torture.[18] If these cases were the only ones in view, there would be no reason to balk at disgust as a moral heuristic. The cases that worry the sceptics are those where no such justifications are forthcoming, such as disgust at same-sex sexual relations.

Here we need to tread carefully. I don't think people should trust their disgust when it comes to homosexual sex. Indeed, I think they should work to rid themselves of the reaction. However, I think we can explain why without throwing out disgust entirely.

Our norms support a way of life, and obedience to them reflects a commitment to it. So when there isn't a straightforward justification of a given norm in terms of harm or fairness, there may still be one in terms of larger social goods that are sustained, at least in part, by adherence to that norm. Granted, these goods—and their connection to the act in question—may not be ones that individuals can readily formulate. Hence, it's sometimes easy to *dumbfound* people about certain disgust-prompting norm violations. Jonathan Haidt has shown that, even when people can't identify the harm involved, they're disinclined to say that consensual, nonprocreative, adult incest is morally permissible.[19] But this is no objection. If moral emotions are instances of fast thinking, then we shouldn't expect to be better at articulating their justifications than we are with respect to *other* instances of fast thinking. Upon seeing my wife's face, I know automatically whether she's upset about something, but I have no idea how to explain that recognitional ability. And that's no reason to think I'm wrong about her emotional state.[20]

So the real question is whether, when there is no straightforward justification of our aversion, it's plausible that our response is sensitive to some larger goods—and whether those are, ultimately, more important than the restriction of freedom we're supporting by condemning the relevant action. That is, we're asking whether the norm supports a way of life worth preserving. In the case of consensual adult incest, this amounts to the question of whether there are sufficiently important goods that depend on using the family/nonfamily distinction to draw a line between those who are and aren't potential sexual partners. In the case of gay sex, this amounts to the question of whether there are sufficiently important goods that depend on using gender or sex to draw a line between those who are and aren't potential sexual partners.

Perhaps there are sufficiently important goods at stake in the case of consensual adult incest. First, the incest taboo is one of the few tools we have to discourage sexual abuse in contexts where oversight is practically impossible—namely, the home. In trying to preserve the view that family relationships are inherently asexual, we try to make the unthinkable, unthinkable—thereby judging that the interests of potential victims outweigh the interests of those who would like to sleep with their consenting, adult family members. Second, and as I've argued elsewhere, it's valuable to have close, long-lasting, socially recognized, and decidedly asexual relationships.[21] Among other things, they create a haven from the complexities created by the mere possibility of sex, freeing us from the norms of conduct that govern relationships that *might* become sexual— norms that regulate our appearance, how we demonstrate affection, and more. Families are the natural context for such relationships, and in preserving the incest taboo, we also preserve a kind of relationship that might otherwise be much rarer. Admittedly, the taboo imposes a burden on some. However, a ban on incestuous sex leaves people with a wide array of potential sexual and/or romantic partners, and thus doesn't seem overly burdensome. Jointly, these considerations might—*might*—justify preserving the taboo.

In the case of gay sex, however, I very much doubt that there are sufficiently important goods at stake. But for present purposes, it doesn't matter whether I'm right about either case. Perhaps *no* larger good is weighty enough to justify condemning the sexual activities of consenting adults. If so, this is no mark against disgust as a moral heuristic. All it would show is that the heuristic shouldn't be applied to sex between consenting adults. The method for reaching this conclusion is simple. If there is no immediate justification of disgust's recommendation, then we should shift our attention to larger goods to which it might be sensitive. And if, after sustained reflection, we don't find any such goods, or we judge them not to be of sufficient worth, then we should dismiss our reaction as confused.

As I've already noted, it's unreasonable to demand that we have the story about social goods before we have a reason to think that the behaviour in question is wrong. Still, the longer it takes to tell the story, the more we should worry about two potential defeaters: first, that we're reacting to a feature of a situation simply because it's a trigger for core disgust, and not because it has some connection to, say, social order (e.g., anal sex repulses us because we're repulsed by faeces, rather than because it somehow damages society); second, that the relevant community's norms are unjustified. So consider sex reassignment surgery and some individuals who find it disgusting. Let's assume that, given their epistemic circumstances, they aren't *epistemically* blameworthy for condemning this procedure. Given as much, I grant that their disgust provides them with some reason for believing that the procedure is wrong. However, in this case both potential defeaters are of concern: the mutilation involved in surgery can be gross, regardless of its purpose, and we might doubt that the social goods created by a norm against surgical transformation are outweighed by the burden placed on those who seek to make such changes to their bodies. (The story is more complicated if individuals ought to know that there aren't adequate responses to these defeaters. Then disgust may never provide them with any reason to condemn sex reassignment surgery. Whether it does depends on the complex web of relationships between our epistemic obligations, available defeaters, and our reasons.)

The upshot is this: According to the proposal that I've developed here, disgust isn't in touch with queer moral properties; it isn't infallible; it doesn't deserve unequivocal respect. It is, however, a valuable moral heuristic—one that's often a good guide to norm violations, and as such can provide us with moral reasons. Granted, disgust tells us nothing about the merits of our community's norms. But that's no objection. Heuristics are mental shortcuts, and even when they lead us aright, they don't explain why their recommendations are correct. So it's perfectly appropriate to expect our norms to require independent justification.[22]

DISGUST AND THE COLLECTION OF BOVINE FOETAL BLOOD

Let's return to the case with which we began: the collection of bovine foetal blood. As we do so, it's worth noting that many standard practices in contemporary concentrated feeding operations (CAFOs) and slaughterhouses are repugnant. And when we consider practices such as debeaking chickens and docking the tails of pigs—which are required by consumer demand for cheap meat, which then drives the decisions of CAFO operators—it seems that we have good reasons to condemn them. We might get there via some considerations about the relative moral importance of obtaining gustatory pleasure and relieving extraordinary suffering.[23] Or, if we prefer, we can reach the same conclusion from the weak principle that sentient animals deserve at least some moral consideration, combined with the observation that current practices fail to afford them even that.[24] So when a person is repulsed by some of the everyday horrors at factory farms, and she employs disgust as a moral heuristic, it's easy to validate the negative assessment it recommends.

But we can't tell an equally straightforward story when it comes to harvesting bovine foetal blood. After all, on the assumption that the foetuses weren't yet sentient, you might well think that utilitarians would need to regard this practice as a reason in favour of slaughter (albeit not a decisive reason), for then the only beings harmed are the cows. Hence, acquiring the means to produce bovine foetal serum — for which the blood is collected — is one more benefit to be weighed against the costs to those cows. Again on the assumption that the foetuses weren't yet sentient, we don't need to worry about the foetuses being treated as mere means. Granted, it may be wrong to treat the cows as mere means, and so you might want to validate someone's disgust by insisting that collecting foetal blood is one more way in which the cows are being used. This may well be part of the story, but I doubt that it's all of it. After all, the reaction seems to be prompted by what the worker does to the foetus. On the account under consideration, the foetus is incidental to the wrong: you might make the same point about harvesting livers or eyes or stomachs. So what else can we say?

Return to the idea that our norms create and preserve a way of life. In some circumstances, our norms make certain kinds of relationships possible. Jerome Neu, for example, makes this observation about friendship:

> The [utilitarian calculus] may miss the importance of "identity", where the identity of the individual is intimately connected with the coherence of a way of life distinguished by the characteristic virtues and vices and patterns of relationship recognized within it. . . . There are in fact a number of ideals in various spheres which make for absolute prohibitions. One must not betray friends, not simply because they might become angry, but because they would no longer be "friends", indeed, the betrayal might reveal that they never were. Certain sorts of loyalty may be necessary to certain sorts of friendship. And those sorts of friendship are valuable.[25]

In light of these points, we might expect people to be disgusted by certain disloyalties — as I suspect they are — not necessarily because the betrayal has such devastating consequences, but because it calls into question the betrayer's status as an insider, as someone who shares the commitments necessary to participate in the relevant sort of relationship. In any case, the lesson from Neu is that when we shift our attention to larger social goods, those goods may be structural; they may concern the kinds of lives we lead.

In this vein, I propose that our norms make certain kinds of *virtues* possible. Consider, for example, the claim that torture is unequivocally wrong, and suppose we face a situation in which a terrorist has planted bombs around the city that are scheduled to go off in a short while, and torture seems to be the only way to locate and defuse them. Might we need to affirm the unequivocal wrongness of torture if we're to be a compassionate people—even as, in this horrific scenario, we go on to torture someone? To insist that we were *justified* in torturing counts against our being people who understand the horror of what we did; it counts against our being people who are moved by suffering wherever it occurs. To insist, rather, that our hands are dirty is to admit that we couldn't live up to an important ideal (even if the fault is the world's, not ours), and being willing to make that admission is partially constitutive of having the virtue. If we make this link between the norm and the virtue, then we may be able to explain the rationale for horrified reactions to arguments in defence of torture. The detractors might well feel the weight of the ticking bomb case against an absolute ban. Still, there's something disturbing about ever thinking that, should we act so cruelly, we could act blamelessly. (Again, the idea isn't that the detractors actually have this in mind. Rather, the thought is that we might have reason to value a rich variety of compassion, and hence to condemn actions that would prevent us from possessing that virtue were we instead to affirm them.)

This, I think, is how we should defend disgust at harvesting foetal blood. It is, in part, justified by this practice failing to provide cattle with the measure of respect they deserve. But it's also warranted by the tension between, on the one hand, an ideal of compassion, and on the other people being prepared to treat new life like *that* (or what would have been new life like *that*). Admittedly, we may not want to pin the lack of virtue—or a corresponding vice—on the individual worker. A host of factors may converge to make this particular job the only live option for the person doing the harvesting, and he may hate his work; hence, it may not be reasonable to think of his character as being marred by his actions. But we might think that management isn't adequately compassionate, or those who run the medical lab that support the practice, or we as consumers who turn a blind eye.

Alternatively, we might follow Paul Woodroof in thinking that *reverence* is a virtue. According to his secular account of this trait, it "is the well-developed capacity to have the feelings of awe, respect, and shame when these are the right feelings to have".[26] And we might say that to be in awe of, and to feel respect for, animal life—and animal bodies, even when dead—is partially constitutive of one version of this virtue. We might see glimmers of this in the impulse towards burying the bodies of companion animals: thanks to our relationship with them, we're moved to honour them in something like the way we would members of our own kind. This variety of reverence asks us to go further, though, and recognize that if we honour their deaths for their sake, then we have reason to honour other deaths too—not, perhaps, by burying each body we come across, but at least by recognizing that something of value was lost when that life was extinguished. Taken this way, harvesting foetal blood is a kind of moral myopia, a failure to see that there is value in lives that aren't immediately related to our own.

These proposals aren't mutually exclusive; indeed, they're mutually reinforcing. That animals deserve respect grounds the call for more demanding conceptions of compassion and reverence, and the virtues themselves give form and content to the respect that animals merit. And with these reasons in place, we can see that disgust justified our condemning the blood collection. It pointed us towards weighing moral considerations against this practice, and against the larger exploitative practice of which it's a part. It served us well as a moral heuristic. [27]

DISGUST AS A MORAL HEURISTIC

The upshot is this: If we are disgusted by the collection of bovine foetal blood, then we have a reason to think that this practice is wrong. This is because disgust is a moral heuristic, and we can, on reflection, validate our initial negative assessment. On the one hand, the practice is worrisome because of the way it treats cattle. On the other, it's a failure to exhibit certain valuable virtues.

Of course, a person need not be able to articulate any of this to acquire a reason to condemn that which they find morally disgusting. It suffices that, upon reflection, these analyses are available. Furthermore, I've not argued that disgust gives a person a decisive reason against collecting foetal blood. If it turns out that we can't fill in the details of the deontological and virtue-based arguments that I've sketched here, then the presumption in favour of disgust might be lost.

But suppose we can. Then the position I've developed explains why we aren't engaged in emotional manipulation when we expose people to the realities of slaughterhouses. Quite the contrary: we're inviting people to see whether their moral commitments—at least as summarized by one moral heuristic—allow them to tolerate standard operating procedures. Thankfully, an increasing number find that they don't.

My proposal about disgust, combined with my application of that proposal to the collection of foetal blood, suggest a general strategy for exploring the merits of our visceral responses to our interactions with nonhuman animals. If no obvious justification of our negative moral assessment is forthcoming, we should switch our attention to less obvious goods that might be at stake: social goods, varieties of relationship, certain virtues. (As before, if none emerges upon reflection, or if they aren't sufficiently valuable, then we should set aside our revulsion. How quickly should we conclude that we've come up empty-handed? I submit that our patience with this process should be guided by how often our disgust has been a good guide in a particular domain. In animal ethics, this probably means taking ample time for our search.) So if we are revolted by some aspect of animal experimentation, or our way of dealing with an invasive species, or the consequences of some new farming technology, there will be times when we should direct our attention away from narrowly utilitarian and rights-based reasoning. Instead, we should consider the kinds of communities we hope to build, the kinds of relationships with animals we hope to have, and the kinds of people we hope to be.[28]

NOTES

1. Timothy Pachirat, *Every Twelve Seconds: Industrialized Slaughter and the Politics of Sight* (New Haven, CT: Yale University Press, 2011), 4.

2. Pachirat, *Every Twelve Seconds*, 79–80. Medical labs purchase foetal blood to make foetal bovine serum, which they use in cell culture. Synthetic alternatives are widely available, and there is evidence that they are actually preferable. There is controversy as to whether some foetuses are capable of feeling pain at the beginning of this process. For more, see Carlo Jochems et al., "The Use of Foetal Bovine Serum: Ethical or Scientific Problem?", *ATLA-Nottingham* 30 (2002): 219–28.

3. A defeasible reason—though that's hardly an objection.

4. Daniel Kelly, *Yuck!: The Nature and Moral Significance of Disgust* (Cambridge: MIT Press, 2011), 147.

5. See, for example, John Kekes, "Disgust and Moral Taboos", *Philosophy* 67 (1992): 431–46; Christopher Knapp, "De-moralizing Disgustingness", *Philosophy and Phenomenological Research* 66 (2003): 253–78; Martha Nussbaum, *Hiding from Humanity: Disgust, Shame and the Law* (Princeton: Princeton University Press, 2004); Peter Singer, "Ethics and Intuitions", *Journal of Ethics* 9 (2005): 331–52; Joshua Greene, "The Secret Joke of Kant's Soul", in *Moral Psychology: Volume III*, ed. Walter Sinnott-Armstrong (Cambridge: MIT Press, 2008), 35–80.

6. See Michael Hauskeller, "Moral Disgust", *Ethical Perspectives*, 13 (2006): 571–602; Dan Demetriou, "There's Some Fetish in Your Ethics", *Journal of Philosophical Research* 38 (2013): 377–404; Alexandra Plakias, "The Good and the Gross", *Ethical Theory and Moral Practice* 16 (2013): 261–78.

7. For a helpful overview, see Paul Rozin, Jonathan Haidt, and C. R. McCauley, "Disgust", in *Handbook of Emotions*, 3rd ed., ed. M. Lewis, J. M. Haviland-Jones, and L. F. Barrett (New York: Guilford Press, 2008), 757–76.

8. Rachel Herz, *That's Disgusting: Unraveling the Mysteries of Repulsion* (New York: W. W. Norton & Company, 2012), 4.

9. J. M. Tybur, D. L. Lieberman, and V. G. Griskevicius, "Microbes, Mating, and Morality: Individual Differences in Three Functional Domains of Disgust", *Journal of Personality and Social Psychology* 29 (2009): 103–22; Mary Kite and Bernard Whitley, "Do Heterosexual Men and Women Differ in Their Attitudes toward Homosexuality? A Conceptual and Methodological Analysis", in *Stigma and Sexual Orientation: Understanding Prejudice Against Lesbians, Gay Men, and Bisexuals*, ed. Gregory M. Herek (Thousand Oaks: SAGE Publications, 1998), 39–61; V. Curtis, R. Aunger, and T. Rabie, "Evidence That Disgust Evolved to Protect from Risk of Disease", *Proceedings of the Royal Society: Biological Science Series B* 271 (2004): S131–S133.

10. Paul Rozin, Linda Millman, and Carol Nemeroff, "Operation of the Laws of Sympathetic Magic in Disgust and Other Domains", *Journal of Personality and Social Psychology* 50 (1986): 703–12.

11. For an overview, see Kelly, *Yuck!*, 11–41.

12. We might think that, rather than narrowing our attention to one species of disgust, we're considering a different phenomenon altogether. For empirical evidence against this view, see Hannah Chapman and Adam Anderson, "Things Rank and Gross in Nature: A Review and Synthesis of Moral Disgust", *Psychological Bulletin* 139 (2013): 300–327.

13. Jonathan Haidt, *The Righteous Mind: Why Good People Are Divided by Politics and Religion* (New York: Pantheon, 2012), 3–4.

14. I teach an ethics class of 380 students every semester. When I tell this story, about half report that the man has done something wrong.

15. Carol Nemeroff and Paul Rozin, "Sympathetic Magical Beliefs and Kosher Dietary Practice: The Interaction of Rules and Feelings", *Ethos* 20 (1992): 96–115; Daniel Fessler and Carlos Navarrete, "Meat Is Good to Taboo", *Journal of Cognition and Culture* 3 (2003): 1–40; Shaun Nichols, "On the Genealogy of Norms: A Case for the Role of Emotion in Cultural Evolution", *Philosophy of Science* 69 (2002): 234–55; Debra Lieberman, John Tooby, and Leda Cosmides, "Does Morality Have a Biological Basis? An Empirical Test of the Factors Governing Moral Sentiments Relating to Incest", *Proceedings of the Royal Society of London. Series B: Biological Sciences* 270 (2003): 819–26; Yoel Inbar et al., "Disgust Sensitivity Predicts Intuitive Disapproval of Gays", *Emotion* 9 (2009): 435–39; Yoel Inbar, David Pizarro, and Paul Bloom, "Conservatives Are More Easily Disgusted Than Liberals", *Cognition and Emotion* 23 (2009): 714–25; Paul Rozin, "The Process of Moralization", *Psychological Science* 10 (1999): 218–21.

16. Joshua Greene, *Moral Tribes: Emotion, Reason, and the Gap Between Us and Them* (New York: Penguin Press, 2013), 23.

17. In making this claim, I'm ignoring certain varieties of sentimentalism according to which emotional experiences can justify moral claims by themselves. But my task would be easier on such views—if emotional experiences *do* justify by themselves, I see no obvious reason why disgust wouldn't.

18. Again, we might think that the term *disgust* is being used loosely here, reporting our disapproval rather than psycho-physical revulsion. For empirical evidence against this view, see Chapman and Anderson, "Things Rank and Gross in Nature".

19. Jonathan Haidt, "The Emotional Dog and Its Rational Tail: A Social Intuitionist Approach to Moral Judgment", *Psychological Review* 108 (2001): 814–34.

20. I suspect that the free-riding problem is a further issue here. Lots of social goods depend on *most* people contributing (in whatever form), but not everyone. Hence, there often won't be any serious harm in one person's not playing along, and the lack of an immediate harm always weakens the case for restricting personal freedom.

21. See Robert William Fischer, "Why Incest Is Usually Wrong", *Philosophy in the Contemporary World* 19 (2012): 17–31.

22. It's interesting to ask whether disgust is a wholly intracommunal response: perhaps there's no reason to expect its reliability beyond the borders of the community, since quite different emotional dispositions may serve to promote social order in different environments. I suspect that some concessions need to be made in this direction, but it can't be the whole story. Insofar as we take some of our moral beliefs to be justified in the face of disagreement, we might likewise trust disgust across communal boundaries. Moreover, given what we know of human nature, there are probably limits to the norms that could preserve social order for any length of time; this may provide the basis for some cross-cultural critique.

23. Alastair Norcross, "Puppies, Pigs, and People: Eating Meat and Marginal Cases", *Philosophical Perspectives* 18 (2004): 229–45.

24. David DeGrazia, "Moral Vegetarianism from a Very Broad Basis", *Journal of Moral Philosophy* 6 (2009): 143–65.

25. Jerome Neu, "What Is Wrong with Incest?", *Inquiry* 19 (1976): 36.

26. Paul Woodruff, *Reverence: Renewing a Forgotten Virtue* (New York: Oxford University Press, 2003), 8.

27. Is it possible to extend this line of argument to show that it's wrong to consume the meat with which harvesting foetal blood is associated? Perhaps. The answer would have two parts: one moral, one psychological. The first would be based on the well-worn observation that (*ceteris paribus*) it's wrong to benefit from wrongdoing. As Jordan Curnutt observes, the Nazis made lampshades from human skin, and that was wrong ("A New Argument for Vegetarianism", *Journal of Social Philosophy* 28 [1997]: 153–72). Moreover, if you happen to acquire one of these lamps now, you shouldn't sell it to the highest bidder. To do so would be to show insufficient respect towards those who were tortured to bring that artefact into existence. More mundanely, if I steal some chocolate from the grocery store, and my wife knows I stole it, she shouldn't say, "Well, I guess I'll enjoy it since it's here". Instead, she should refuse to eat it and insist that I pay for what I took. The second, psychological answer is based on the idea that disgust transfers: if x is disgusting, and x is associated with y, then y becomes disgusting too. In the present case, this means that meat becomes repugnant—and thus wrong—because of its association with the collecting of foetal blood. Here, too, we might think of disgust as a moral heuristic that helps us avoid profiting from evil. Incidentally, this proposal fits neatly with the view that disgust marks community boundaries. Suppose that we construe our disgust in this case as responding to an absence of respect, or compassion, or reverence. Then it draws a line between two visions of how life should be lived, and in being disgusted someone might find that he was wrong about the form of life he embraces. He might have thought that he could be respectful, compassionate and reverent while eating meat. But as it turns out, he can't—even by his own lights.

28. Thanks to Elisa Aaltola, Steve Bein, John Hadley, Audrey McKinney, Jimmy McWilliams, Burkay Ozturk, Alexandra Plakias, Heidi Savage, and a group of very attentive students at SUNY Geneseo for their help with this chapter.

TEN

Hume on Animals and the Rest of Nature

Angela Coventry and Avram Hiller

> Like Darwin after him, Hume has a powerful way of demythologizing the idea that humans have some magical capacity that distances them as a species from the rest of creation. [1]

The concept of intrinsic value, roughly that a thing has value for its own sake, has traditionally and controversially [2] been central in environmental ethics. It is often held that a satisfactory environmental ethic rests on whether a defensible concept of intrinsic value can be articulated to ground human obligations towards elements of nonhuman nature as well as to nature as a whole. [3] According to J. Baird Callicott, whether or not nature has intrinsic value is "the defining problem for environmental ethics". [4] After all, if there is no intrinsic value attached to nature and the value of nature consists only in its instrumental value to human beings, then environmental ethics itself is not a distinct domain or discipline. Instead, environmental ethics is a species of applied ethics, just another particular "application of human-to-human ethics" like that of bioethics or business ethics. [5]

Callicott's account of intrinsic value draws from David Hume and Charles Darwin in an effort to develop Aldo Leopold's holistic "land ethic". Leopold's land ethic "implies respect for fellow-members" and for the "biotic community" that includes soils, waters, plants and animals. [6] Leopold extends moral consideration not only to individual members of the natural world but also to ecosystems as wholes. [7] Callicott argues that Leopold's land ethic has "philosophical foundations" and a "pedigree" in the history of Western moral philosophy. [8] In a series of influential works,

Callicott elaborates a "Humean/Darwinian bio-empathetic moral meta-physic" that is grounded in moral sentiments that are naturally selected.[9] The upshot is that there is no objective intrinsic value in the world; rather, value is grounded in the subjective feelings of observers that are then "projected" onto the relevant "natural objects or events" in the world.[10] That is, we project value not only onto fellow humans but also onto nonhuman animals as well as the ecological system as a whole. Callicott argues that this type of subjectivism will not be radically relativistic because humans' common evolutionary heritage will ensure that differences in valuing will be limited.

Callicott's view has been subject to many criticisms. A number of commentators have argued that Callicott's Humean/Darwinian metaethic fails to support his first-order claims favouring environmental preservation.[11] Many critics have also claimed that there is little basis in Hume's work for this interpretation.[12] We claim that although Callicott's account does need supplementation, it is nevertheless on the right track. This chapter develops a Humean environmental metaethic to apply to the animal world and, given some further considerations, to the rest of nature. Our interpretation extends Hume's account of sympathy, our natural ability to sympathize with the emotions of others, so that we may sympathize with not only human beings but also animals, plants and ecosystems. Further, we suggest that Hume has the resources for an account of environmental value that applies to nonhuman animals, nonsentient elements of nature as well as nature as a whole even without the appeal to sympathy. One consequence of this approach is that the reasons for promoting animal welfare need not be restricted to "sentientist" reasons.

Callicott focuses primarily on giving a Humean metaethic for a holistic environmental ethic. Our own route proceeds first through animal ethics, which is an obvious candidate for a Humean view since it is not hard to see that humans may have sympathy for sentient animals. After doing so, we give considerations that extend this Humean animal metaethic to the rest of nature. It is perhaps unsurprising that Callicott fails to take this route in developing his Humean account. In his early work, Callicott argues explicitly against individualistic animal ethics since it conflicts with holistic environmental ethics.[13] For instance, a concern for ecosystemic flourishing is fully consistent with (and in many cases requires) gruesome killings of predators by prey. Thus, in line with Callicott's early position, one who is overly sympathetic with the well-being of individual animals may be unable to properly respect the ecosystem as a whole. Even though in later work Callicott argues for common ground between environmentalists and animal rights activists, he remains sceptical of the fundamentality of claims that we should respect individual animals.[14] But his first-order communitarian commitments make Callicott's development of a Humean metaethic more difficult than it need be.

By beginning with animal ethics, our development of a Humean environmental metaethic takes an easier route.[15]

CALLICOTT'S HUMEAN/DARWINIAN ACCOUNT

Callicott's main idea is that a Humean-Darwinian account of human feelings of benevolence can explain how we can feel sympathy for both individuals within nature as well as the whole of nature. The starting point is Darwin's account of the origin and evolution of ethics in the 1871 work *Descent of Man, and Selection in Relation to Sex*. Darwin thought that social instincts lead an "animal to take pleasure in the society of its fellows, to feel a certain amount of sympathy with them", and to help them out.[16] Ethics first arises to promote the solidarity of human societies, upon which depends the human survival and reproductive success of the individual members of society. As Darwin says, "No tribe could hold together if murder, robbery, treachery, etc., were common", and the disintegration of the tribe means that the survival and reproductive success of its members would be doomed.[17] As such, "actions are regarded by savages . . . as good or bad" only insofar as they "affect the welfare of the tribe—not that of the species, nor that of an individual member of the tribe".[18] Darwin thinks that this conclusion backs up the belief that ethics is "derived from the social instincts, for both relate at first exclusively to the community".[19]

Callicott then traces Darwin's view back to Hume's theory of the moral sentiments in which "there also runs a strong strain of holism".[20] On Hume's view we have "sympathy for our fellows" and we are also "naturally endowed with a sentiment the object of which is society itself".[21] In support of his interpretation, Callicott quotes a passage from the 1751 *Enquiry Concerning the Principles of Morals*[22] when Hume insists that "we must renounce the theory which accounts for every moral sentiment by the principle of self-love", and that we "must adopt a more publick affection, and allow that the interests of society are not . . . entirely indifferent to us" (EPM 5.2.17).[23] Callicott interprets this to mean that we ought to have concern for the well-being of society as a whole as well as concern for the individual members of society. Callicott also emphasizes passages in which Hume says things such as the "benevolent principles of our frame engage us on the side of the social virtues" and that "everything that promotes the interests of society must communicate pleasure, and what is pernicious give uneasiness".[24] Both Hume and Darwin, he points out, recognized that some moral sentiments, such as loyalty and patriotism, relate exclusively and specifically to society.[25]

The Humean/Darwinian framework provides a subjectivist sort of intrinsic value that ultimately depends upon human valuers and their feelings or sentiments.[26] Callicott claims, "There can be no value apart from an evaluator . . . all value is as it were in the eye of the beholder [and] therefore, is humanly dependent".[27] He says that terms such as *good, evil, beauty, ugliness, right,* and *wrong* would cease to apply if all human consciousness happened to be "annihilated at a stroke".[28] That is to say, all intrinsic value is "anthropogenic" — generated by humans and "humanly conferred", although it is "not necessarily homocentric", as value extends beyond human beings.[29]

Callicott recognizes the concern that an account of intrinsic value grounded in human sentiments may lead to relativism. Certainly, not everyone values old-growth forests. Some see no value in an old-growth forest except for its lumber value — one might say that they miss the forest not for the trees, per se, but for the board feet of timber. However, if value is based upon human reactive attitudes, then are there interpersonal grounds upon which one claims that it is wrong to exploit a forest for its maximum timber value and destroy an ecosystem in so doing? Callicott responds to this kind of criticism by claiming that differences in attributions of intrinsic value are due to differences in individuals' factual understanding of ecological processes. Callicott discusses at length how reading Leopold's *Sand County Almanac* gave him a greater understanding of mountain ecology and changed his attitude towards wolf hunting. Wolves kill deer, and when deer population increases, flora become severely depleted. After seeing these effects, Leopold decided that it is wrong to hunt wolves. This kind of conversion is important for Callicott's purposes, because it shows that making the wrong judgements about how to treat the nonhuman world can be reduced (at least in this case) to committing an error in factual judgement about the consequences of one's action. Hence, there is still a genuinely normative aspect to his theory.[30]

It is plausible to suppose (and *A Sand County Almanac* provides a good case study) that those who have studied the complexity of biotic systems are likely to have an appreciation and respect for them. Just as learning more about the lives of people in distant places often has the effect of making one more respectful of them, learning more about complex ecological relationships will make one more inclined to view biotic systems as being morally considerable. If this is correct, then those who believe that biotic communities have no value have either false beliefs or an inadequate understanding of how the biological world, of which they are a part, works, and this is why Callicott's account can be taken to be genuinely normative. Moreover, Callicott believes that Leopold provides reasons why nonhuman species, biotic communities, and ecosystems should be valued intrinsically. Of wildflowers and songbirds, Leopold writes that "these creatures are members of the biotic community, and if (as I believe) its stability depends on its integrity, they are entitled to continuance".[31]

Callicott's view requires considerable convergence of human judgement under circumstances of a good understanding of natural ecological processes, and this might be overly optimistic. If appreciation for nature is a natural feature of all humans, then why has there been such enormous variation between different people in different places, or different epochs, concerning their valuing of nature? To respond, Callicott invokes a Darwinian moral psychology.[32] The basic idea is that individuals in the far past who destroyed their natural environments would have been unable to pass their genes down through the generations, and so those who have the greatest reproductive fitness are those who did not destroy their environments. And so, somehow, it is encoded into our genes for us to wish to promote the flourishing of the environment.

The majority of the criticism directed at Callicott's environmental metaethic concerns the use of Hume's theory of moral sentiments and not Darwin's evolutionary account, and the former will be our focus as well. As stated above, many commentators have claimed that Hume's philosophy does not support the land ethic. Partridge even thinks that Humean moral sentiments actually "alienate humans from nature".[33] While we can extrapolate from sympathy with concrete others to consider the public interest at large, it is difficult to conceive, on Hume's view, how we can sympathize with or take moral concern in society as a whole, over and above its individual members.[34] Critics have also pointed out that it is difficult to see how we can extend moral concern to inanimate objects such as trees, soils and waters. According to Valls, these simply are not the sorts of things for which we can have an independent moral concern, and so it seems difficult to incorporate such things under the Humean progress of sentiments.[35]

Despite all these concerns regarding Callicott's assumptions, the Humean environmental ethic approach is promising. The next section develops a Humean metaethic for the specific case of animal ethics. To situate our position, we survey first Hume on animals and the relevant interpretative options.

HUME ON ANIMAL MORALITY

Hume makes frequent comparisons between human and animal nature. Sometimes he emphasizes the similarity between them. He says that animals are "endowed with thought and reason as well as men", that the mechanism of sympathy "takes place among animals, no less than among men", and that animals are capable of the same passions of love, hatred, fear, anger, courage, grief, envy, malice and pity as humans (THN 1.3.16; 2.2.12/EMPL 592). At other times Hume emphasizes the differences between humans and animals.[36] Animals have no moral sense or the capacity to make moral judgements. In the *Treatise* he says that "incest in the human species is criminal" but that the same actions in animals "have not the smallest moral turpitude" (THN 3.1.1.25). In another notorious passage, Hume says that animals are exempt from the rules of justice. He imagines a species of "creatures, intermingled with men, which, though rational, were possessed of such inferior strength, both of body and mind, that they were incapable of all resistance" and claims that "we should be bound by the laws of humanity, to give gentle usage to these creatures, but should not, properly speaking, lie under any restraint of justice" (EPM 3.1.18/EMPL 467–68).[37] At the end of the passage he says that this is "plainly" the situation of humans with regard to nonhuman animals (EPM 3.1.18/EMPL 467–68). This suggests that the rules of justice can only apply to relations between equal persons and are not applicable in the relations between human and purportedly inferior creatures. For Hume, then, justice does not apply to nonhuman animals. Given that Hume understands the scope of justice so narrowly to include only property rights, all he really means is that animals cannot own property (although, by the law of humanity,[38] animals require our mercy and compassion).[39]

As there is a great deal of dispute over Hume's attitude towards animal morality and an array of interpretations in the secondary literature, before we outline our own position, it will be instructive to summarize this literature. Some scholars claim that Hume denies moral status to animals. In "Moral Animals: Humans Beings and the Other Animals", Christine Korsgaard takes Hume's view to imply that we owe animals nothing at all and we may treat them however we like.[40] Other scholars allow that while animals may be legitimate objects of our moral concern, they are not moral agents. Antony Pitson claims that animals are "incapable of sharing the same community" as humans.[41] Pitson does not deny that animals share some moral features in common with humans, such as sympathy, but he emphasizes that there are significant differences that deny animals the status of moral agents.[42] Angus Taylor also claims that Hume "excludes animals from the moral community".[43] Aaron Garrett claims that "there is no obligation between men and brutes" and that for Hume the consanguinity of animal and human passion cannot be the basis of a moral duty".[44]

Some scholars allow that animals are moral agents to a certain extent. For instance, Beauchamp claims that Humean animals are "in some degree moral agents, however minor those degrees might be" because they exhibit qualities constituting virtues.[45] Other commentators do not think that animals are moral agents but instead aim to show how moral consideration can still be extended to include animals. Boyle maintains animals exhibit Humean virtues and that acts of animal reason may inspire moral approval or approval in us, so animals can "be the subjects of our moral evaluation".[46] Annette Baier claims that even though the duties of justice are not owed to animals, the law of humanity will "cover our treatment of animals", and so "moral wrongs" can be inflicted on them.[47] Driver agrees: animals deserve moral status by the duty of humanity, and the mistreatment of animals violates a law of humanity rather than the law of justice.[48] She details how in Hume's account of humanity, kindness, and particularly "kindness to those who are vulnerable" plays an important role in sustaining society and that virtuous people in society will treat animals well.[49] Most recently, Andrew Valls defends Baier's interpretation. He emphasizes that while Hume withholds the protection of justice from animals, he affirms that humans still have duties towards animals based on humanity. According to Valls, even though Hume places animals outside of justice, this does not mean that humans' treatment of them is outside morality itself, and so on "a broader conception of justice, where that concept covers more of morality", it is "compatible with Hume's view to say that animals are entitled to just treatment".[50]

It seems reasonable enough to suppose that a general Humean framework provides an extensive conception of justice that can be applied to animals. After all, Hume thought that "the boundaries of justice" will continue to expand in accordance with the expansiveness of our viewpoints, and that history, experience and reason "sufficiently instruct us in this natural progress of human sentiments" (EPM 3.1.21).[51] The inclusion of moral duties towards animals might naturally be considered as part of the "gradual enlargement" of the domain of justice (EPM 3.1.21). However, it might be questioned as to whether the sentiment of humanity would be enough to develop a genuine account of justice required for an animal ethic. Korsgaard notes that on Hume's view there are no obligations towards animals, although the law of humanity may "restrain us from treating them too badly".[52] In "Just Like All the Other Animals of the Earth", Korsgaard argues that while "most people seem to hold that we should not kill or hurt the animals unless we have a good reason, but also that any reason except malicious fun is probably good enough" and that "in the same way, Hume's 'laws of humanity' do not clearly forbid us to use the other animals in any way that we might find convenient". In response to Korsgaard, Driver provides a Humean defence of humanity. Extending Hume's "framework", she notes that animals "have a kind of society with us", and "we interact with pets and other domesticated animals".[53] This relationship sets up a "separate class of artificial norms" that governs the interactions between humans and animals.[54] On the Humean view, then, we may extend our positive duty to aid those who are suffering to include animal suffering, but this duty is confined only to those animals closely connected to us. There is no positive duty to aid animals that do not have a connection with us such as wild animals, although we do at least have a negative duty not to cause animal suffering.[55]

Driver's defence of the Humean law of humanity is limited as a theory of animal ethics. A more comprehensive account would have to include sentiments and duties towards animals with no personal connection to us in addition to those who are close to us, for environmentalists are concerned with the treatment of both domesticated and wild animals, where the relation of distance should not affect the level of human concern.[56] Driver suggests that something like benevolence might incline us to aid animals not close to us, but she does not develop the point and is content to allow that we have a duty to refrain from harming animals that are not close to us. But positive duties to relieve animal suffering regardless of personal relationships or distance are required to develop the kind of animal ethic that most of those who are interested in animal ethics demand. Certainly, while we love and value the nonhuman members of our immediate family, such as the cats and dogs who share our homes, there is a great distance from the lives of billions of factory farmed animals, animals used in experimentation, animals used for clothing, and animals used in the entertainment industry and kept in zoos. These are presumably issues relevant to the development of an ethics of animals. We show that a Humean can provide such an account.

On Hume's account, moral sentiments for others are based in sympathy. Sympathy is a natural mechanism in human nature by which we "receive by communication" the "inclinations and sentiments" of others resembling us so that one's idea of another's emotion (say, my idea of your happiness), when vivid enough, is actually converted into the experience of the emotion itself (THN 2.1.11.2, 4–8). Hume recognizes that it is natural for us to sympathize more greatly with those closest to us, meaning that it is easier to relate to and connect with someone who is similar and close to you. Our ability to sympathize thus varies with the differences in the relations between ourself and to others: our spatial and temporal distance to other persons, the degree of resemblance others have to us, and whether relations of causality exist between ourself and others, such as our being related as family members or as close friends. Recent research has supported the notion that it is also much easier to sympathize with someone you recognize, understand and identify with.[57]

To compensate for variation in the observer's sympathies resulting from physical or temporal closeness to or distance from the person judged, Hume recommends contemplation of the person or action from a common perspective or general point of view (EPM 9.1.6). These sorts of corrections are "common" to all of our senses (THN 3.3.1.16). If we did not correct our own perspective and assume some sort of common standard in our everyday interactions with others, communication would be difficult, and we would run into constant conflicts with others (THN 3.3.1.16). So we consider a general point of view in which the character or action of the person is examined from the standpoint where it appears the same to every person "without reference to our particular interest" (THN 3.1.2.4; 3.3.1.30). As Elizabeth Radcliffe explains, if we understand that "our sentiments are influenced by our particular perspectives", we can "compensate for our relation to others by considering how we would feel when the influence of relations is eliminated".[58] It is only when "we fix on some steady and general point of view" that in fact moral sentiments are felt (THN 3.3.1.15–16). The consideration of person or action in general is what "causes such a feeling or sentiment as denominates it morally good or evil" or produces "that particular feeling or sentiment, on which moral distinctions depend" (THN 3.1.2.4; 3.3.130). Sympathy allows us to continue to feel pleasure or displeasure from the consideration of the characters of persons or actions considered from the general point of view. We must take up the general point of view for the sympathetic pleasant or unpleasant feelings to cause a corresponding pleasant or unpleasant moral sentiment that marks the presence of virtue or vice.[59]

Next, consider that our sympathy may be extended to animals. This has been defended by many authors in recent literature. In *The Age of Empathy*, de Waal directly builds on Darwin's account of sympathy as an instinct and develops empathy as an ability designed to care about those closest to us (e.g., family, friends and partners), but shows that can be extended to also include other species. Harrison observes that our fundamental ability to respond to the emotional expressions of others can be extended to other species, and Bradshaw and Paul suggest that concern for animals may derive from an "evolved human trait".[60] Luke emphasizes "the depth of the human-animal connection" and claims that the capacity to respond and feel sympathy for animals is a "deep and recurring feature of humans".[61] Several studies have indicated that sympathy towards animals is connected to sympathy towards humans.[62] Research suggests that those less sensitive to the mistreatment of animals tend to exhibit less sympathy towards other people, and that the lack of ability to sympathize is the underlying reason for violence towards both humans and animals.[63] Certainly more research needs to be done, but it is highly likely that one can have sympathetic feelings towards animals as well as humans.

As previously noted, Hume thought that the strength of the sympathetic communication of sentiments is subject to variation and depends upon the degree of resemblance as well as the distance between the observer and the person with whom he or she sympathizes. Hume does emphasize the resemblances between humans and animals: both experience pain and pleasure, possess reason[64] and the passions and are capable of sympathy.[65] Given this, along with the fact that because of sympathy we infer the feelings of others by their behaviours and the fact that animals express their feelings in ways similar to those of humans, we can sympathize with animals when they experience pain or pleasure. Increased understanding of our similarity to animals will heighten our feelings of sympathy towards animals. Studies indicate that our sympathy for different species tends to increase with phylogenetic relatedness to humans.[66] But it does not follow from this that we cannot sympathize at all with all types of wild animals or animals in distant places. Note also that a sign of a declining species may often get plenty of attention, concern and even at times positive outcomes.[67] In addition, considerable resources are devoted to animal rescue. Luke reminds us of the 1988 plight of three California gray whales off the coast of Alaska. The ice holes through which the whales were surfacing to breathe were in the process of freezing over, which would result in the whales drowning.[68] There was widespread and deep concern for the well-being of the whales among people, and the rescue attempt ultimately cost $5.8 million. If we can have sentiments about domesticated cats and our pet goldfish, then surely we can also relate our sentiments to wild animals such as tigers or whales. If we care deeply for our fluffy rabbit, we might feel pain and distress when we learn about some of the cruel chemical treatments and surgical operations performed on millions of rabbits around the world in scientific experiments.

As we have seen, Hume is aware that we do sympathize to a greater degree with those close to us than we do with those that are further removed, but the fact remains that we can and do sympathize with those that are further removed from us, including animals. This is done by taking up the general point of view. When we adopt the general point of view and from that position contemplate the quality or character of another that has a tendency to produce good for others or humanity itself or nonhuman animals, and whose operation produces, or is expected to produce, pleasure, we approve of it, as we sympathize with the feelings of those affected. A recent example is the overwhelming outpouring of admiration and approval of the recent video posted online of Tara the cat, whose quick intervention saved a little boy from a dog attack in Bakersfield, California. In nearly all of the news reports, Tara the cat is deemed a hero.[69]

Further, given that humans and animals both strive to avoid pain, we feel disapprobation towards those who are malicious; for example, those who inflict or condone the infliction of pain and suffering on both humans and animals, and we deem their motives and character to be vicious and consider them morally blameworthy. From a Humean point of view, then, it is morally wrong to inflict pain and suffering on any animal whether close to us or far away, domestic or wild. The only relevant differences between our relationships with domesticated and wild or distant animals are those of degree of distance, resemblance and causality, and thus we can still sympathize with animals that are exploited far away from us and deem poor treatment of them to be immoral. In sum, if we allow that our sympathy extends to animals, and if we are capable of taking up the general point of view, then we can be moved by the plights of animals' suffering whether those animals are domesticated or wild, or close to us or far away from us. Since this concern can be seen as an intrinsic valuing of these animals, this view provides the groundwork for humans to have positive duties to relieve such cases of animal suffering, like a duty to do something about some of the unnecessary suffering of rabbits used in experiments in human cosmetics. In short, we might broaden the scope of sympathy, and our resulting moral emotions are what ultimately move us to act compassionately towards animals on the Humean view.

One problem for a Humean account of value in animal ethics is that it is questionable exactly *which* sentiments play the proper role in determining one's moral judgement. Many natural processes are distasteful to many humans in many ways, and many humans take delight in many natural processes.[70] According to Serpell, the animal's appearance, how attractive and cute the animal is seen to us, as well as phylogenetic closeness affects the level of emotional response shown towards it.[71] Bradshaw and Paul emphasize the interactions between the animals' appearance (i.e., its level of attractiveness or "cuteness") and cultural factors that determine the degree and to what extent we relate emotionally to animals and to which species.[72] So exactly which sentiments should be identified as the particularly normative, value-bestowing ones? For example, some animals are viewed by most as being ugly, such as naked mole rats, aye-ayes, and cockroaches. We do not delight in seeing these creatures. But does these animals' unattractiveness make them less valuable than comparable animals that are more attractive, such as rabbits, ringtail lemurs, and butterflies? Human sentiments are influenced by a lot of peculiarities, and many of them seem too ad hoc and contingent upon which to base a normative theory.

But this problem may also be overcome by appealing to the general point of view. Hume thinks sympathy also "has a great influence on our sense of beauty" and recommends we "fix on some steady and general points of view" to correct our judgements about beauty. These sorts of corrections are common to all the senses (THN 3.3.3.6; 3.3.1.16). An object that tends to produce pleasure is called beautiful, and one that produces pain is called disagreeable or deformed. Sympathy allows the production of pleasure in a spectator as the result of the production of pleasure in the possessor of a beautiful thing. Hume thinks that the usefulness of an object increases its beauty, and he gives a number of examples, including the strength of a horse (THN 3.3.1.8). While we may not immediately delight at the appearance of certain sorts of creatures, it is certainly possible that a greater understanding of how the animal's unique physical features help it to survive and its integral role in the system of nature might alter our judgement about their appearance. For example, one's immediate reaction of disgust at the appearance of certain sorts of bats might be lessened once one understands the function of their features and their importance in controlling the insect population.

Concerns have been raised that Callicott's Humean environmental ethic may not provide the kind of convergence needed for a proper environmental ethic. But in the case of animal metaethics, if the foregoing is correct, such concerns are lessened. Of course, not every person values nonhuman animals. The degree of variation, given the right kinds of information about nonhuman animals, is not as extensive as the difference in how much different people value nonsentient aspects of nature. There is considerable convergence among people that nonhuman animals matter. For instance, a prominent study of American attitudes shows widespread agreement that nonhuman animals matter.[73] In the next section, we consider whether a Humean account can extend sympathy so as to embrace not only other human beings and animals but also nonsentient things like plants and ecosystems, and we suggest that a Humean account of value may even extend to nonhuman animals, the nonsentient parts of nature and ecosystems without sympathy.

A HUMEAN ENVIRONMENTAL ETHIC?

We have focused primarily on providing a Humean metaethic that shows that nonhuman animals are, in principle at least, morally considerable. However, there are other resources in Hume's sentimentalism—resources to which Callicott and others do not appeal—which support an extension of moral consideration to other aspects of the nonhuman world.

As Valls has shown, several of Callicott's critics have pointed out that aesthetic considerations are morally relevant from a Humean point of view.[74] If we do value and appreciate these aesthetic aspects of nature, they may provide "reasons and motives for preserving it".[75] Hume allows that we are affected with pleasure by inanimate objects in the world such as houses, ships and chimneys (THN 2.2.5.16). He pays special attention to features of the natural world that "delight us", such as rich soils and a "happy climate" (THN 3.3.1.20). Sunshine or "well-cultivated plains" communicate to us a "secret joy and satisfaction" (EPM 6.1.22). Grand features in the natural world such as a vast ocean, an "extended plain", a "wide forest" or "a vast chain of mountains" do "excite in the mind a sensible emotion", and this "admiration . . . is one of the most lively pleasures, which human nature is capable of enjoying" (THN 2.2.8.4). The advantages attached to natural objects increases our admiration. He says "that nothing renders a field more agreeable than its fertility" and that a "plain, overgrown with furze and broom, may be, in itself, as beautiful as a hill cover'd with vines or olive-trees" (THN 2.2.5.18/ 3.3.1.8).

This is all made possible by sympathy. Hume gives the example of a person who shows us with particular care the layout of a convenient house. The beauty is evident in the house and this gives us pleasure, but also by the communication of sentiments we also sympathize with the proprietor of the house: we "enter into his interest" and "feel the same satisfaction, that the objects naturally occasion in him" (THN 2.2.5.16). Hume extends this observation to objects such as tables, chairs, coaches, saddles and ploughs. The beauty of these kinds of objects is "chiefly derived from their utility", and this advantage concerns the owner alone and interests the spectator via sympathy only (THN 2.2.5.17). Features of nature such as the fertility of soils, bright sunshine and the vast plains "delight us by a reflection on the happiness they would afford the inhabitants" (THN 3.3.1.20). The Humean view can allow that sentiments to preserve or destroy certain kinds of inanimate objects and features of nature are the sorts of things that can be morally considerable given their fundamental relations to humans.

Furthermore, sentiments towards the preservation or destruction of society as a whole can themselves be morally considerable given that society is necessary for the subsistence of the human species. Human life relates to and depends on the elements of nature and the ecological system in fundamental and complex ways. Hume argues that we depend on society to survive, and we want to advance it (EMPL 480/THN 3.2.2.24). Accordingly, everything "that promotes the interests of society must communicate pleasure" and moral approval, whereas "what is pernicious give[s] uneasiness" and is morally blameworthy (EPM 5.2.46). All the virtues that have a "tendency to the public good", such as justice and loyalty, "derive all their merit from our sympathy with those, who reap any advantage from them" (THN 3.3.6.1).

The nonhuman components of our environment—animals and natural features such as the rivers, soils, oceans, even the societal system as a whole—are then capable of engaging our sympathy via pleasure and becoming objects of moral standing on the Humean view. A Humean view might well allow, as Haught suggests, that "we are warranted in projecting some kinds of intrinsic values to objects that have instrumental value or are subjectively satisfying".[76] Even if the origins of our interest in such objects is entirely instrumental, our interest can and in many cases does extend to an intrinsic valuing. This is not due to any necessary connection, so to speak, between usefulness and intrinsic goodness, but even if the intrinsic valuing somehow owes its origins to instrumental valuing, such a transference does not comprise any sort of mistake.

There may even be resources in Hume's account to develop a sentimentalist account of moral regard to nature *without* extending sympathy to it. To explain, we draw on Frierson's compelling case that sympathy with nonsentient nature is possible within Adam Smith's ethics.[77] *Contra* Callicott, who finds "little ethical holism" in Smith's moral philosophy, Frierson shows the possibility of extending Smith's account of sympathy, "and thereby benevolence and justice", to nature.[78] Frierson also shows how Smith can accommodate similar attitudes towards nature without any extension of sympathy. He appeals to Smith's account of sympathy and duties towards the dead to show how "Smith provides a model for how to account for similar attitudes towards nature".[79] This is "important in the context of environmental ethics", according to Frierson, because it "dramatically expands the scope of sympathy" beyond sentient creatures since the "dead are not human, not sentient, and not even living".[80]

There is a lot of debate about the similarities and differences between Hume and Smith on sympathy. Frierson explains that the main difference is that Hume emphasizes "that one sympathizes with the *actual passions* of the object of one's sympathy", whereas Smith's "account of sympathy includes sufficient examples to show that sympathetic feelings are based not on the actual feelings of another".[81] For Smith, sympathy depends on how one feels when "one imagines oneself in the position of the other, and that feeling will often be quite different from what that other feels".[82] There is not the space to compare Hume and Smith on sympathy in detail, but it is worth noting that Hume might have the resources to adopt a similar approach. If so, then it might also be possible on Hume's account that one might have attitudes and duties towards nonhuman animals, parts of nonsentient nature and the ecological system as a whole without the requirement of sympathy. Frierson acknowledges in the twenty-fifth footnote of "Adam Smith and the Possibility of Sympathy with Nature" that there are some examples wherein "Hume seems to suggest that one can sympathize without sympathizing with actual feelings of another". Hume describes, for example, being present at the "more terrible operations of surgery":

> 'Tis certain, that even before it begun, the preparation of the instruments, the laying of the bandages in order, the heating of the irons, with all the signs of anxiety and concern in the patient and assistants, would have a great effect upon my mind, and excite the strongest sentiments of pity and terror. (THN 3.3.1.7)

This example of the observer strongly resonating with the feelings of the patient during the preparation of instruments in anticipation for a surgical operation supports the possibility of extending Hume's account of sympathy to nonhuman aspects of nature.

Moreover, Hume admits that when we apply principles of correction to our feelings, we find that our feelings do not often correspond entirely to our considered judgements. He says that the "judgment corrects or endeavours to correct the appearance", but that "it is not able entirely to prevail over sentiment" (EPM 5.2 n.1). He therefore allows that our passions "do not always follow our corrections" and that our passions "do not readily follow the determination of our judgment" (THN 3.3.1.21, 17).

Nevertheless, the correction of our sentiments is good enough to serve its purpose for our everyday social interactions with other people. Hume says that the correction is "sufficient to regulate our abstract notions, and are alone regarded, when we pronounce in general concerning the degrees of virtue and vice" (THN 3.3.1.21). He writes that even though

> the heart takes not part entirely with those general notions, nor regulates all its love and hatred, by the universal abstract differences of vice and virtue, without regard to self, or the persons with whom we are more intimately connected; yet, have these moral differences a considerable influence, and being sufficient at least for discourse, serve all our purposes in company, in the pulpit, on the theatre, and in the schools. (EPM 5.2)

Consequently, Hume's theory does not require that our feelings need to correspond precisely to the moral standards we adopt and espouse in discourse. Hume even suggests that moral judgements can occur without the presence of actual feelings:

> We blame equally a bad action, which we read of in history, with one performed in our neighbourhood the other day: The meaning of which is, that we know from reflection, that the former action would excite as strong sentiments of disapprobation as the latter, were it placed in the same position. (THN 3.3.1.18)

This has the advantage of broadening the scope of a Humean environmental ethic. Now it may be possible to defend environmental values towards not only animals but also inanimate objects such as trees and marshes, as well as the whole of nature, without the sole appeal to sympathy with nature.

One further point worth noting, especially in the context of the other chapters in this book, is that this also entails that our reasons for caring for animals (and even other humans) need not depend exclusively on their status as fellow sentient beings. We may appreciate all animals for their beauty and for their contributions to the ecosystems of which they are parts.

One might still argue that the kind of moral standing on this Humean view is a purely instrumental value, and thus does not provide the kind of warrant for intrinsic moral consideration of the environment that is desired by Callicott and other environmental philosophers. There are three forms of response to this. First, we might abandon the intrinsic/instrumental value distinction. One could adopt a view, such as that of Bryan Norton, who seeks to undermine the distinction between intrinsic and instrumental value, and claims that arguments in favor of environmental preservation should be cast in terms of anthropocentric reasons.[83] Second, one might claim that sentiments favouring environmental preservation have become so entrenched within us that even in specific cases where there is no human benefit of a feature of the environment or even of a far-flung ecosystem as a whole, we would continue to value the environment and desire its preservation, all things considered. For example, it seems that even if the last person (as in Richard Sylvan's famous thought experiment from "Is There a Need for a New, an Environmental, Ethic?") derives pleasure out of destroying the last remaining trees, there still seem (to many people, at least) to be moral reasons why he is wrong to do so.

Third, we can accept that Hume himself did not accept an extension of intrinsic ethical consideration to ecosystems, but we may still use the resources of the metaethical system he develops, with its nonrelativist sentimentalist projectivism, to create a *neo-Humean* environmental meta-ethic in the same spirit as Callicott's. This might be done in a variety of ways. The fact is that many humans—especially those who have studied ecology—nowadays do have sentiments favouring ecosystems, and this may be enough to ground an ascription of intrinsic value to the natural world. Hume did recommend that the expression and scope of such feelings of sympathy and moral sentiments depend on how far our reason and understanding informs them, so it makes sense that the Humean environmental ethic would be open to revision of sentiments in light of new empirical information about the interrelatedness of natural beings in ecological science. In this spirit we hope to have shown in this chapter that there is no reason to limit Humean moral sentiments to the human species.[84]

NOTES

1. Tom Beauchamp, "Hume on the Nonhuman Animal", *Journal of Medicine and Philosophy* 24, no. 4 (1999): 322–35, 332.

2. Some scholars have argued that we ought to drop the term *intrinsic value* from environmental ethics altogether; see Andrew Light, "Contemporary Environmental Ethics: From Metaethics to Public Philosophy", *Metaphilosophy* 33 (2002): 426–49; Bruce Morito, "Intrinsic Value: A Modern Albatross for the Ecological Approach", *Environmental Values* 12 (2003): 317–36; Bryan Norton, "Why I Am Not a Nonanthropocentrist: Callicott and the Failure of Monistic Inherentism", *Environmental Ethics* 17 (1995): 341–58; and Anthony Weston, "Beyond Intrinsic Value: Pragmatism in Environmental Ethics", in *Environmental Pragmatism*, ed. Andrew Light and Eric Katz (London: Routledge, 1996), 285–306. For a recent defence of intrinsic value, see Katie McShane, "Why Environmental Ethics Shouldn't Give up on Intrinsic Value", *Environmental Ethics* 29 (2007): 43–61.

3. See Jim Cheney, "Intrinsic Value in Environmental Ethics: Beyond Subjectivism and Objectivism", *The Monist*, 75, no. 2 (1992): 227–35; Holmes Rolston III, *Environmental Ethics* (Philadelphia: Temple University Press, 1988), 4, 197; and J. Baird Callicott, "Intrinsic Value, Quantum Theory, and Environmental Ethics", *Environmental Ethics* 7 (1985): 257–75, 261.

4. J. Baird Callicott, *Beyond the Land Ethic: More Essays in Environmental Philosophy* (Albany, NY: SUNY Press, 1999), 241.

5. J. Baird Callicott, "Intrinsic Value in Nature: A Metaethical Analysis", *Electronic Journal of Analytic Philosophy* 3 (1995), http://ejap.louisiana.edu/EJAP/1995.spring/callicott.1995.spring.html (accessed 30 April 2014). See also Richard Routley (Sylvan), "Is There a Need for a New, an Environmental, Ethic?", reprinted in *Environmental Philosophy*, ed. Michael Zimmerman et al. (Saddle River, NJ: Prentice Hall, 2001): 17–25; Holmes Rolston III, "Is There an Ecological Ethic?", *Ethics: An International Journal of Social, Political, and Legal Philosophy* 18, no. 2 (1975): 93–109; and Tom Regan,

"The Nature and Possibility of an Environmental Ethic", *Environmental Ethics* 3, no. 1 (1981): 19–34.

6. Aldo Leopold, *A Sand County Almanac*, reprinted in *A Sand County Almanac with Essays on Conservation from Round River* (New York: Ballantine Books, 1970), 204.

7. Leopold, *A Sand County Almanac*, 239.

8. Callicott, *Beyond the Land Ethic*, 66–67.

9. J. Baird Callicott, *In Defense of the Land Ethic: Essays in Environmental Philosophy* (Albany: State University of New York Press, 1989), 152, and "The Land Ethic", in *A Companion to Environmental Philosophy*, ed. Dale Jamieson (Oxford: Blackwell, 2001), 204–17, 205.

10. Callicott, *In Defense of the Land Ethic*, 147. Rolston in *Environmental Ethics* defends an alternative account of intrinsic value where value is literally a property of entities of the world.

11. See, for instance, Bryan G. Norton, "Why I Am Not an Nonanthropocentrist" and Ernest Partridge, "Ecological Morality and Nonmoral Sentiments", *Environmental Ethics* 18 (1996): 149–63.

12. See, for example, Alan Carter, "Projectivism and the Last Person Argument", *American Philosophical Quarterly* 41, no. 1 (2004): 51–62; James Fieser, "Callicott and the Metaphysical Basis of Ecocentric Morality", *Environmental Ethics* 15 (1993): 171–80; Paul Haught, "Hume's Projectivist Legacy for Environmental Ethics", *Environmental Ethics* 28, no. 1 (2006): 77–96; Yeuk-Sze Lo, "Non-Humean Holism, Un-Humean Holism", *Environmental Values* 10 (2001): 113–23, and "Making and Finding Values in Nature: From a Humean Point of View", *Inquiry* 49, no. 2 (2006): 123–47; Partridge, "Ecological Morality and Nonmoral Sentiments"; Andrew Valls, "Hume, Justice and the Environment", in *Engaging Nature: Environmentalism and the Political Theory Canon*, ed. Peter Cannavo and Joseph H. Lane Jr. (Cambridge: MIT Press, 2014); Gary Varner, "No Holism without Pluralism", *Environmental Ethics* 13 (1991): 175–79; and Jennifer Welchman, "Hume, Callicott, and the Land Ethic: Prospects and Problems", *Journal of Value Inquiry* 43 (2009): 201–20.

13. J. Baird Callicott, "Animal Liberation: A Triangular Affair", *Environmental Ethics* 2, no. 4 (1980): 311–38.

14. See J. Baird Callicott, "Animal Liberation and Environmental Ethics: Back Together Again", *Between the Species: An Online Journal for the Study of Philosophy and Animals* 4, no. 3 (1988): 163–69.

15. For an account of sentimentalism and animal ethics, see Elisa Aaltola's "The Rise of Sentimentalism and Animal Philosophy", chapter 12 of this volume.

16. Charles Darwin, *The Descent of Man, and Selection in Relation to Sex* (New York: Appleton, 1871), 69.

17. Darwin, *Descent of Man*, 89.

18. Darwin, *Descent of Man*, 92–93.

19. Darwin, *Descent of Man*, 93.

20. Callicott, "Environmental Ethics".

21. Callicott, *In Defense of the Land Ethic*, 126.

22. The following abbreviations will be used for Hume's works: EMPL (*Essays, Moral, Political, and Literary*, revised edition), ed. Eugene Miller (Indianapolis: Liberty Fund, 1985); EPM (*An Enquiry Concerning the Principles of Morals*), ed. Tom Beauchamp (Oxford: Oxford University Press, 1998); and THN (*A Treatise of Human Nature*), ed. David F. Norton and Mary J. Norton (Oxford: Oxford University Press, 2007). References to the *Enquiry* and *Treatise* cite book, chapter, section, and paragraph. References to the *Essays* cite page numbers only.

23. Quoted in Callicott, "Environmental Ethics" and "The Land Ethic", 208.

24. Quoted in Callicott, "The Land Ethic", 209.

25. Callicott, "The Land Ethic", 209.

26. J. Baird Callicott, "Non-anthropocentric Value Theory and Environmental Ethics", *American Philosophical Quarterly* 21 (1984): 299–309, 305.

27. Callicott, "Non-anthropocentric Value Theory", 325.

28. Callicott, *In Defense of the Land Ethic*, 193–94.

29. J. Baird Callicott, "Rolston on Intrinsic Value: A Deconstruction", *Environmental Ethics* 14 (1992): 129–43, 132, 129.

30. Callicott, *In Defense of the Land Ethic*, 115.

31. Leopold, *A Sand County Almanac*, 210.

32. Callicott, *Beyond the Land Ethic*, 107–8.

33. Partridge, "Ecological Morality and Nonmoral Sentiments", 149–50.

34. See Varner, "No Holism without Pluralism", and Welchman, "Hume, Callicott, and the Land Ethic", 205.

35. Valls, "Hume, Justice and the Environment", part 3.

36. For a recent account of the similarities and differences between human and animal cognition, see David Premack, "Human and Animal Cognition: Continuity and Discontinuity", *Proceedings of the National Academy of Sciences* 104, no. 35 (2007): 13861–67.

37. There is a lot of debate about this passage. For discussion, see Arthur Kuflik, "Hume on Justice to Animals, Indians and Women", *Hume Studies* 44, no. 1 (1998): 53–70, and Joyce L. Jenkins and Robert Shaver, "'Mr. Hobbes Could Have Said No More'", in *Feminist Interpretations of David Hume*, ed. Anne Jaap Jacobson (University Park: Pennsylvania State University Press, 1992), 137–55.

38. We shall suppose that Hume uses the term *humanity* more or less synonymously with *benevolence*. On this point, see Remy Debes, "Humanity, Sympathy, and the Puzzle of Hume's Second *Enquiry*", *British Journal for the History of Philosophy* 15 (2007): 27–57, 29, and Jenkins and Shaver, "'Mr. Hobbes Could Have Said No More'", 546.

39. This point is made by Julia Driver, "A Humean Account of the Status and Character of Animals", in *The Oxford Handbook of Animal Ethics*, ed. Tom Beauchamp (Oxford: Oxford University Press, 2011), 144–71, 160, and Valls, "Hume, Justice and the Environment", part 2.

40. Christine Korsgaard develops a Kantian account of animal ethics in "A Kantian Case for Animal Rights", in *Animal Law: Developments and Perspectives in the 21st Century*, ed. Margot Michel, Daniela Kühne and Julia Hänni (Switzerland: Dike Publishers, 2012), 3–25.

41. Antony E. Pitson, "The Nature of Humean Animals", *Hume Studies* 19 (1993): 301–16, 312.

42. Pitson, "The Nature of Humean Animals", 311. See also Antony E. Pitson, "Hume on Morals and Animals", *British Journal for the History of Philosophy* 11, no. 4 (2003): 639–55, 639; Knut Erik Tranoy, "Hume on Morals, Animals, and Men", *Journal of Philosophy* 56, no. 3 (1959): 94–103; Denis Arnold, "Hume on the Moral Difference between Humans and Other Animals", *History of Philosophy Quarterly* 12 (1995): 303–16; Michael J. Seidler, "Hume and the Animals", *Southern Journal of Philosophy* 15, no. 3 (1977): 361–72; and A. T. Nuyen, "Hume on Animals and Morality", *Philosophical Papers* 27, no. 2 (1998): 93–106. For a good breakdown of the similarities and differences between these interpretations, see Deborah Boyle, "Hume on Animal Reason", *Hume Studies* 29, no. 1 (2003): 3–28, 27n.27.

43. Angus Taylor, *Animals and Ethics: An Overview of the Philosophical Debate* (Peterborough, ON: Broadview Press, 2009), 46.

44. Aaron Garrett, "Anthropology: The 'Original' of Human Nature", in *The Cambridge Companion to the Scottish Enlightenment*, ed. Alexander Broadie (Cambridge: Cambridge University Press, 2003), 79–93, 85.

45. Beauchamp, "Hume on the Nonhuman Animal", 328.

46. Boyle, "Hume on Animal Reason", 4, 20.

47. Annette Baier, *Postures of the Mind: Essays on Mind and Morals* (Minneapolis: University of Minnesota Press, 1995), 147, 149.

48. Driver, "A Humean Account of the Status and Character of Animals", 163, 166.

49. Driver, "A Humean Account of the Status and Character of Animals", 165.

50. Valls, "Hume, Justice and the Environment", part 2.

51. See Peter Singer, *The Expanding Circle: Ethics and Sociobiology* (New York: Farrar, Straus, and Giroux, 1981).

52. Christine Korsgaard, "Moral Animals: Humans Beings and the Other Animals", http://www.people.fas.harvard.edu/~korsgaar/CMK.MA3.pdf (accessed September 25, 2014), 26.

53. Driver, "A Humean Account of the Status and Character of Animals", 163.

54. Driver, "A Humean Account of the Status and Character of Animals", 163.

55. Driver, "A Humean Account of the Status and Character of Animals", 164. See Claire Palmer, *Animal Ethics in Context* (New York: Columbia University Press, 2010), for a lengthy defence of this position, though not on Humean grounds.

56. John A. Fischer, "Taking Sympathy Seriously: A Defense of Our Moral Psychology toward Animals", *Environmental Ethics* 9, no. 3 (1987): 197–215, 200.

57. Frans De Waal, *The Age of Empathy: Nature's Lessons for a Kinder Society* (New York: Three Rivers Press, 2009), and Birgitta Forsman, *Animal Experimentation* (Stockholm: Almqvist and Wiksell International, 1992).

58. Elizabeth Radcliffe, "Hume on Motivating Sentiments, the General Point of View, and the Inculcation of Morality", *Hume Studies* 20, no. 1 (1994): 37–58, 43.

59. For recent neuroscience on sympathy and empathy, see Jean Decety and Kalina J. Michalska, "Neurodevelopmental Changes in the Circuits Underlying Empathy and Sympathy from Childhood to Adulthood", *Developmental Science* 13, no. 6 (2010): 886–99, esp. 886. Sympathy and empathy are often used interchangeably, although it is thought that there are important differences between them.

60. M. A. Harrison and A. E. Hall, "Anthropomorphism, Empathy, and Perceived Communicative Ability Vary with Phylogenetic Relatedness to Humans", *Journal of Social, Evolutionary, and Cultural Psychology* 4, no. 1 (2010): 34–48, and J. W. S. Bradshaw and E. S. Paul, "Could Empathy for Animals Have Been an Adaptation in the Evolution of Homo Sapiens?", *Animal Welfare* 19 (2010): 107–12, 107. For discussion of the relevant literature, see Elisabeth Tjärnström, *Decision Making and the Role of Empathy in Animal Ethics Committees (AECs)* (Uppsala: SLU, Dept. of Animal Environment and Health, 2013).

61. Brian Luke, "Justice, Caring, and Animal Liberation", *Between the Species: An Online Journal for the Study of Philosophy and Animals* 8, no. 2 (1992): 100–8, 107. See also Fischer, "Taking Sympathy Seriously", and Boyle, "Hume on Animal Reason", 24.

62. For example, F. R. Ascione, "Enhancing Children's Attitudes about the Humane Treatment of Animals: Generalisation to Human Directed Empathy", *Anthrozoös* 5 (1992): 176–91; N. Taylor and D. T. Signal, "Empathy and Attitudes to Animals", *Anthrozoös* 18, no. 1 (2005): 18–27; and E. S. Paul, "Empathy with Animals and with Humans: Are They Linked?", *Anthrozoös* 13, no. 4 (2000): 194–202. For an overview of the relevant literature, see Tjärnström, *Decision Making and the Role of Empathy in Animal Ethics Committees*, 24.

63. Tjärnström, *Decision Making and the Role of Empathy in Animal Ethics Committees*, 24, and S. McPhedran, "A Review of the Evidence for Associations between Empathy, Violence and Animal Cruelty", *Aggression and Violent Behavior* 14 (2009): 1–4.

64. There is a lot of debate about the differences and similarities between human and animal reasoning in Hume's philosophy; see Beauchamp, "Hume on the Non-Human Animal", and Boyle, "Hume on Animal Reason", for discussion. For intellectual context, see Peter Kail, "Leibniz's Dog and Humean Reason", in *New Essays on David Hume*, ed. Emanuele Ronchetti and Emilio Mazza (Milan: FrancoAngeli, 2007), 65–80.

65. Most recently, Marc Bekoff and Jessica Pierce detail the "distribution of cognitive empathy in different species" in their *Wild Justice: The Moral Lives of Animals* (Chicago: University of Chicago Press, 2009), 123f.

66. See, for example, Harrison and Hall, "Anthropomorphism, Empathy, and Perceived Communicative Ability".

67. Fischer, "Taking Sympathy Seriously", 201.

68. Luke, "Justice, Caring, and Animal Liberation", 106.

69. The video of the incident is posted on YouTube, accessed on 30 June 2014 at https://www.youtube.com/watch?v=Y6GQR3Ym5M8.

70. This topic has received a great deal of attention in the literature on environmental aesthetics; see especially the papers in part III of Allen Carlson and Sheila Lintott, ed., *Nature, Aesthetics, and Environmentalism: From Beauty to Duty* (New York: Columbia University Press, 2008).

71. J. A. Serpell, "Factors Influencing Human Attitudes to Animals and Their Welfare", *Animal Welfare* 13, no. 1 (2004): 145–51.

72. Bradshaw and Paul, "Could Empathy for Animals Have Been an Adaptation?", 109.

73. Willet Kempton, James Boster, and Jennifer Hartley, *Environmental Values in American Culture* (Cambridge, MA: MIT Press, 1996), chapter 5.

74. Valls, "Hume, Justice and the Environment", part 3; Carter, "Projectivism and the Last Person Argument", 26; Fieser, "Callicott and the Metaphysical Basis of Ecocentric Morality", 173; and Partridge, "Ecological Morality and Nonmoral Sentiments".

75. Valls, "Hume, Justice and the Environment", part 3.

76. Haught, "Hume's Projectivist Legacy", 93. See also D. A. Lloyd Thomas, "Hume and Intrinsic Value", *Philosophy* 65 (1990): 419–37.

77. Patrick Frierson, "Adam Smith and the Possibility of Sympathy with Nature", *Pacific Philosophical Quarterly* 87, no. 4 (2006): 442–80, and "Applying Adam Smith: Towards a Smithian Environmental Virtue Ethics", in *New Voices on Adam Smith*, ed. Eric Schliesser and Leonidas Montes (London: Routledge, 2006).

78. Callicott, "The Land Ethic", 209; Frierson, "Adam Smith and the Possibility of Sympathy with Nature", 479.

79. Frierson, "Adam Smith and the Possibility of Sympathy with Nature", 453, 455.

80. Frierson, "Adam Smith and the Possibility of Sympathy with Nature", 453.

81. Frierson, "Adam Smith and the Possibility of Sympathy with Nature", 450–51.

82. Frierson, "Adam Smith and the Possibility of Sympathy with Nature", 450.

83. Bryan Norton, "Integration or Reduction: Two Approaches to Environmental Values", in *Environmental Pragmatism*, ed. Andrew Light and Eric Katz (New York: Routledge, 1996): 105–38.

84. Thanks to Adrian Bardon, Stavroula Glezakos, P. J. E. Kail, Ralph Kennedy, Win Lee, Emilio Mazza, Christian Miller and Andrew Valls for very useful feedback and/or discussion on earlier versions of this chapter. Thanks also to the editors Elisa Aaltola and John Hadley for helpful comments on a more recent draft.

ELEVEN

The Politicization of Animal Love

Tony Milligan

The case for animal rights has always been political, typified by a call not just for the recognition of moral rights but also for the enactment of legal protection through the political process. However, the explicitness of the theme of the political in recent years constitutes a turn away from a conception of animal rights as an ethical issue in a restrictive sense.[1] Understandably, opinions differ about just how novel this political turn has been, about just how it can best be understood, and about how fruitful it will be as a guide to action. What follows will use the idea of the turn, and an inclusive way of making sense of it, in order to say something about why we should be interested not just in concepts such as justice, civility and citizenship but also in the concept of love. And although my appeal here is only to love, the direction in which the appeal points is towards the need for a more inclusive attitude towards the emotions. Appeals to the latter, to shame and joy, guilt and love, should be an integral part of the political narratives that we deploy in order to support a change in human-animal relations. More specifically, I will address the idea that at least some animals are potential citizens in order to draw out a political dimension of love for animals. In making this move, I am claiming that two familiar attempts to go beyond the core, established conceptual repertoire of animal advocacy (first, a move into a more political vocabulary and, secondly, a move into a more affective vocabulary) should be brought closer together. However, because concepts have a history, and because the concept of citizenship in particular carries a heavy historical weighting in favour of the human, I shall be using the idea of potential citizenship as a placeholder, as a stand in for some future, and better, political classification. Such a classification will perform many of the key, nonanthropocentric functions of citizenship and thereby help us to see other creatures as having interests that should not only be considered but also be considered as part of the common good.[2]

TWO WAYS OF ARTICULATING "THE POLITICAL TURN"

Talk about a "political turn" emerges out of two kinds of dissatisfaction on the part of animal advocates. On the one hand, it emerges out of dissatisfaction with a perceived narrowness of discourse, a conviction that familiar ways of addressing matters (ways that have their provenance especially in Peter Singer, Tom Regan and Gary Francione) fail to do justice to the complexity of human-animal relations.[3] On the other hand, it also emerges out of dissatisfaction with a restricted level of impact that the established discourse has had upon the overall pattern of animal harms. Localized gains have been won, but there has been a failure to secure a satisfactory level of change or even broad popular support for changes that overstep the bounds of piecemeal welfare reform. As Donaldson and Kymlicka put matters, conventional animal rights theory "has virtually no resonance amongst the general public".[4] Their guiding hope, and that of others associated with the political turn, is not that a change of discourse will suddenly allow the end goals of animal liberation to be secured (it appears that nothing will do that), but rather that such a change will allow the advocacy of at least some worthwhile goals to move closer to the political mainstream. The turn has thus been associated with positions that endorse the value of piecemeal reform, with or without a commitment to some ultimate form of animal liberation.

But just how broadly or narrowly *should* we construe the idea of a political turn? Just how far do we need to shift from a conceptually more restricted Singer or Regan/Francione–type discourse? As a partial response to this query, I will set up a contrast that should bear a recognizable relation to the familiar and favoured options. There is, first, what I will call the *narrow scope* option of treating the turn as a movement from a restrictive rights discourse towards a more inclusive theory of interspecies political justice and/or citizenship. Arguments may then be had about how Rawlsian this inclusive theory of justice should be and about the extent to which citizenship should be articulated in communitarian or liberal terms. Tensions between the dominant liberal conceptions of justice and our illiberal practice in relation to animals may then be highlighted and used to good effect, and a broadened account of political justice may then be inscribed within an overall account of democratic legitimacy.[5] This is, I will take it, a useful and productive approach, one that can generate important insights. Secondly, there is what I will call the *broad scope* option. This involves treating the political turn as an opportunity to open up the discourse to a far broader range of concepts (and in particular "thick" concepts) that are embedded in everyday discourse, that are related to our human affectivity and have a political dimension that is not always given its due, in part because use of the concepts in question does not translate without remainder into talk about rights or justice.

While key texts such as Donaldson and Kymlicka's *Zoopolis*, with its call for mixed human/nonhuman citizenship, can be read as an instance of the narrow scope option (indeed, they explicitly situate an affective turn as an alternative to the political turn), in practice this text spills over into broad scope, into what Donaldson and Kymlicka refer to as "an exercise in expanding the moral imagination to see animals not solely as vulnerable and suffering individuals but also as neighbors, friends, cocitizens, and members of communities ours and theirs".[6] The language here, although perhaps owing more to Donaldson than Kymlicka, connects up to the tradition of Martha Nussbaum, Cora Diamond and Iris Murdoch, a tradition in which moral imagination is closely tied to concepts such as love and attention to the particular. In practice, I suspect that nobody adheres strictly and exclusively to a narrow scope option. A conceptual broadening beyond the familiar terms of political discourse is the unacknowledged, and perhaps now unavoidable, norm.

In what follows, I will explicitly favour broad scope for two reasons: (1) the alternative, while illuminating, ultimately amounts to trading one narrow discourse for another; and (2) the broad scope option is better placed to address the felt, emotional, dimensions of human life and may therefore be better placed to perform a motivating role. And here I will take it that feeling, motivation and rational agency do not fall apart from one another. The emotions that help to shape our actions are best understood as affective, but also conative and cognitive states for which good, justifying reasons can often be given.

POLITICIZING LOVE

More specifically, I will suggest that, alongside familiar political concepts such as justice, citizenship and rights, a politicized concept of love can be a useful part of the animal advocates' conceptual toolkit. This is not to be confused with the claim that talk about love can and ought to displace talk about rights because the latter is part of a discredited Enlightenment project.[7] Nor is the idea of politicizing love to be confused with the more modest, and plausible, strategic claim, advanced by Donaldson and Kymlicka, that people who love animals are "key allies" for animal advocacy,[8] or with the claim that animal liberation ought to be expounded on the basis of sentimentality rather than reason, a contrast posed by Singer as a justification for exiling talk about fondness and love from successive editions of *Animal Liberation*.[9] Instead, my claim is that in some contexts where the standing of animals is at stake, love may function as a concept that integrates with and enriches, rather than supplants, our regular political repertoire. This is a point that at least some animal rights activists have, in recent years, shown some sympathy.[10]

As a further clarification, while the idea that love can have a political dimension has not figured prominently in a great deal of recent political theory, it is nonetheless familiar in the writings of Plato, Aristotle, Saint Augustine, Tolstoy, Gandhi, Simone Weil, Hannah Arendt and Jacques Derrida, all of whom present variant ways of politicizing love. One of the more obvious and familiar ways of doing so is to follow Tolstoy and Gandhi by building a requirement for love into the theory of civil disobedience such that the political agent who engages in the latter, in defence of human liberties or animal rights, must act in ways that express love for their enemies, for humanity at large, or for all sentient beings. However, this is a particularly demanding way of politicizing love; such demandingness need not be a feature of all of the ways in which love, and politics, entwine.[11] A less demanding example, with particular relevance to the case of animals, is the inclusion of love within ecological discourse. From Aldo Leopold's *A Sand County Almanac* (1949) onwards, the legitimacy of love for the natural, for various nonsentient things, has been used to underpin claims of value that are, in turn, used to legitimate political action. A recent example of this is the appeal to a concept of *oikophilia*, love for home, which runs through Roger Scruton's *Green Philosophy* (2012). For Scruton, *oikophilia* is, above all, an attachment that serves as a motive for action. But the attachment is emphatically local. Our true home is always some particular *here* (specifically, a *here* with a distinctive history). Moreover, my *here* will not be the same as everyone else's. *Oikophilia* is explicitly set out by Scruton as a politicized concept of love, one that can be used in order to combat notions of international planning and centralized environmental control, where the latter rests upon universal considerations such as a shared humanity.

Oikophilia sits in the background of Scruton's defence of fox hunting, not merely an instance of respect for tradition but an instance of motivation by *love of place*. This will not endear him to animal rights advocates. However, we can learn a great deal from such an appeal to love for the natural, although perhaps Holmes Rolston captures a more readily appropriated form of ecological concern when he writes that "we humans too belong on the planet; it is our home, as much as for all the others . . . But the glistening pearl in space may not be something we want to possess, as much as a biosphere we ought to inhabit with love".[12] Rolston approvingly quotes Boutros Boutros-Ghali at the close of the Earth Summit in 1992 in order to show the way in which such talk can enliven political discourse at the highest level: "The Spirit of Rio must create a new mode of civic conduct. It is not enough for man to love his neighbor;

he must also learn to love his world".[13] The emerging literature that seeks to make a parallel move in the case of animals, an appeal to love as a central ethical concept, is to be encouraged. It can also help to reshape, or at least constrain, the role of love for the nonsentient (whether we think in terms akin to Scruton or Rolston).

The most prominent instances of a shift in this direction are discussions of animal love that have appeared over the past couple of decades within the feminist tradition. Deborah Slicer, for example, has drawn upon Iris Murdoch to suggest that "loving attention" should be the basis of ethical relations with what is radically other—that is, with animals and nonsentient things.[14] Murdoch is a particularly good source here, not simply because of her unconventional brand of philosophical sophistication but also because of the way in which love for the nonhuman, for places, things and fellow creatures (dogs especially) figure regularly in her novels. The proper direction of attention, for Murdoch, is outwards, away from the self. For Slicer, such attention to what is other helps to situate the importance of love.

However, problems about the articulation of animal love and its ethical and/or political role have also emerged. From a similarly feminist and care perspective, Chris Cuomo and Lori Gruen adopt a diametrically opposite approach.[15] Rather than appealing to love for what is radically other, they use love to challenge the binary contrast between human and nonhuman. Love is taken to be something that animals, as well as humans, deserve. Their hope is that this will expand our "moral orientation" and reduce our sense of otherness and "moral distance". Kennan Ferguson, writing outside of the feminist tradition but with clear influences from the latter, is slightly sceptical about the viability of this inclusive, distance-eliminating move given the fickleness of humans: many pet lovers are also untroubled meat eaters. Instead, Ferguson places emphasis more directly upon a familiar kind of anti-Enlightenment critique and seeks to politicize animal love as an alternative to reliance upon deliberative reason. He hopes to bring into focus "the unacknowledged possibilities of animal/human relations" while retaining a conception of love as an attitude towards particulars rather than an attitude towards *types* of creatures.[16] Ferguson's option does not exclude the possibility of eating, or owning, animals that we do not love. In this respect, it captures the ethical importance of relations to animals as discrete particular beings but, for rights advocates, it will seem grossly underconstrained and insufficiently challenging to the status quo.

Ferguson's approach may then seem to confirm suspicions about love talk as insufficiently radical or insufficiently proximate to considerations that can be turned into suitable legislation. Indeed, his project is to show that imbalance and inequality (of the sort that exists in relations between owners and their pets/companion animals) may be loving rather than pernicious. Therefore, the wholesale extinction of pets (as a means of eliminating their oppression) or an ending of human control over nonhumans is not a suitable political goal. "People's love of dogs does not necessitate them, or anyone else, to stop eating other animals, to give dogs equal legal and civic protections, or to place the suffering of distant, unknown humans above their pet's needs and pleasures".[17] I suspect that this quickly puts us into territory where loving relations with particular animals functions, in part, as a thin attempt to compensate for the other wrongs that we sanction and permit. Those who enjoy a good steak, and even those who carry out intrusive animal experimentation, can be the most loving pet owners.

Kathy Rudy executes much the same compromise on a larger scale in *Loving Animals*. Like Ferguson, Rudy appeals to love as an alternative to rights on familiar anti-Enlightenment grounds. But she goes much further than Ferguson, who does at least stress our protection for those we love. Rudy treats love for particular animals as consistent with experimentation upon those very same animals given the belief that they would understand and consent if only they could do so. Similarly, for Rudy, we get to kill those we love for consumption but only on the understanding that they would want to return something to us. This involves a spiritual conception of sacrifice and purity of motive, themes that emerge towards the end of Rudy's text. A question mark may then be placed over the conception of love that is in play. It looks very different from the kind of love that is ordinarily in play between humans. After all, we do not think it acceptable to sacrifice the life of a loved one for anything other than a matter of the deepest importance, and certainly not for culinary pleasure. The conspicuous absence of restrictions about such matters in Rudy's account of loving animals is at least partly the result of her decision to treat rights attributions and talk about love as mutually hostile, competing rather than overlapping discourses. For Rudy, when love enters, negative rights (not to be eaten or experimented upon) simply drop out of the picture. By contrast, I shall argue below that citizenship has a neglected conceptual connection to love and that rights of various sorts (both negative and positive) go hand in hand with citizenship. Rights talk and love talk work best when they work together, without an elimination of one by the other and without a reduction of one to the other.

It is, admittedly, tempting to think otherwise and to contrast a loving approach towards others with a citizen approach. Iris Murdoch has alluded to just this point as a fundamental feature of the liberal stance. "Liberal political thought posits a certain fundamental distinction between the person as citizen and the person as moral-spiritual individual". Love attaches to the other *qua* moral-spiritual individual rather than *qua* citizen. In Murdoch, the distinction is cautiously drawn: "We are not as real, whole, persons identical with this fictitious citizen, nor are we essentially divided between the two roles".[18] Yet the point is pressed home. Murdoch, who places so much emphasis upon love as the heart of ethics, and who is drawn upon by feminist scholars who wish to politicize animal love, is herself cautious about any attempted politicization of the concept. Jan Bransen has pressed this division more firmly by arguing that others are worthy of something better than merely being regarded as fellow citizens; they are worthy instead of a loving attitude.[19] The view is tempting, but what it brings into play is a pared-back and decidedly liberal conception of citizenship, one that can be associated with legal rights of residency and return, together with entitlement, to participation in the electoral process. This is a conception of citizenship that is all too familiar as a feature of legal discourse. It is also bloodless in the sense of being minimal in terms of what is required in order to see the other as a fellow citizen. While Bransen's intuition about what we owe to others seems plausible, I will suggest that we can more effectively articulate his insight by bringing citizenship and love closer together, or rather, bringing them back together, where they belong. In short, love matters politically not just because the personal can be political but also because citizenship matters. However, citizenship is best understood in broadly Aristotelian terms, with a focus not upon voting entitlement or residency and return (although these too may be included) but upon the sharing of a life and the consideration of interests as part of a common good.

ARISTOTLE AND POLITICAL FRIENDSHIP

Notoriously, Aristotle connected citizenship and (loving) friendship but, because of the depth of the bond of friendship, claimed that we can only have a limited number of true friends. This looks like a plausible generalization about friendship and about human moral psychology. However, we may then wonder why citizenship and friendship are related at all. We may wonder what Aristotle had in mind when he claimed that friendship holds states together (*Nicomachean Ethics* 1155a). Minimally (drawing upon both the *Nicomachean* and the *Eudemian Ethics*), he seems to have held that the political community is constituted by networks of moral agents who are bound together by bonds of personal friendship and by bonds of a broader political friendship (*philia politike*) as well as bonds of other sorts. And while this brings into play an idea of political friendship that may not be identical to friendship in the familiar sense, it is not entirely unlike the latter. Indeed, our familiar understanding of what personal friendship entails will be shaped by an understanding of what Aristotle can possibly have meant by "political friendship". As instances of *philia*, both will involve some manner of love.

On a charitable reading of *philia politike*, Aristotle's point does not seem to be that all members of a political community must be intimately involved, on a one-to-one basis, with each other. Indeed, the relation of personal friendship involves a connection of a deep sort that positively precludes such breadth. Rather, the point concerns the role that is played by networks of agents who are bound together through shared activity, mutual interest and above all through *identification*, where the latter is understood in a specific sense: we identify with a friend of the truest sort because such a friend is, figuratively, another self. This makes our loving concern for them different from the merely benevolent concern that we may happen to have for strangers, acquaintances or the members of generations. We would no more deliberately and wantonly harm our truest friends than we would deliberately engage in self-harm. We desire that our friends, or at least our true friends, flourish, and that they do so for their own sake.

If there are enough bonds of this type, overlaid and interconnecting with one another across a political community, it will, no doubt, foster a sense of solidarity, a sense of belonging with and acting with one another. I will take it that this is partly constitutive of the elusive phenomenon of *philia politike*. There are, of course, dangers built into this communitarian picture. We may wonder about how to secure interconnection rather than rivalry and about whether a network of friendships could ever be so extensive that it included all of those who are entitled to be regarded as fellow citizens. When Aristotle links citizenship and friendship (of a sort that requires love in the sense of *philia*), there always seems to be a danger of exclusion, a danger of alienation on the part of those who are left out and who do not seem at all like another self. We may know enough about large communities to believe that there will be a substantial number of people who fall through this particular net. Even so, the Aristotelian position does not require utopia. There is no need to posit the practicality of an all-inclusive loving community in order to acknowledge and to sympathize with the insight that there is a connection between regarding others as fellow citizens and regarding them as, at least potentially, participants in friendships of some sort, and hence as potentially loving and/or loved agents. To view others as potential citizens, on a broadly Aristotelian account, requires only that there be no barrier to viewing them as suitable recipients of love by someone within the political community, if not by ourselves then by someone else. By contrast, those who cannot be loved, who are seen as utterly unlovable, will also be agents with whom we cannot share our interests, political projects, lives and sense of belonging. There are some obvious examples of the latter: agents who *could not be* regarded as fellow citizens because they have been guilty of evil beyond vice. On a realistic view of Hitler, we could not regard him as a suitable fellow citizen (likewise for Pol Pot, Joseph Stalin and Jack the Ripper).

But just why should we follow Aristotle in this exclusionary construal of citizenship and love? Why not *simply* connect up citizenship with respect (as, indeed, Donaldson and Kymlicka, and many others, do)? Why not say that we cannot regard such people as fellow citizens because "to treat someone as a citizen involves facilitating and enabling their political agency", and this is precisely what we *refuse* to do in the case of those who are, in some important sense, morally lost?[20] The most obvious reason why this is not strong enough is that seeing others as fellow citizens involves more than enabling their political agency, it also involves seeing that their interests are worth sharing and promoting. Those who are beyond a defensible love are also beyond such sharing and promoting. To see others as beyond a defensible love is precisely to see them as agents whose well-being should not be promoted by ourselves or by any sovereign body to which we owe allegiance. They cannot form part of "the people" in whose interests an authoritative sovereign body should claim to speak and act.

Treating a perceived *unlovability* in this way, as a barrier to the recognition or perception of the other as a fellow citizen, is my suggested route to the politicization of love, and it is a route that is very different from the Tolstoy and Gandhi path of loving our enemies. It is very different, too, from attempts to use talk about love to supplant talk about rights. It is, however, close to the Aristotelian-derived view that has been advanced by Jacques Derrida in *The Politics of Friendship* (1994), a critique of contemporary liberalism's neglect of *fraternity* as integral to an adequate conception of democracy. Derrida's point is that liberalism has steadily pared away at the conception of liberty, equality and fraternity in a way that diminished liberty and equality by excluding fraternity. Indeed, this move is partly constitutive of contemporary liberalism, and free-market liberalism would make no sense without it.

This paints a picture of love, and acceptance of the *lovability* of particular others, as central to political life. It also paints a picture of a tempting and worrying sort. Tempting, because it provides a warmed-up or full-blooded conception of what it takes to accept another as a fellow citizen. Worrying, because it may seem too demanding and, in particular, too demanding for nonhuman creatures if we find it difficult to relate to them in other than hostile or defensive ways. Perhaps a requirement for love might exclude some nonhuman creatures from citizenship even if we might otherwise be persuaded to accept them as members of a mixed political community, as beings whose interests are considered *as* part of the common good. And here we may be inclined to follow Donaldson and Kymlicka and point out that because assisted and enabled agency is required for some human citizens, there seems to be no particularly good reason to deny that nonhuman animals could, and perhaps should, in some cases be accepted as fellow citizens. They, too, may stand in need of similar enabling and advocacy, but this is not an automatic disqualifier.

Even so, an appeal to suitability as a recipient of love may be the source of a deeper concern (at least with regard to love of the kind that flourishes in the context of friendship). It is premised, on a strict Aristotelian account, upon the entitlement of the other to be seen realistically as another self. This sounds and is demanding. Only beings who could share our hopes, dreams and convictions could ever play such a role. Even a dog could not do so. While fellow creatures of many sorts might share our activities, lives and interests, they could not do so in this more demanding sense. Accordingly, on a strictly Aristotelian account, other animals, infants and various humans who have done nothing wrong could never truly be that other self who merits the name of friend. This is Aristotle's own dominant view about animals (represented, for example, at *Nicomachean Ethics* I, ix, 32–35 and *Politics* III, ix, 32–35), although he says different things about animals in different places. It is also a view to which I have made concessions in the past but that I now regard as simply mistaken.[21] It is a view that will automatically lead us to doubt whether *they* could be bound to *us* by the bonds of political friendship that join the members of a good political community together.

As a saving response, we may point out that Aristotle always allowed for lesser forms of friendship based upon mutual usefulness and pleasure rather than identification. He also seems to have regarded *philia politike* as itself an instance of utility friendship. This would still permit the relevant exclusions of particular, morally abhorrent humans while retaining an openness to political friendship between humans and nonhumans. However, such a saving move does not do justice to the idea that some commentators on *philia* have discerned in Aristotle, the idea that utility friendship aspires to be friendship of a more robust sort. Put otherwise, utility friendship makes sense only against the background of some possibility of pleasure-based and ultimately identification-based friendship. And this possibility is what allows it to qualify not as a purely mercenary connection but as a genuine instance of friendship. It is also what gets lost in translation when *philia politike* is reduced to some conception of mere "civic friendship", which is amenable to incorporation in, say, a Rawlsian account of the political community.

Alternatively, we may simply challenge the Aristotelian formulation that a friend, or a true friend, or a friend of the best sort, ought to be seen as another self. If understood loosely, as a highly figurative way of expressing fraternity, a way that would not automatically exclude the nonhuman, it is perhaps unobjectionable. But if it is understood more restrictively and more literally, it looks obviously and demandingly egocentric, tending even towards the narcissistic claim that looking at a friend is like holding up a mirror (Cicero, *De Amicitia*, vii, 23). Understood thus, friendship that requires unselfishly caring for the other for his or her own sake would make no sense.

ANIMALS AND CONTEMPORARY PHILOSOPHY OF LOVE

Even with a modified version of Aristotelian *philia*, one that removes such narcissism, the temptation to indulge in some manner of human-elevating restriction, when it comes to both citizenship and the subject of love, is considerable. And so Aristotle's own suspicion about the inclusion of animals may return. This same suggestion can be seen in contemporary work on the philosophy of love where restrictions agreed upon by advocates of competing positions regularly premise suitability as an object of love upon the possession of a shared humanity (a view set out by Raimond Gaita), or, relatedly, upon the possession of Kantian personhood (a view associated with Bennett Helm, Niko Kolodny, David Velleman and, more recently, Troy Jollimore).[22]

While the agency of nonhuman animals is acknowledged in at least some of the above, they are denied the standing of creatures who are suitable recipients of love in the full and proper sense.[23] This will also rob animals of any possibility that they might qualify as suitable fellow citizens or as members of a genuinely mixed political community understood in terms that borrow heavily from the concept of the citizen. In the context of discussions about love, such exclusion characteristically takes two forms: one concerns loving and the other concerns being loved. On the one hand, there is weak denial, an acceptance that animals can perhaps be loved but rejection of the view that they can love in return (in the philosophically deep and interesting sense of love). Harry Frankfurt advanced this view.[24] On the other hand, there is strong denial, a rejection of the view that animals can either love or be loved, again in the philosophically deep or interesting sense, a view advanced by Bennett Helm, Nikko Kolodny and, with reservations, Troy Jollimore.[25]

It is slightly odd that the stronger form of such exclusion has not been met with an equally strong opposition given that (1) it seems to conflict in obvious ways with the Darwinian emphasis upon human/nonhuman continuity by turning human love into something radically discontinuous from bonding among our fellow creatures; and (2) it seems to conflict with the familiar phenomenology of our human love for nonhuman animals. Here we may point to the joy that we humans take from sharing parts of our lives with nonhuman animals. However, there may be many root sources of joy. By contrast, there is only one root source of grief. That humans grieve over the loss of at least some animals is perhaps the best indication of the genuineness and depth of our love for such creatures. Indeed, it is difficult to accept such grief as genuine unless we are also prepared to accept that it emerges out of, and is the price that we pay for, love.

Even so, in spite of the difficulties of matching up strong denial with our familiar experiences of loving and being loved by other creatures, there is, nonetheless, a clear rationale for the position. It draws upon an assumption about reciprocation: what we can love (in the deep sense) and what we can have reasons to love is regularly taken to be some other being who can return our feelings. David Velleman put this point rather well by saying that what the heart responds to is another heart.[26] More recently, Troy Jollimore has made the same point by claiming that "the special opportunity that love for persons affords us is the opportunity to care about something that can care about us. It is because our loved ones care whether or not we care that our caring about them matters in the fullest possible sense".[27]

If we bring together weak denial (animals cannot love us) and this assumption about reciprocation (we can only truly and deeply love beings who are in principle capable of returning our love), strong denial will then be entailed (i.e., animals can neither love us nor be appropriately loved by us). But what if one or both of the assumptions in play here misfire? They are certainly open to dispute. The ecologically minded, drawing upon the centrality given to love for the natural, are likely to deny that the potential for real (nonfigurative) reciprocation is in any way a basic requirement for a genuine and deep love. We may love hills, areas of woodland, or our local bit of the forest, and some of us do so in a truly deep way, but without any prospect of a return. As with animals, the best evidence for the genuineness of such love again seems to be the fact that grief seems to follow upon loss and destruction.[28] However, we may not need to make any such eco-minded claim in order to make room for a legitimate love for at least some particular nonhuman animals. On its own, weak denial (the view they can't love us) is every bit as problematic and vulnerable as the assumption about reciprocation.

More precisely, claims that animals, although capable of certain kinds of bonding and affection, cannot love (or at least they cannot do so in the right way), are usually based upon a return to the Aristotelian idea of identification with the other. Given a realistic appraisal of their cognitive limitations, it is taken to be impossible for animals to identify with others in a genuine and deep manner. And while we may not hold that identification must involve seeing someone as another self in the restrictive and narcissistic sense, something akin to identification in a more minimal sense does seem to be required for love as opposed to other caring responses such as mere benevolence. When we love another, we connect our interests with their interests and adopt attitudes towards their hopes and fears. However, it is not clear that nonhuman animals are capable of the kind of identification that is integral to and partly constitutive of love.

What the dispute here will ultimately turn upon is our understanding of what a good story about loving identification must involve. Frankfurt and Helm tell variations of one kind of story: identification involves second-order desires, desires with regard to the first-order desires that we have for the well-being of the other. And so, when we love someone, we want him or her to flourish for his or her own sake, and we also want to continue to have this desire for his or her flourishing. As we might expect, this turns out to be exclusionary because it is difficult to find evidence for second-order desires among nonhumans, a point made long ago by Frankfurt.[29] As a simplification, I will assume that Frankfurt was right and that for the most part animals do not form second-order desires and so cannot identify with others in this sense, or in any related and even more cognitively demanding sense.

However, there is a different kind of story that may be told about identification, one that keeps love's desires resolutely at the first-order level and that appeals not to a hierarchy of desires, but to the conditionality of desires, to the way in which, when we love, the satisfaction of all sorts of first-order desires become conditional upon the satisfaction of a desire for the well-being of another. The formation of desires of this sort clearly does, in some sense, involve a deep connection to, or identification with, the other. It is equally clear that it falls within the capabilities of many (but not all) nonhuman animals. When the core desire in question, the desire for the well-being of the other, can no longer be satisfied (for example, as a result of the death of the other), all sorts of commonplace desires can no longer be fulfilled and a radically demotivated state ensues. This is what grief involves, and it is a state that can be observed and documented among both humans and many nonhumans.

Given that a satisfactory account of identification can be given in these terms, and that there is no need to reach for something more cognitively demanding, there is no good reason to deny that animals can care intimately for, and thereby identify with, others in the way that is required for love. And given that animals can love, then even should we retain a requirement that suitable recipients of love must in turn be capable of reciprocation, there will still be no good reason to deny that we can defensibly love the animals in question. In which case, a plausible account of love may be reconciled with what we have known all along about the genuineness and depth of our human feelings for particular, nonhuman others. With acceptance of this idea in place, viewing fellow creatures as fellow citizens will no longer be excluded by a politicization of love along broadly Aristotelian lines. Rather, the fact that we can love them, and that they can love us, will make animals exceptionally good candidates for membership in such a shared community. Here we see the beginnings of an account of how a greater politicization of animal rights theory and an appeal to affective and emotional concepts can be brought together.[30]

NOTES

1. For prominent examples of this political shift, see Siobhan O'Sullivan, *Animals, Equality and Democracy* (Basingstoke: Palgrave Macmillan, 2011); Robert Garner, *The Political Theory of Animals Rights* (Manchester: Manchester University Press, 2005);

Alasdair Cochrane, *An Introduction to Animals and Political Theory* (Basingstoke: Palgrave Macmillan, 2010).

2. I refer here to "other creatures" and not to "all other creatures". The restricted quantification is intentional.

3. For criticism of Singer's conception of rational, unsentimental deliberation, see Cathryn Bailey, "On the Backs of Animals: The Valorization of Reason in Contemporary Animal Ethics", *Ethics and the Environment* 10, no. 1 (2005): 1–17, as well as Sue Donaldson and Will Kymlicka, *Zoopolis* (Oxford: Oxford University Press, 2011), 3.

4. Donaldson and Kymlicka, *Zoopolis*, 4–5.

5. For examples of articulations of what justice requires, see O'Sullivan, *Animals, Equality and Democracy*, and Robert Garner, *A Theory of Justice for Animals* (Oxford: Oxford University Press, 2013).

6. Donaldson and Kymlicka, *Zoopolis*, 24.

7. Kathy Rudy, *Loving Animals: Toward a New Animal Advocacy* (Minneapolis: Minnesota University Press, 2011), 192.

8. Donaldson and Kymlicka, *Zoopolis*, 10.

9. Peter Singer, *Animal Liberation* (London: Pimlico, 1995), x, uses scare quotes around "animal lover" in a way that suggests that it is more of a charge of sentimentality and misplaced attachment than a description.

10. Kim Stallwood's recent, partly autobiographical, *Growl: Life Lessons, Hard Truths, and Bold Strategies from an Animal Advocate* (Brooklyn, NY: Lantern Books, 2014), 137–52, sets out the author's own shift from rejection of "animal lover" as a slur to endorsement of the idea that an openness to love is a crucial part of animal advocacy.

11. Tony Milligan, *Civil Disobedience: Protest, Justification and the Law* (London and New York: Bloomsbury, 2013), 78–81.

12. Holmes Rolston, *A New Environmental Ethics* (New York: Routledge, 2013), 222.

13. Rolston, *New Environmental Ethics*, 195.

14. Deborah Slicer, "Your Daughter or Your Dog? A Feminist Assessment of the Animal Research Issue", *Hypatia* 6, no. 1 (1991): 108–24, 111.

15. Chris Cuomo and Lori Gruen, "On Puppies and Pussies: Animals, Intimacy, and Moral Distance", in *Daring to Be Good: Essays in Feminist Eco-Politics*, ed. Bat-Ami Bar On and Ann Ferguson (New York: Routledge, 1998), 29–42, 140.

16. Kennan Ferguson, "I [Heart] My Dog", *Political Theory* 32, no. 3 (2004): 373–95, 384.

17. Ferguson, *My Dog*, 391.

18. Iris Murdoch, *Metaphysics as a Guide to Morals* (London: Penguin, 1993), 357.

19. Jan Bransen, "Loving Attitude and Citizen Attitude", in C. Maurer, T. Milligan and K. Pacovska, *Love and Its Objects* (Basingstoke: Palgrave Macmillan, 2014), 143–59.

20. Donaldson and Kymlicka, *Zoopolis*, 58.

21. See Tony Milligan, "Dependent Companions", *Journal of Applied Philosophy* 26, no. 4 (2009): 402–13, and Cynthia Townley, "Animals as Friends", *Between the Species* 10 (2010), for a plausible criticism.

22. Raimond Gaita, *A Common Humanity* (London: Routledge, 2000); Bennett Helm, *Love, Friendship and the Self* (Oxford: Oxford University Press, 2010); Niko Kolodny, "Love as Valuing a Relationship", *The Philosophical Review*, 112, no. 2 (2003): 135–89; David Velleman, "Love as a Moral Emotion", *Ethics* 109, no. 2 (1999): 338–74; Troy Jollimore, *Love's Vision* (Princeton: Princeton University Press, 2011).

23. For a fuller exploration of these issues, see Milligan, "Animals and the Capacity for Love", in Christian Maurer, Tony Milligan and Kamila Pacovska, *Love and Its Objects* (New York: Palgrave Macmillan, 2014), 211–25.

24. Harry G. Frankfurt, *Reasons of Love* (Princeton: Princeton University Press, 2004).

25. Kolodny, "Love as Valuing a Relationship", 135–89; Helm, *Love, Friendship and the Self*; Jollimore, *Love's Vision*.

26. Velleman, "Love as a Moral Emotion".

27. Jollimore, *Love's Vision*, 122.

28. Phyllis Windle, "The Ecology of Grief", *Bioscience* 42, no. 5 (1992): 363–66.

29. See Harry G. Frankfurt, "Freedom of the Will and the Concept of a Person", *Journal of Philosophy* 68, no. 1 (1971): 5–20, for the claim that animals cannot have second-order desires. The claim is for the most part defensible, but the tone of his treatment of animals belongs to an earlier era of human thought.

30. Earlier versions of the chapter were presented at the Cosmopolitan Animals event in London in 2012 and at the Manchester Centre for Political Theory (MAN-CEPT) workshop on "The Political Turn in Animal Rights" at the University of Manchester in 2013. Thanks for improving comments go to participants in the discussion at both events, and particularly to Steve Cooke, Les Mitchell, Alasdair Cochrane and Rob Garner for helping to clarity my ideas about the "turn", as well as to John Hadley and Elisa Aaltola for more detailed suggestions.

TWELVE

The Rise of Sentimentalism and Animal Philosophy

Elisa Aaltola

Sentimentalism is undergoing a powerful revival in moral psychology and metaethics. The impetus for this revival is founded upon the claim that emotions play a necessary part in moral agency. One of the first advocates of this revival was Martha Nussbaum, who has suggested throughout her work that moral decision making must include an emotive component; in fact, without emotion, one cannot speak of "moral understanding".[1] Many have repeated this claim, and recently, for instance, Alice Crary has argued that reason-based judgement—although "a philosopher's fixation"[2]—forms only one aspect of moral agency, the more foundational aspect being formed by emotions. Perhaps the most well-known contemporary defender of sentimentalism is Jesse Prinz, who maintains that emotions and the type of intuitive sentiments that they echo are the basis of moral decision making. Prinz puts forth the arguement, in line with Nussbaum, that a person who grasps the Kantian or utilitarian ramifications of a given act, but has no emotion, does not truly understand the potential wrongness of that act. On these grounds, he makes a bold claim: "Emotions are both necessary and sufficient for moral judgment".[3]

Of course, the roots of sentimentalism go back to David Hume, according to whom morality originates from evaluations based on rudimentary reactions towards such emotions as joy and suffering, and our sympathetic capacity to form impressions and thereafter ideas concerning the emotions of other individuals.[4] Indeed, many contemporary authors refer to Hume as a still relevant inspiration, while criticizing the rival Kantian stance, which famously claimed reason rather than emotion to facilitate moral agency. Thus, Patricia Churchland, according to whom emotions are at the epicentre of moral ability, argues in favour of the Humean account, and claims that "Kant's conviction that detachment from emotions is essential in characterizing moral obligation is strikingly at odds with what we know about our biological nature".[5] Similarly, Victoria McGeer posits that values are "fundamentally rooted in the depth and quality of one's affective life",[6] and goes on to say, "I claim in a broadly Humean way that we human beings are moral beings . . . because of our affective natures".[7]

Animal ethics has not been immune to this turn towards the sentiment. Indeed, already the heyday of sentimentalism—eighteenth- and nineteenth-century humanitarianism—included a drastic upsurge of moral arguments on behalf of nonhuman animals,[8] and it can even be argued that sentimentalism shares common roots with the birth of the animal welfare movement.[9] However, the ties between sentimentalism and animal ethics were cut during the 1970s and 1980s, when the "first generation of animal ethics", most notably Peter Singer and Tom Regan, sought to explicitly distance proanimal arguments from emotions. The motivations for doing so were quite understandable, considering the negative connotations gained by "sentimentalism" in the twentieth century. Largely positivist emphasis on rational analysis, verification, objectivity and propositional language meant that during this era, emotions were viewed as a faulty way of approaching moral considerations or (within emotivism), when combined with morality, rendered the latter into sheer vocalizations of one's subjective affect. This split between sentimentalism and animal ethics was not, however, long lived.

Animal ethics has seen, within its "second generation", a sharp critique of reason-centred moral theory, formulated particularly through the viewpoint of feminist considerations. In line with Genevieve Lloyd,[10] care theorists suggest that the history of philosophy, up to the present day, is marred by the tendency to unduly prioritize reason due to its links to the masculine identity—that is, philosophers have tended to be men, who overtly emphasize the faculty that is celebrated as the core of masculinity. According to this thesis, animal ethics has also been guilty of favouring the more "masculine" emphasis on reason, detachment and logics instead of paying heed to emotions. Following suit, Josephine Donovan and Lori Gruen, among others, have wished to bring forward emotive thinking as the feminine alternative thus far largely ignored—for them, animal ethics must include a sentimental focus.[11] Next to care theorists, also various other philosophers from different paradigmatic backgrounds have similarly brought forward the role of emotion in animal ethics. For Mary Midgley, emotions must form an integral part of approaching other sentient beings,[12] Ralph Acampora has discussed "corporal compassion",[13] and Cora Diamond has fitted her Wittgensteinian stance on other animals with the notion of "fellow-feeling".[14]

However, animal ethics has not yet taken a stance on, or made use of, the latest research on sentimentalism that is quickly accumulating in both philosophy and fields such as social psychology, psychiatry and neurostudies. More importantly, although sentimentalism has reserved a place in some of the second-generation approaches to animals, the majority of contemporary animal ethics has remained staunchly orientated towards rationalism. The aim of this chapter is to explore recent philosophical and empirical studies on sentimentalism in the context of animal ethics. Can the revival of sentimentalism shed new light on the normative relation between humans and other animals? More importantly, what are the metaphilosophical and metaethical implications of the recent revival of sentimentalism, when considered in the animal context?

SENTIMENTALISM IN MORAL PSYCHOLOGY AND EVERYDAY ANIMAL ETHICS

Humean sentimentalism gains support from empirical studies—in fact, the rise of empirical considerations has arguably been the main incentive behind the sentimentalism revival. Following evolutionary, biological, ethological, psychological and neurological research, it is claimed with increasing frequency that moral judgement is often based on something much more immediate than Kantian rationality. The argument is that although people do resort to reasoning, this happens usually in surplus to their immediate and affect-laden normative responses. That is, reason enters the scene after the initial normative stance is formulated and tends to be used mainly in cases of conflict, contradictions or efforts of persuasion: "Moral reasoning matters, but it matters primarily in social contexts in which people try to influence each other and reach consensus with friends and allies".[15] Indeed, following Jerome Kagan's groundbreaking claim, according to which reasoned argument is used only superficially as a kind of epiphenomenon, Jonathan Haidt maintains that reason is a mere servant of emotion, and its use is limited to post hoc justification.[16] Thereby, reason surfaces as a technical tool with which to overcome potential divergence or fissures—not as the foundational and necessary basis of moral evaluation or even deliberation.

Instead of reason, it is emotion that sparks morality. Haidt goes so far as to argue that "emotion is a significant driving force in moral judgment"[17] and "emotions are in fact in charge of the temple of morality".[18] Indeed, Haidt has maintained that morality consists largely of automated responses, and particularly emotive and stereotyping elements, the first of which serves a primary role. Therefore, we are bound by affective, evaluative associations, which are immediate, taking place before any conscious reflection or deliberation. This "social intuitionist model" maintains that moral judgements are based on intuitions, which are characterized as "the sudden appearance in consciousness, or at the fringe of consciousness, of an evaluative feeling (like-dislike, good-bad) about a character or actions of a person, without any conscious awareness of having gone through steps of search, weighing evidence, or inferring conclusions".[19] To cut the story short, people have culturally produced stereotypes, which intertwine with emotive responses, and as a result an immediate sense of "good" and "bad" (our "social" or "moral" "intuition") is formed. In order to alter the ensuing morality, one needs to address the underlying stereotypes and emotions. This means that change in moral beliefs happens primarily via the social sphere, which affects our automated, affective responses and thus pushes forward new intuitions.

Sentimentalism has clear explanatory power in the context of moral judgements concerning nonhuman animals. Everyday animal ethics are often based on emotive responses, which again are guided by socially constructed meanings, and which remain wholly unreflected. Importantly, however, this does not apply only or primarily to proanimal advocacy, but rather to typically anthropocentric notions concerning the human-animal relation.

How other animals are valued is arguably grounded—at least to a significant extent—on cultural stereotypes and particularly various emotions that are linked to those stereotypes. There is some recent evidence to support this claim. As it comes to cultural influences, it has been discovered that the desire for in-group belonging motivates people to endorse meat eating in a meat-eating society; furthermore, when people witness animals being exploited in their own culture, they are prone to attribute less sentience and cognition to those animals in order to downplay the need for moral concern.[20] Moreover, it has been confirmed that viewing animals as "meat" (a culturally produced schema) will similarly lead to seeing less sentience, cognition and thereby value in nonhuman animals.[21] Perhaps the clearest example of the power of cultural stereotypes is categorization, within which animals are labelled as "pets", "food animals", and so on. Research indicates that "food animal", like "meat", is a schema, which enables one to concentrate on viewing the animal as food while downplaying other considerations, such as the animal's capacity to suffer.[22] In short, the cultural stereotype "food animal" includes human-centred factors such as taste, while ignoring animal-centred factors such as sentience, cognition or moral value. Thereby, the desire for social inclusion, together with conceptual schemas, lead to cultural stereotypes of animals as less sentient, less cognitive and less valuable. Indeed, cultural and social influence has been found to strongly correlate with meat eating.[23] These influences intertwine with emotions. Arguably, negative emotions such as disgust and contempt are routinely applied to other animals, ranging from pigs to rats, and following Haidt's social intuition model, these emotions are linked to culturally produced stereotypes of pigs and rats as dirty, ugly, greedy and cognitively incapable. Following suit, research shows that disgust towards animals, based on presumed ugliness and deviation from the norm, are strong predictors of meat eating[24]; in conclusion, "those individuals consuming the most meat were more disgust sensitive".[25] Crucially, these negative emotions go on to affect moral judgements concerning pigs and rats—judgements which may exist wholly beyond any rational reflection.

On these grounds, it appears that reason serves a limited role in everyday animal ethics—a matter perhaps best manifested in the "meat paradox", within which people tend to simultaneously love and eat nonhuman animals.[26] That is, the ambiguous and paradoxical nature of moral conceptions concerning other animals reveals the restricted use of logical, clarifying reason. Arguably (and again following Haidt's model), reason tends to serve a function only when emotive responses exist in a conflict (watching *Babe* and eating bacon), or when one needs to justify one's beliefs to others. Moreover, we often choose, post hoc, the type of reasoned accounts that best serve our own emotive responses: those with negative emotions may favour contractual takes on other animals, whereas those with positive emotions may find Singer-Regan accounts highly persuasive. In short, Haidt's "social intuitionist model" is relevant in explaining moral attitudes towards nonhuman animals, as emotive and stereotyping responses unaccompanied by rational reflection—a seemingly standard path to making sense of animality.

These considerations pose uncomfortable questions for academic animal ethics. First of all, although the feminist care tradition in animal ethics has been eager to underline sentimentalism as the guide towards a more ethical take on other animals, it is worth bearing in mind that current anthropocentrism is, in itself, largely sentimental. The crucial mistake is to presume that sentimentalism includes only positive emotions, or that it leads to a world filled with equality, care and solidarity. As emphasized by sentimentalists, positive emotions are only half the story, and negative emotions tend to play a powerful role in determining moral judgements.[27] Animal ethics and philosophy should consider more carefully just how relevant a role disgust, hate, anger, contempt, pride and other similar emotions play in determining anthropocentric attitudes towards animals. Moreover, care theorists would do well to consider whether positive emotions may also spark hierarchical and dualistic takes on nonhuman animals, as, for instance, love or concern for one's closest may imply relative indifference towards those more distant from oneself—the typical example being a person who "loves" her dog while wearing fur. Indeed, some feminist authors on "love" for animals have suggested that it can quite feasibly walk hand in hand with eating other animals,[28] thus confirming the "meat eaters paradox". What emerges as clear, therefore, is that sheer emphasis on emotion is not sufficient: we need to specify what types of emotions are morally relevant. That is to say, in a world filled with sentimental anthropocentrism, care needs to be taken in mapping out the links between moral agency and emotion—sheer, generic advocacy of the latter may be nothing short of counterproductive.

Secondly, and more importantly, if reason is mainly used post hoc, what purpose does particularly analytical animal ethics serve? Is it restricted to writings that those rare philosophers, who are interested in rationally exploring the human-animal relation, direct to other similarly minded philosophers—that is, does it remain hopelessly secluded in the ivory tower of academic rationalism, separated from the world at large, which remains vehemently sentimentalist? Is analytical animal ethics able to persuade the broader public? Of course, one option is to suggest that even if moral judgement is largely, de facto, based on emotion, we ought to make it more reason based. Perhaps the *ideal* form of morality is grounded on reason, and thereby one's task is to rid oneself of the shackles of emotion and become more reason orientated. Quite evidently, the role of academic animal ethics is not simply to communicate given normative judgements to others, but also to explore these judgements via the viewpoint of reason—the ideal that so often remains missing from everyday morality. However, although this argument has a kernel of truth to it (rational analysis still holds relevance, especially when that of emotions is recognized), even contemporary rationalists Jeannette Kennett and Cordelia Fine acknowledge that sidelining the de facto role of emotion is a mistake.[29] Simply put, even if reasoned analysis is needed, completely ignoring the de facto level renders that analysis pragmatically irrelevant. This is arguably one of the most significant metaphilosophical problems faced by animal ethics: not only is animal ethics metaethically naïve in its ignorance of basic moral psychology, but it may also remain hopelessly unpragmatic when focused solely on reasoned, theory-dependent analysis.

Therefore, attention needs to be focused on the relevance of emotions in general as well as the role played by specific emotions. Before exploring the latter issue (which emotions form a fruitful basis for animal philosophy?), it is worthwhile to spend a little longer with the first (are emotions relevant?).

THE RATIONALIST BACKLASH

Not all agree with the rediscovered prominence of emotion. Kennett and Fine, among other defenders of rationalism, argue that automated responses are evident when judgement is made spontaneously, under limited time, or when self-regulation is low. Yet if these obstacles are avoided, people tend to behave according to their conscious, reasoned beliefs, which correct and curtail automated responses, and it is only in these instances that one can speak of "moral judgment": "Genuine moral judgments are those that are regulated or endorsed by reflection".[30] Here, Kennett and Fine refer to a distinction between "reason trackers" (those who can note and follow reasons) and "reason responders" (those who respond to reasons as reasons).[31] Reason trackers can depend upon automation alone, whereas reason responding is a slow, deliberative task. According to Kennett and Fine, affective responses are often reason tracking, and thus we simply follow emotion without being able to offer further analyses of why our actions are right. Yet this does not constitute morality *proper*. Following Frankfurt's famous distinction into first- and second-order volition, Kennett and Fine maintain that only reason responding counts are "normative". Thus, mere automated responding cannot be considered "moral judgment" in the true sense of the word: "The real moral judgment is ultimately the one that the agent can reflectively endorse".[32]

Kennett and Fine also offer psychiatric evidence for their case. They refer to psychopathy, which as a personality disorder includes the incapacity to distinguish between "moral" and "convention" transgression, and which therefore is characterized as a condition that lacks moral agency (in short, psychopaths cannot grasp the concept of "morality"). According to Kennett and Fine, psychopaths are not excluded from the sphere of moral agency on the basis of emotion defects, but because they "don't appear to understand that moral claims are reasons claims and so it can be argued that they are not capable of genuine moral judgment".[33] Elsewhere, Kennett argues that psychopaths tend to be deficient in reflective thought, reasoned planning and internal conflict resolution. Therefore, she suggests that they are lacking *executive functioning* (higher-order capacity for self-regulation, evaluation and planning), which in plain terms undermines their rational ability. This, again, Kennett argues, explains their incapacity for moral agency, which in her mind has far-reaching implications: it is lack of reason that paves the way to amorality.[34] Another personality type used as an example by Kennett and Fine is autism, which is characterized as lacking particularly empathy (an emotive state often underlined by sentimentalism), and which is nonetheless also characterized as including the capacity for moral agency. According to Kennett and Fine, it is precisely the rational ability of autistic individuals that constitutes their moral agency—their deficiency in empathy, on the other hand, proves sentimentalism wrong.[35] On the grounds of these two cases, Kennett elsewhere argues, "Only individuals who are capable of being moved directly by the thought that some consideration constitutes a reason for action can be conscientious moral agents".[36]

On the basis of this debate, can it be decided whether the Singer-Regan or the care theory approach has the winning card? One option is to

point out that the conception of "moral judgment" advanced by rationalists is precisely what sentimentalists are criticizing. According to sentimentalism, "moral judgment" must be redefined in order for the concept
to do justice to emerging research concerning moral deliberation. What
Kennett and Fine are doing is simply restating the Kantian status quo,
without offering further reasons as to why this status quo ought to be
accepted—in other words, why ought one be a reason responder in order
to count as a moral agent? More importantly, the presumption that reason responding is a purely rational task is undermined by recent empirical studies—instead of cool reflection, it may be emotive responses that
pave the way for moral deliberation. This, again, points towards a non-
dichotomic understanding of reason and emotion, wherein the latter affects the former on a foundational level, and which renders traditional
rationalism ungrounded. Briefly, the notions of "moral judgment" and
"reason responding" are challenged by sentimentalism, and require reconfiguration.

   Kennett and Fine may also be hasty in their interpretation of psychopathy and autism. Whereas antisocial personality disorder does include
poor executive functioning[37] and deficient intellectual skills,[38] this may
not be the case with psychopathy. Indeed, recent research suggests that
psychopaths appear not to have lessened abilities in intelligence, IQ or
even executive functioning[39]; if anything, many appear to have higher
than average executive functioning.[40] Those characterized as "primary
psychopaths" are grandiose, emotionally detached and yet coolly calcula-
tive when it comes to serving their own ends. It is precisely their well-
developed capacity for rationality that defines their ability to manipulate
and control others—in this category of psychopathy, emotive defects are
combined with high rational ability.[41] This category presents a counter-
case for Kennett and Fine's depiction: primary psychopaths excel in rationality while lacking in empathy. Following the criteria set by Kennett
and Fine, these individuals would pass the test of moral agency, and yet
they appear to be the epitome of amoral monstrosity.

   Also, the example of autism faces difficulties. Most importantly, it is
not specified which form of empathy autistic individuals are said to be
lacking in. Adam Smith (a contemporary namesake of the famous historical figure) argues that autistic individuals are deficient in cognitive empathy (the capacity to mind-read in a detached manner) while their affective empathy (the capacity to emotively resonate with others) is perhaps
even higher than average. If, indeed, autistic individuals have high levels
of affective empathy, this may explain their wish to withdraw from social
settings: resonating strongly with the emotions of others may be too
much to bear, particularly in the absence of the ability to mind-read.[42]
Importantly, it may be precisely this ability to experience affective empathy that supports moral agency in autistic individuals—perhaps they are
not moral agents because of their ability to reason alone, but (also) be-

cause of affective empathy. Moreover, quite crucially, psychopaths suffer from the opposite problem: they master cognitive empathy, but are lacking in affective empathy.[43] This could suggest that it is their lack of precisely affective empathy that undermines their capacity for moral agency. Therefore, the case of psychopathy suggests that reason alone does not suffice, and that affective empathy may be required for moral agency, and the case of autism strengthens the claim: it may be lack of empathy that renders the former so prone to moral transgressions, and the latter so keen to follow moral norms.[44]

Hence, although Kennett and Fine use psychopathy and autism to support a rationalist take on moral agency, these two disorders may in fact support sentimentalism. Moreover, even if (as Kennett and Fine suggest) emotive responses can be corrected via reason, and be based on reasoned deliberation, one may argue that choosing given reasoned beliefs may, again, be grounded on emotive responses: to use their example of racist reactions, one may choose to correct them on the basis of rational beliefs on racial equality, because one has chosen those beliefs on the account of, for example, affective empathy towards others. Jesse Prinz has supported this stance. According to Prinz, evidence suggests that moral judgements tend to be emotional in nature: not only are emotions reactions based on moral judgements (we have negative feelings towards moral wrongs), but they also impact or constitute that judgement, whereby, for instance, negative emotions lead to negative moral evaluations. Prinz emphasizes that people tend to follow their moral judgements even when no rational justification can be found to support them, and he locates the impetus for doing so in emotions: therefore, emotions take priority over reason and can be the sole source of judgements.[45] This offers a convincing counterargument against Kennett and Fine. Although reason may motivate moral judgements, it may do so because of a prior emotive response.

Therefore, there are good grounds to support sentimentalism. Sentimentalism appears to explain the felt immediacy and even irrationality of moral judgement, as well as the amorality of psychopaths, together with the morality of autistic individuals. Although the defenders of rationalism suggest that moral agency is based on the ability to step back away from emotive responses and become an analytical, reflective "reason responder", a creature capable of entering the metalevel, the claim here is that such stepping back is often superfluous or post hoc, with emotion acting as the ultimate foundation of moral deliberation and justification. A sentimentalist definition of moral judgement is not necessarily resistant to the role played by reason, but places emotion as the necessary component of moral agency. This is highly relevant from the viewpoint of the type of metaethics or moral psychology often deployed in animal ethics: the rationalistic stance of much of contemporary animal ethics[46] appears, quite simply, as suspect.

Moreover, the contemporary discussion on rationalism holds promise of illuminating de facto animal ethics, as employed in everyday practices. First, it strengthens the claim that emotions affect even reasoned responses toward nonhuman animals: if Prinz is correct, those anthropocentric attitudes, which are celebrated as coolly "rational", from utilitarian defences of hunting to contractual defences of animal agriculture, may in fact be wholly sentimental on a foundational level. In other words, the debate points towards the need to reflect on the type of emotions that may affect seemingly rational arguments concerning human relations with other animals. Second, the debate opens up interesting interpretations of cultural attitudes regarding nonhuman animals. Perhaps the type of ethos most celebrated in the nonhuman context is, on a collective level, something akin to cultural psychopathy, with its desire to manipulate, control and violate other animals in order to serve human benefit, often perceived as "naturally" superior. Furthermore, perhaps the most fruitful way to combat such rational egoism is not rational, detailed defences of the logical order, akin to cultural or philosophical autism, but rather a stance explicitly inclusive of emotion. In other words, moral psychology may shed light not only on the role played by emotions but also on the character of our culture and philosophy.

This leads us to the second theme, mentioned earlier: Which specific emotions ought to be centralized in animal philosophy? Due to space restrictions, only one candidate—affective empathy—will be explored next.

VARIETIES OF EMPATHY

As seen above, sentimentalism is the de facto grounds for much of everyday morality. However, here emphasis is on the descriptive: how people tend to make moral judgements. The issue of how they ought to make those judgements, were they to follow the ethos of what we understand "morality" to be, is often left without due attention. Is anger, hate, disgust or love the way forward? Or is some other emotion the basis for moral agency *proper*? One interesting option is empathy. Empathy emerges as an obvious candidate when taking into account the emphasis placed on sentience (or "experiencing one's good") within animal ethics; also as suggested above, the cases of psychopathy and autism point towards its relevance.

Literature on empathy, whether it be philosophical, social psychological, psychiatric or neuroscientific, tends to use the term *empathy* without further specifications—therefore it is discussed as a broad umbrella term. A more careful analysis reveals that there are four definitions of empathy, which hold interest from the viewpoint of philosophy and moral psychology: *cognitive empathy* (ability to mind-read), *affective empathy* (ability to resonate with others), *projective empathy* (ability to project one-self to the position of others) and *embodied empathy* (ability for bodily, expressive intersubjectivity).[47] Out of these, cognitive and affective empathy in particular have gained attention, and those careful enough to notice varieties of empathy have noted that the distinction between the two may also be significant in the context of moral agency—an issue which brings us back to the case of psychopathy.[48]

Cognitive empathy facilitates social fluency, and can heighten such fluency to a point where one is capable of easily detecting what others are thinking or feeling, thereby furthering competitiveness in relation to and manipulation of those others up to Machiavellian levels. Affective empathy, on the other hand, rests on resonation, and can feed emotional attunement, prosocial behavior, other-directedness and even altruism, whereby one shares emotive states of others and is primarily concerned for the well-being of those others.[49] Thereby, cognitive empathy can co-exist with and further immoral (or, indeed, amoral) behavior (thus offering a fertile ground for anthropocentrism), whereas affective empathy appears to be connected to moral agency. Can affective empathy even be positioned as a criterion for moral agency?

What emerges as relevant here is our definition of "morality". If we accept that moral agency requires a sense of *other-directedness* (the well-being of creatures external to oneself is considered to have significance regardless of the utility of those creatures for oneself) and *openness* (other beings are approached as their own independent and specific entities),[50] positioning affective empathy as the criterion for moral agency appears solid. This is because affective empathy, in its facilitation of shared experience, sparks both other-directedness and openness towards others: it introduces us to the specificity and independence of those others, while inviting instant concern for their well-being. Indeed, affective empathy is inherently other-directed and open, since resonation renders the specificity and independence of others manifest on an experiential level, and forces one—on an equally experiential level—to come face to face with their flourishing. It is on these grounds that affective empathy has been argued to constitute the necessary criterion for moral agency.[51]

In order to make this more evident, it is worthwhile to go back to the philosophy of Hume, who emphasized the links between affective empathy and moral agency. Using the term *sympathy* synonymously with contemporary usages of *affective empathy*, Hume argued that it consists of one witnessing impressions of another individual (for instance, bodily expressions of suffering), forming ideas concerning these impressions ("suffering"), and again undergoing similar impressions in oneself (thereby resonating with the suffering of another). It ought to be emphasized that here resonation reserves a foundational role, as minds can be "mirrors to one another, not only because they reflect each others' emotions but also because those rays of passions, sentiments and opinions

may be often reverberated".[52] Resonation can gain such an intense degree that one almost feels as if one is undergoing the original emotion;
thereby it can contain "such a degree of force and vivacity, as to become
the very passion itself, and produce an equal emotion, as any original
affection".[53] Importantly, for Hume, sympathy (affective empathy) forms
the fundamental grounds for moral agency, as it enables us to pay heed
to not only our own emotive states that go on to constitute values but also
those of others. Indeed, Hume calls sympathy (affective empathy) the
most striking ability found in humanity, thereby undermining the popular notion that rationality is humanity's hallmark of excellence: "No quality of human nature is more remarkable, both in itself and in its consequences, than that propensity we have to sympathize with others, and to
receive by communication their inclinations and sentiments, however
different from, or even contrary to our own".[54] Hume's stance is strikingly similar to contemporary takes on affective empathy, which have manifested that direct, immediate resonation does indeed commonly take
place between individuals.[55] It has also offered much fuel to contemporary defenders of sentimentalism. The simplified message is this: morality consists of things mattering to us, and things matter because we *feel*
they matter. Affective empathy enables us to resonate with this "feel" in
others too, thereby—in quite a straightforward manner—likewise making their good and bad bear a normative impact.

Arguably, Hume got it right: resonation with the emotions or experiences of another being is a remarkable capacity, most importantly because it sparks the type of moral concern and commitment that neither
any other emotive state nor rationality—taken on their own—can
achieve. In regard to other emotive states, the threat of egoism and partiality remains the inevitable risk, as emotions tend to make us hate or
love others primarily on the grounds of how those others are related or
affiliated to us. In regard to rationality, optimizing similarly serves egoism and bias, and detachment is a poor facilitator of care and concern.
Affective empathy offers a fruitful solution that avoids these pitfalls. In
its grips, wholly partial love or hate, let alone detached or optimizing
reason, is harder—if not impossible—to sustain. In short, it forces one to
become in the most immediate sense possible familiar with the emotions
and experiences of others, regardless of their affective relation or optimal
utility to oneself.

More broadly, the debate between sentimentalism and rationalism
would benefit from taking into consideration the role played by affective
empathy: perhaps it offers a way out from the loggerhead situation between the two parties. Neither sheer emotion nor rationality suffice, for
in order to constitute "morality", both need to be grounded on affective
information concerning the mental contents of other individuals. Of
course, anger, love and reasoned analysis may play a part, and arguably
in many cases should play a part, but they should be based upon and

motivated by the primary route towards understanding the inner states and ultimately the individuality of others—affective empathy.

On these grounds, it is here suggested that contemporary animal ethics should take sentimentalism more extensively into account as a meta-ethical standpoint. If emotions, and particularly affective empathy, form the necessary (even if not the only) basis for moral agency and judgement, issues such as the value, moral status, rights and treatment of nonhuman animals cannot be decided upon sheer rational analysis. Rather, the baseline on which such analysis must be structured on is our affective resonance with other animals and its moral thickness: it is via affective empathy that value emerges, and reason reserves a position only in mapping out the various implications that stem from that empathy. Indeed, in line with sentimentalists, it can be maintained that one does not truly "understand" the moral status of other animals, if one merely follows, say, a utilitarian logic.

BECOMING SENTIMENTAL

One final issue needs to be raised: What of those, who approach animals rationally, and cannot resonate with rats and pigs? If affective empathy is what we ought to pronounce in ourselves, how can it be cultivated in our relations with other animals? This ties back to the issue of cultural stereotypes as—next to emotion—the other factor behind intuition. As suggested earlier, normative, societal change will only happen with the change of cultural stereotypes and the forms of emotions they are intertwined with. How, then, can we seek to advocate a more empathic approach towards other animals—an approach that will derail existing stereotypes linked to animality?

Another classic author on empathy (who like Hume also used the term *sympathy*), Adam Smith, may provide a solution to this question. Smith underlined the notion of projective empathy, within which one projects oneself into the position of another with the aid of imagination. Hence, Smith argued, "As we have no immediate experience of what other men feel, we can form no idea of the manner in which they are affected, but by conceiving what we ourselves should feel in the like situation".[56] Thereby, one seeks to simulate how oneself would feel in the position of another, which forms an important distinction in comparison to Humean resonation: one does not reverberate with the emotions of another, but undergoes one's own emotions, appropriate for the context of the other. Smith clarifies that our senses "never did, and never can, carry us beyond our own person, and it is by the imagination only that we can form any conception of what are his sensations . . . it is the impressions of our own senses only, not those of his, which our imaginations copy".[57] Now, although projective empathy suffers from various limitations in the context of moral agency,[58] it may nonetheless provide an important tool for learning affective empathy.

In practice, this means that it may be helpful to imagine what the context (living conditions, etc.) of other animals is, what their physiology is like, how they may sense things—in short, what type of emotions and experiences they may have in specific contexts. Of course, the difference and specificity of other animals is to be taken into account, and thereby projective empathy would not here mean simply projecting human egos into the position of nonhuman animals; rather, the aim would be to use imagination in order to spark affective responses in oneself. Arguably, many struggle to feel affective empathy towards animals due to cultural processes and meanings—the type of stereotypes emphasized earlier by Haidt—and rehearsing projective empathy may provide a countermeasure with which to realize that there indeed are billions of beings around us whose subjective states are not entirely inaccessible to us.

Another method is to use the fourth form of empathy—embodied empathy. Its advocates, Dan Zahavi at the forefront, have suggested that empathy requires and rests upon intersubjectivity—a state within which one approaches another being as a minded subject, with whom one can instantly communicate via expressive means. Resting particularly on the phenomenology of Merleau-Ponty, this approach brings forward the body as expressive of a mind, arguing that individuals can achieve a mode of being within which the other party is instantly comprehended and communicated with prior to any inference. Thus, Zahavi argues, "Expressive movements and behavior is soaked with the meaning of the mind; it reveals the mind to us".[59] Sheer resonation is replaced by intersubjective expressivity and communication. The model offered by Zahavi allows one to question whether one truly cannot empathize with other animals—instead of incapacity, the problem would seem to involve the lack of open, expressive intersubjectivity. That is, one may not have approached other animals as minded beings, with whom one can enter into an intersubjective relation. The task at hand, then, would not be the use of projection, but rather encaging oneself in states of mutual attunement with other animals—that is, getting familiar with pigs and rats. A perfect case in point here would be that of the cognitive ethologist Barbara Smuts, who has offered detailed accounts of learning to perceive the animal viewpoint precisely via such attunement—using the example of spending extensive periods of time with wild baboons, she argues that concrete intersubjective interaction with nonhuman animals opens the door for "learning a whole new way of being in the world—the way of the baboon".[60]

Therefore, by facilitating openness to the subjectivity of other animals, concrete interactions with those animals may help to teach us affective empathy—that is, becoming more open to expressive communication holds promise of enabling resonation.[61] Learning empathy towards nonhuman others, then, would rest on coming, with an intersubjective approach, face to face with pigs and rats, cows and pigeons.

The implication is that varieties of empathy are needed in order to alter and shape anthropocentric cultural stereotypes and emotions intertwined with them, from disgust to anger and love—the type of stereotypes and emotions that tend to predetermine everyday animal ethics. It is by imaginatively projecting ourselves into the at times alien experiential worlds of other animals, and by entering into intersubjective states with them, that resonation with and concern towards their subjectivity may begin to take flight.

CONCLUSION

The revival of sentimentalism as a metaethical stance poses uncomfortable questions for much of contemporary animal ethics, heavily rooted in the tradition of rationalism. In particular, utilitarianism, deontology, contract theory and, to some extent, virtue ethics have been applied to the nonhuman context, with the starting premise being that it is rational analysis that will reveal or construct the moral status of other animals. The basic claim of sentimentalism—that it is first and foremost emotion that renders us into moral beings—questions the very basis of this approach. From the viewpoint of sentimentalism, it is not reason but emotion that will reveal or construct the moral significance of pigs and rats. The feminist care tradition within animal ethics has paid some attention to the role of emotions, as have philosophers like Mary Midgley and Ralph Acampora. However, these explorations have not investigated with care the metaethical and moral psychological debate concerning sentimentalism, or the contemporary research that exists on the role played by reason and emotion.

An analysis of the metaethical debate reveals that there are good grounds for sentimentalism, and contemporary empirical research offers support for this conclusion. In particular, affective empathy emerges as a prime criterion for moral agency and judgement, and acts as a third alternative between reason-based animal ethics, which can remain hopelessly unpersuasive and detached, and care theory, which can remain hopelessly idealistic in its presupposition that emotions as a generic group offer fruitful grounds for zoocentrism, equality and justice. As such, affective empathy constitutes an arable metaethical ground on which to work new landscapes for animal philosophy.

NOTES

1. Martha Nussbaum, *Upheavals of Thought: The Intelligence of Emotions* (Cambridge: Cambridge University Press, 2001).

2. Alice Crary, *Beyond Moral Judgment* (Cambridge, MA: Harvard University Press, 2009), 10.

3. Jesse Prinz, "The Emotional Basis of Moral Judgments", *Philosophical Explorations* 9, no. 1 (2006): 29–43, 36.

4. David Hume, *A Treatise on Human Nature* (London: Penguin, 1969).

5. Patricia Churchland, *Brainstorm* (Princeton: Princeton University Press, 2010), 175.

6. Victoria McGeer, "Varieties of Moral Agency: Lessons from Autism (and Psychopathy)", in *Moral Psychology, vol. 3: The Neuroscience of Morality*, ed. W. Sinnott-Armstrong (Cambridge, MA: MIT Press, 2007), 247.

7. McGeer, "Varieties of Moral Agency", 247.

8. James Turner, *Reckoning with the Beast: Animals, Pain, and Humanity in the Victorian Mind* (Baltimore: Johns Hopkins University Press, 1980).

9. Turner, *Reckoning with the Beast*. One philosophical example of this line of thinking was Schopenhauer, who urged for the extension of compassion to other animals partly on the account that compassion is the key ingredient in "humanity": "He, who appears to be without compassion, is called inhuman; so 'humanity' is often used as its synonyme". Arthur Schopenhauer, *On The Basis of Morality* (New York: Dover Publications, 1985), 89.

10. Genevieve Lloyd, *The Man of Reason: "Male" and "Female" in Western Philosophy* (Minnesota: University of Minnesota Press, 1993).

11. Lori Gruen, "Empathy and Vegetarian Commitments", in *The Feminist Care Tradition in Animal Ethics: A Reader*, ed. J. Donovan and C. J. Adams (New York: Columbia University Press, 2007), 333–43; Josephine Donovan, "Attention to Suffering: Sympathy as a Basis for Ethical Treatment of Animals", in *The Feminist Care Tradition in Animal Ethics: A Reader*, ed. J. Donovan and C. J. Adams (New York: Columbia University Press, 2007), 174–97.

12. Mary Midgley, *Animals and Why They Matter* (Athens: University of Georgia Press, 1983).

13. Ralph Acampora, *Corporal Compassion* (Pittsburgh: University of Pittsburgh Press, 2006).

14. Cora Diamond, "Eating Meat and Eating People", in *Animal Rights: Current Debates and New Directions*, ed. C. R. Sunstein and M. C. Nussbaum (London: Routledge, 2005), 93–107.

15. Joshua Greene and Jonathan Haidt, "How (and Where) Does Moral Judgment Work?", *Trends in Cognitive Sciences* 6 (2002): 517–23, 517.

16. Jonathan Haidt, "The Moral Emotions", in *Handbook of Affective Sciences*, ed. R. J. Davidson, K. R. Scherer, and H. H. Goldsmith (Oxford: Oxford University Press, 2003).

17. Greene and Haidt, "How (and Where) Does Moral Judgment Work?", 522.

18. Jonathan Haidt, "The Emotional Dog and Its Rational Tail: A Social Intuitionist Approach to Moral Judgment", *Psychological Review* 108 (2001): 814–34, 815.

19. Haidt, "The Emotional Dog and Its Rational Tail", 816.

20. B. Bratanova, S. Loughnan and B. Bastian, "The Effect of Categorisation as Food on the Perceived Moral Standing of Animals", *Appetite* 57 (2011): 193–96, 194.

21. Bratanova et al., "The Effect of Categorisation as Food on the Perceived Moral Standing of Animals", 196.

22. Bratanova et al., "The Effect of Categorisation as Food on the Perceived Moral Standing of Animals", 196.

23. M. Ruby and S. Heine, "Too Close to Home: Factors Predicting Meat Avoidance", *Appetite* 59 (2012): 47–52.

24. Ruby and Heine, "Too Close to Home".

25. D. Fessler, A. Arguello, J. Mekdara, and R. Macias, "Disgust Sensitivity and Meat Consumption: A Test of an Emotivist Account of Moral Vegetarianism", *Appetite* 41 (2003): 31–41, 37.

26. Bratanova et al., "The Effect of Categorisation as Food on the Perceived Moral Standing of Animals".

27. Jonathan Haidt, Paul Rozin, Laura Lowery and Sumio Imada, "The CAD Triad Hypothesis: A Mapping between Three Moral Emotions (Contempt, Anger, Disgust) and Three Moral Codes (Community, Autonomy, Divinity)", *Journal of Personality and Social Psychology* 76 (1999): 574–86.

28. Kathy Rudy, *Loving Animals* (Minnesota: University of Minnesota Press, 2011).

29. Jeannette Kennett and Cordelia Fine, "Will the Real Moral Judgment Please Stand Up?", *Ethical Theory and Moral Practice* 12 (2009): 77–96.

30. Kennett and Fine, "Will the Real Moral Judgment Please Stand Up?", 78.

31. This distinction is from Karen Jones, "Emotion, Weakness of Will and the Normative Conception of Agency", in *Philosophy and the Emotions*, ed. A. Hatzimosyis (Cambridge: Cambridge University Press, 2003), 181–200.

32. Kennett and Fine, "Will the Real Moral Judgment Please Stand Up?", 93.

33. Kennett and Fine, "Will the Real Moral Judgment Please Stand Up?", 86.

34. Jeannette Kennett, "Do Psychopaths Really Threaten Moral Rationalism?", *Philosophical Explorations* 9 (2006): 69–82.

35. Kennett and Fine, "Will the Real Moral Judgment Please Stand Up?"

36. Jeannette Kennett, "Autism, Empathy and Moral Agency", *Philosophical Quarterly* 52 (2002): 340–57, 357.

37. Alex Morgan and Scott Lilienfeld, "A Meta-Analytic Review of the Relation Between Antisocial Behavior and Neuropsychological Measures of Executive Function", *Clinical Psychology Review* 20 (2000): 113–36.

38. Kent Kiehl, "A Cognitive Neuroscience Perspective on Psychopathy: Evidence for Paralimbic System Dysfunction", *Psychiatry Research* 15 (2006): 107–28.

39. Kiehl, "A Cognitive Neuroscience Perspective"; M. Mahmut, J. Homewood and R. Stevenson, "The Characteristics of Non-Criminals with High Psychopathy Traits: Are They Similar to Criminal Psychopaths?", *Journal of Research in Personality* 42 (2008): 679–92.

40. Andrea Glenn, Robert Kurzban and Adrian Raine, "Evolutionary Theory and Psychopathy", *Aggression and Violent Behaviour* 16 (2011): 371–80.

41. B. Hicks, K. Markon, C. Patrick, R. Krueger and J. Newman, "Identifying Psychopathy Subtypes on the Basis of Personality Structure", *Psychological Assessment* 16 (2004): 276–88.

42. Adam Smith, "Cognitive Empathy and Emotional Empathy in Human Behaviour and Evolution", *The Psychological Record* 56 (2006): 3–21.

43. R. J. Blair, "Fine Cuts of Empathy and the Amygdala: Dissociable Deficits in Psychopathy and Autism", *Quarterly Journal of Experimental Psychology* 61 (2008): 157–70.

44. For a more detailed discussion, see Elisa Aaltola, "Affective Empathy as Core Moral Agency: Psychopathy, Autism and Reason Revisited", *Philosophical Explorations* 17 (2014): 76–92.

45. Jesse Prinz, "The Emotional Basis of Moral Judgments".

46. One of the most eloquent defences of this stance can be found in Christine Korsgaard, "Fellow Creatures: Kantian Ethics and Our Duties to Animals", in *The Tanner Lectures on Human Values* (Ann Arbor: University of Michigan, 2004).

47. Elisa Aaltola, "Varieties of Empathy and Moral Agency", *Topoi* 33 (2014): 243–53.

48. See, for instance, Blair, "Fine Cuts of Empathy and the Amygdala".

49. Smith, "Cognitive Empathy and Emotional Empathy".

50. Aaltola, "Varieties of Empathy and Moral Agency".

51. Aaltola, "Varieties of Empathy and Moral Agency". One important element supportive of this conclusion is the manner in which affective empathy facilitates one to comprehend the individuality of other beings: if we accept that one of the most primary and foundational grounds for individuality is "qualia", the Nagelian experience of "what it is like", which allows us to have a viewpoint into this world, it

becomes evident that resonating with the qualia of others enables one to become, in a very immediate and tangible sense, aware of their individuality and ultimately personhood. Thus, affective empathy renders perception of individuality possible—arguably a key ingredient in moral agency.

52. Hume, *A Treatise on Human Nature*, 414.

53. Hume, *A Treatise on Human Nature*, 367.

54. Hume, *A Treatise on Human Nature*, 367.

55. Jean Decety and Philip Jackson, "A Social-Neuroscience Perspective on Empathy", *Current Directions in Psychological Science* 15 (2006): 54–58.

56. Adam Smith, *The Theory of Moral Sentiments* (London: Penguin Books, 2009), 13.

57. Smith, *The Theory of Moral Sentiments*, 13.

58. Most notably, it rests on an atomistic epistemology—see Dan Zahavi, "Simulation, Projection and Empathy", *Consciousness and Cognition* 17 (2008): 514–22.

59. Zahavi, "Simulation, Projection and Empathy", 520.

60. Barbara Smuts, "Encounters with Animal Minds", *Journal of Consciousness Studies* 8 (2001): 293–309, 295.

61. It should be noted that whereas projective empathy faces the risk of anthropomorphism, embodied empathy emphasizes the difference of others, thereby facilitating a more zoocentric approach. This is because, as Zahavi underlines, expressiveness continuously presents us with cues we fail to grasp, and thus accentuates the otherness and difference of the other being (see Dan Zahavi, "Expression and Empathy", in *Folk Psychology Re-Assessed*, ed. D. Hutto and M. Ratcliffe [Dordrecht: Springer, 2007], 25–40). Hence, by entering into intersubjective encounters with other animals, we may not only learn affective empathy in relation to them but also become poignantly reminded of their difference.

Further Reading

BOOKS

Regan, Tom. *The Case for Animal Rights*. Berkeley: University of California Press, 1983. The first full-length explication of a nonconsequentialist theory of animal rights based upon the idea of respect for inherent value.

Regan, Tom. *The Case for Animal Rights*. 2nd ed. Berkeley: University of California Press, 2004. Important for the revised introduction. Regan addresses a number of objections; most significantly, he reiterates that inherent value is a metaphilosophical "postulate" (a fact lost on many commentators). His discussion of positive duties calls into question the recent claim by Donaldson and Kymlicka that "traditional" animal rights theory is an exclusively negative rights theory.

Singer, Peter. *Animal Liberation*. 2nd ed. London: Pimlico, 1995. First edition published in 1975. This book represents the first flowering of the philosophical seed planted by Bentham. The first chapter is an interest-based argument for extending the principle of equality to sentient nonhuman animals. It is interesting to speculate whether the popular appeal and enduring significance of *Animal Liberation* is a function of its philosophical argument or its evocative descriptions of conditions inside factory farms and research laboratories.

Singer, Peter. *Practical Ethics*. 2nd ed. Cambridge: Cambridge University Press, 1993. First published in 1979. Significant for a "species-blind" utilitarian argument for ecosystem protection in which Singer attacks biocentrism by saying, to the effect, "I can imagine what it feels like to be a possum drowning, but I have no idea what it feels like to be a tree with its roots flooded". *Practical Ethics* is also important for Singer's discussion of the harm of death, a topic he only briefly touches upon in *Animal Liberation*.

BOOKS: ADDITIONAL REFERENCES

Aaltola, Elisa. *Animal Suffering: Philosophy and Culture*. Basingstoke: Palgrave MacMillan, 2012.

Acampora, Ralph R. *Corporal Compassion: Animal Ethics and Philosophy of Body*. Pittsburgh: University of Pittsburgh Press, 2006.

Adams, Carol. *Sexual Politics of Meat: A Feminist-Vegetarian Critical Theory*. New York: Continuum, 1990.

Agar, Nicholas. *Life's Intrinsic Value: Science, Ethics and Nature*. New York: Columbia, 2001.

Benton, Ted. *Natural Relations: Ecology, Animal Rights and Social Justice*. London: Verso, 1993.

Birke, Lynda. *Feminism, Animals and Science: The Naming of the Shrew*. London: Open University Press, 1994.

Calarco, Matthew. *Zoographies: The Question of the Animal from Heidegger to Derrida*. New York: Columbia, 2008.

Callicott, J. Baird. *In Defense of the Land Ethic: Essays in Environmental Philosophy*. Albany, NY: SUNY Press, 1989.

Carruthers, Peter. *The Animals Issue: Moral Theory in Practice*. Cambridge: Cambridge University Press, 1992.

Cavalieri, Paola. *The Animal Question: Why Nonhuman Animals Deserve Human Rights*. Oxford: Oxford University Press, 2001.

Cavalieri, Paola, et al. *The Death of the Animal: A Dialogue*. New York: Columbia University Press, 2009.

Cavell, Stanley, et al. *Philosophy and Animal Life*. New York: Columbia, 2008.

Clark, Gillian, trans. *Porphry: On Abstinence from Killing Animals*. Ithaca: Cornell University Press.

Clark, Stephen R. L. *The Moral Status of Animals*. Oxford: Oxford University Press, 1977.

Cochrane, Alasdair. *Animal Rights without Liberation: Applied Ethics and Human Obligations*. New York: Columbia, 2012.

Coetzee, J. M., et al. *The Lives of Animals*. Princeton: Princeton University Press, 1999.

Cohen, Carl, and Tom Regan. *The Animal Rights Debate*. New York: Rowman & Littlefield, 2001.

DeGrazia, David. *Taking Animals Seriously*. Cambridge: Cambridge University Press, 1996.

Dombrowski, Daniel. *Babies and Beasts: The Argument from Marginal Cases*. Chicago: University of Illinois Press, 1997.

Donaldson, Sue, and Will Kymlicka. *Zoopolis: A Political Theory of Animal Rights*. Oxford: Oxford University Press, 2011.

Dunayer, Joan. *Speciesism*. Derwood: Ryce Publishing, 2004.

Francione, Gary. *Introduction to Animal Rights: Your Child or the Dog?* Philadelphia: Temple University Press, 2000.

Francione, Gary, and Robert Garner. *The Animal Rights Debate: Abolition or Regulation*. New York: Columbia University Press, 2010.

Franklin, Julian H. *Animal Rights and Moral Philosophy*. New York: Columbia University Press, 2006.

Frey, R. G. *Interests and Rights: The Case against Animals*. Oxford: Clarendon Press, 1980.

Gaita, Raimond. *The Philosopher's Dog*. Melbourne: Text Publishing, 2002.

Garner, Robert. *A Theory of Justice for Animals: Animal Rights in a Nonideal World*. Oxford: Oxford University Press, 2013.

Gruen, Lori. *Ethics and Animals: An Introduction*. New York: Cambridge University Press, 2011.

Haraway, Donna J. *When Species Meet*. Minneapolis: University of Minnesota Press, 2008.

Hursthouse, Rosalind. *Ethics, Humans and Other Animals: An Introduction with Readings*. London: Routledge, 2000.

Jamieson, Dale. *Morality's Progress: Essays on Humans, Other Animals, and the Rest of Nature*. Oxford: Oxford University Press, 2002.

Linzey, Andrew. *Animal Theology*. London: SCM Press Ltd., 1993.

Malamud, Randy. *Reading Zoos: Representations of Animals and Captivity*. New York: New York University Press, 1998.

McKenna, Erin, and Andrew Light. *Animal Pragmatism: Rethinking Human and Nonhuman Relationships*. Bloomington: Indiana University Press, 2004.

McMahan, Jeff. *The Ethics of Killing: Problems and the Margins of Life*. Oxford: Oxford University Press, 2002.

Merchant, Carolyn. *The Death of Nature: Women, Ecology and the Scientific Revolution*. San Francisco: Harper & Row, 1980.

Midgley, Mary. *Animals and Why They Matter*. Athens: University of Georgia Press, 1983.

Milligan, Tony. *Beyond Animal Rights: Food, Pets and Ethics*. London: Continuum, 2010.

Noske, Barbara. *Beyond Boundaries: Humans and Animals*. Montreal: Black Books, 1997.

Nussbaum, Martha C. *Frontiers of Justice: Disability, Nationality and Species Membership*. London: Belknap Press of Harvard University, 2006.

Oliver, Kelly. *Animal Lessons: How They Teach Us to Be Human*. New York: Columbia University Press, 2009.

Palmer, Clare. *Animal Ethics in Context*. New York: Columbia, 2010.

Passmore, John. *Man's Responsibility to Nature*. London: Duckworth & Co. Ltd., 1974.

Pluhar, Evelyn. *Beyond Prejudice: The Moral Significance of Human and Nonhuman Animals*. Durham: Duke University Press, 1995.

Plumwood, Val. *Environmental Culture: The Ecological Crisis of Reason*. New York: Routledge, 2002.

Rachels, James. *Created from Animals: The Moral Implications of Darwinism*. Oxford: Oxford University Press, 1990.

Rodd, Rosemary. *Biology, Ethics and Animals*. Oxford: Clarendon Press, 1990.

Rollin, Bernard E. *Animal Rights and Human Morality*. New York: Prometheus Books, 1992.

Rolston, Holmes. *Environmental Ethics: Duties to and Values in the Natural World*. Philadelphia: Temple University Press, 1988.

Rowlands, Mark. *Animals Like Us*. London: Verso, 2002.

Ryder, Richard. *Painism*. London: Centaur Press, 2001.

Salt, Henry. *Animals' Rights Considered in Relation to Social Progress*. London: Centaur Press, 1980. First published in 1882.

Sapontzis, Steven. *Morals, Reason and Animals*. Philadelphia: Temple University Press, 1987.

Scruton, Roger. *Animal Rights and Wrongs*. London: Continuum, 2000.

Singer, Peter. *The Expanding Circle: Ethics and Sociobiology*. Oxford: Clarendon Press, 1981.

Sorabji, Richard. *Animal Minds and Human Morals: The Origins of the Western Debate*. London: Duckworth, 1993.

Steiner, Gary. *Animals and the Moral Community: Mental Life and Moral Status*. New York: Columbia, 2008.

Taylor, Angus. *Animals and Ethics: An Overview of the Philosophical Debate*. 3rd ed. Peterborough, Ontario: Broadview Press, 2009.

Taylor, Paul. *Respect for Nature*. Princeton, NJ: Princeton University Press, 1986.

Tyler, Tom. *Ciferae: A Bestiary in Five Fingers*. Minneapolis: University of Minnesota Press, 2012.

Varner, Gary. *In Nature's Interests? Interests, Animal Rights, and Environmental Ethics*. New York: Oxford University Press, 1998.

Warren, Mary Anne. *Moral Status: Obligations to Persons and Other Living Things*. Oxford: Clarendon Press, 1997.

Wise, Steven. *Drawing the Line: Science and the Case for Animal Rights*. Cambridge, MA: Perseus Books, 2002.

Wolfe, Cary. *What Is Posthumanism?* Minneapolis: University of Minnesota Press, 2010.

Zamir, Tzachi. *Ethics and the Beast*. Princeton: Princeton University Press, 2007.

EDITED COLLECTIONS

Armstrong, Susan J., and Richard G. Botzler, ed. *The Animal Ethics Reader*. New York: Routledge, 2003.

Atterton, Peter, and Matthew Calarco, ed. *Animal Philosophy: Ethics and Identity*. New York: Continuum, 2011.

Beauchamp, Thomas, and R. G. Frey, ed. *The Oxford Handbook of Animal Ethics*. New York: Oxford University Press, 2011.

Bekoff, Marc, ed. *Encyclopaedia of Animal Welfare and Animal Rights*. Westport: Greenwood Press, 1998.

Castricano, Jodey, ed. *Animal Subjects: An Ethical Reader in a Posthuman World*. Waterloo: Wilfried Laurier University Press, 2008.

Hargrove, Eugene C., ed. *The Animal Rights/Environmental Ethics Debate: The Environmental Perspective*. New York: State University of New York Press, 1992.

Jamieson, Dale, ed. *Singer and His Critics*. London: Blackwell, 1999.

Kalof, Linda, and Amy Fitzgerald, ed. *The Animals Reader: The Essential Classic and Contemporary Writings*. Oxford: Berg Publishers.

Light, Andrew, and Holmes Rolston III, ed. *Environmental Ethics: An Anthology*. Oxford: Blackwell, 2003.

Linzey, Andrew, and Dorothy Yamamoto, ed. *Animals on the Agenda: Questions about Animals for Theology and Ethics*. Chicago: University of Illinois Press, 1988.

Lurz, Robert W. *The Philosophy of Animal Minds*. Cambridge: Cambridge University Press, 2009.

Palmer, Clare, ed. *Animals Rights*. London: Ashgate, 2008.

Regan, Tom, and Peter Singer, ed. *Animal Rights and Human Obligations*. Englewood Cliffs, NJ: Prentice Hall, 1976.

Singer, Peter, ed. *In Defense of Animals: The Second Wave*. Oxford: Blackwell, 2006.

Smulewicz-Zucker, Gregory R. *Strangers to Nature: Animal Lives and Human Nature*. Lanham, MD: Lexington Press, 2012.

Sunstein, Cass, and Martha Nussbaum, ed. *Animal Rights: Current Debates and New Directions*. Edited by Cass R. Sunstein and Martha C. Nussbaum. Oxford: Oxford University Press, 2004.

Wolfe, Cary, ed. *Zoontologies: The Question of the Animal*. Minneapolis: University of Minnesota Press, 2003.

Index

223

Notes on Contributors

Elisa Aaltola is senior research fellow in philosophy at the University of Eastern Finland. She has been working on animal ethics and animal philosophy for a number of years, and she has written numerous articles in journals such as *Environmental Ethics, Environmental Values* and *Philosophical Explorations*. Her publications include four books on animal philosophy, most recently *Animal Suffering: Philosophy and Culture* (2012).

Jonathan Beever is a postdoctoral scholar at The Rock Ethics Institute at Penn State University. He works primarily at the intersection of environmental and bioethics but also has interests in contemporary continental philosophy and semiotics. Jonathan has received several fellowships and grants, and has published numerous articles and edited books. He has taught a variety of undergraduate and graduate courses in philosophical and research ethics.

Angela Coventry is associate professor of philosophy at Portland State University. She is the author of two books: *Hume's Theory of Causation: A Quasi-Realist Interpretation* (2006) and *Hume: A Guide for the Perplexed* (2007). In addition, she has published several articles and book reviews in journals such as *Hume Studies, Locke Studies, Logical Analysis, History of Philosophy, History of Philosophy Quarterly, Mind* and *The European Legacy*.

Nicolas Delon is assistant professor/faculty fellow in enviromental studies and animal studies at the NYU Department of Enviromental Studies. He received his PhD in philosophy from Université Paris 1 Panthéon-Sorbonne in 2014. Before his PhD, Nicolas studied at the University of Picardie in Amiens, Columbia University, Université Paris 1, and Ecole normale supériere. Nicolas works in animal ethics and wrote a dissertation defending *A Contextual Theory of the Moral Status of Animals*. He has recently published in the *Proceedings of the Aristotelian Society*.

Robert William Fischer is an assistant professor of philosophy at Texas State University. He writes about issues in applied ethics and epistemology. His work has appeared in *Synthese, American Philosophical Quarterly, Philosophy in the Contemporary World* and *Southwest Philosophy Review*.

Elizabeth Foreman is an assistant professor of philosophy at Missouri State University (PhD, UNC-Chapel Hill, 2008). She specializes in ethics, with research interests in normative ethics (especially the role of moral attitudes in ethical theory) and applied ethics (especially nonhuman animal welfare). Her work in these areas has been published in *Ethical Theory and Moral Practice, Journal of Animal Ethics* and *Between the Species*.

John Hadley is a lecturer in philosophy in the School of Humanities and Communication Arts at the University of Western Sydney. He was formerly lecturer in Communication Ethics in the School of Communication and a lecturer in philosophy in the School of Humanities and Social Sciences at Charles Sturt University. His work has appeared in journals such as *Political Studies, Journal of Applied Philosophy, Ethics and the Environment, Environmental Values* and the *Journal of Social Philosophy*.

Avram Hiller is an associate professor of philosophy at Portland State University. He works in environmental ethics as well as epistemology and other areas of analytic philosophy. Recent work includes *Consequentialism and Environmental Ethics* (coedited with Leonard Kahn and Ramona Ilea, 2014) and papers in *Public Affairs Quarterly, Ethics, Policy, and Environment, Logos and Episteme* and *Essays in Philosophy*.

Tony Milligan lectures in philosophy at the University of Hertfordshire and is the author of *Beyond Animal Rights* (2011), *Love* (2012) and *Civil Disobedience: Protest, Justification and the Law* (2014) as well as coeditor of *Love and Its Objects* (2014). His work focuses upon the ways in which an understanding of love, the virtues and otherness can feed into practical ethics.

Jonathan D. Singer is currently a PhD candidate in philosophy at DePaul University. He specializes in phenomenology (especially the philosophy of Maurice Merleau-Ponty) and ethics, and he has been published in *Between the Species* and *Pli: The Warwick Journal of Philosophy*.

Morten Tønnessen is an associate professor of philosophy at the University of Stavanger (Norway). His research interests include biosemiotics, environmental ethics and human-animal studies. He coedited *The Semiotics of Animal Representations* (2014) with Kadri Tüür and is coeditor in chief of *Biosemiotics*. Tønnessen is chair of Minding Animals Norway. He has an academic blog: http://utopianrealism.blogspot.com/.

Zipporah Weisberg is the Abby Benjamin Postdoctoral Fellow in animal ethics in the department of philosophy at Queen's University (Kingston, Canada). She specializes in critical animal studies, critical theory and continental philosophy.

Wayne Williams is a lecturer in philosophy and director of undergraduate studies at the School of Politics, Philosophy and International Studies at the University of Hull. His research interests are in animal ethics, meta-ethics and applied philosophy, and he is currently finishing his doctoral thesis on animal rights and violent activism.

Jason Wyckoff is an associate instructor of philosophy at the University of Utah, and he previously held appointments at Marquette University and the University of Colorado. His work has appeared in *Hypatia, Revue Internationale de Philosophie, History of Political Thought, Sophia, Southwest Philosophy Review* and *The Southern Journal of Philosophy*. He holds a PhD from the University of Colorado and a JD from Georgetown University Law Center.